1001 BEST Internet Sites For Educators

Mark Treadwell

Arlington Heights, Illinois

The author has made every attempt to provide accurate and current information regarding educational sites on the Internet; however, the Internet changes rapidly. Frequently, sites alter their addresses or their contents, undergo reconstruction, cease to be updated, or are removed completely. The author and publisher assume no responsibility for alterations, omissions, or errors, nor do they assume any liability for damages resulting from the use of this information.

This book is supported by the Web sites <http://teachers.work.co.nz>, and <http://www.teachers.work.com>.

1,001 Best Internet Sites for Educators
Second Edition

Published by SkyLight Professional Development
A Pearson Education Company
2626 S. Clearbrook Dr., Arlington Heights, IL 60005
800-348-4474 or 847-290-6600
Fax 847-290-6609
info@skylightedu.com
http://www.skylightedu.com

President: Carol Luitjens
Managing Editor: Chris Jaeggi
Senior Acquisitions Editor: Jean Ward
Project Coordinator: Donna Ramirez
Cover Designer and Illustrations: David Stockman
Book Designer: Bruce Leckie
Formatters: David Stockman and Donna Ramirez
Production Supervisor: Bob Crump

LCCCN 2001086745
ISBN 1-57517-440-5

2876V
Item Number 2338

Z Y X W V U T S R Q P O N M L K J I H G F E D C B A
09 08 07 06 05 04 03 02 01 15 14 13 12 11 10 9 8 7 6 5 4 3 2

There are
one-story intellects,
two-story intellects, and
three-story intellects with skylights.

All fact collectors, who have no aim beyond their facts, are
one-story minds.

Two-story minds
compare, reason, generalize,
using the labors of the fact collectors
as well as their own.

Three-story minds
idealize, imagine, predict—their best illumination comes from above,
through the skylight.

—Oliver Wendell Holmes

Contents

Introduction

How to Use this Resource Guide

Each Internet site included in this book relates to the main curriculum area that the site addresses and how the site can be used in the classroom. Each review is intended as a guide only. Because of the dynamic nature of the Internet, content and presentation can, and do, change without warning. For this reason, the reviews are not a guarantee of the quality and content of the site, because the site may have changed after the review was written.

The ratings for each site refer to the following quality and content criteria. These are overall ratings, as often both quality and content vary through the site.

★★★★★ Both the quality of content and presentation are exemplary. The material presented includes multiple learning styles and modes of approach. The material is interactive, based on sound pedagogy, and is very well researched. The site is easy to navigate, and content is presented using a number of different media.

★★★★ Both the quality of content and presentation are exemplary and much of the material provides interactive feedback to the student or teacher. The material is based on sound pedagogy. The content of the site is well referenced, and the reading ages are appropriate.

★★★ The content is acceptable and is suitable for the levels specified. The presentation of material is variable, but the site is easy to navigate and has a consistent format. Links to additional sites are included that provide backup to the information presented.

★★ The site is worthy of inclusion in the classroom program, because it includes information that is specific to niche areas of study. The information is factual and correct although the presentation style may not optimize the learning process. Some assistance from the teacher will be necessary to maximize the benefit of using the site.

★ The site contains information that provides good support to additional material. The material is text- and image-based and may be very specific or brief. Individual elements make the site valuable, but it should not be viewed as a complete treatise on the subject.

Teacher Alert! Some material within the site is not suitable for some or all students. Please review the site before using with students.

Safety on the Internet

This is the paramount concern of both staff and parents. Schools providing Internet access to students must ensure that systems and policies are in place to manage the use of the Internet so that students do not access information that is inappropriate or use information inappropriately.

It is important that teachers teach the moral and ethical responsibilities in using the Internet. This includes discussion of copyright issues, cutting and pasting, plagiarism, and correct bibliographic referencing, as well as accessing sites that are inappropriate. When teachers have the time, they can allow students to debate the issues rather than have the teacher arbitrarily instigating "thou shalt not" rules.

Teachers can follow four basic guidelines:

- The school must have an Acceptable Use Policy (AUP). A generic policy, copyright-free for schools to adapt to their needs, is available in the section below. An electronic copy can be sent on request. Send your request to <AUP@work.co.nz>. The AUP must be reviewed at six-month intervals and be made available to parents or caregivers of all students using the Internet in the school.
- The use of filtering software is recommended, especially when the Internet is used in places where individual monitoring is not possible (e.g., libraries). The software is relatively inexpensive and is effective when set up correctly. Software titles such as Net Nanny and Cyber Patrol (now part of the SurfControl family) are tried and true products. Alternatively, you may use services such as Family Net <http://www.family.net> that filter the content at the ISP level, providing the school prefiltered content.
- Always ensure that computers with Internet access are placed in an open and public environment. Avoid placing computers in small rooms or behind screens. Placing computers in open spaces can sometimes distract other students not using the computers, but safety must be a priority.
- Schools may choose to have an Internet license system where parents (or caregivers) sign an agreement for their child to access the Internet. This is usually a small laminated card with the school name, the student's name, and a parent (or caregiver) signature. The card is placed on top of the computer whenever the student uses the Internet. No card equals no Internet use.

If these strategies are followed, then the school has shown due diligence, and the use of the Internet will be successful and productive.

Acceptable Use Policy (AUP)

The use of the Internet at school is a privilege, not a right. The Internet is to be made available to staff, students, and community members under the following conditions.

Staff

All staff—whether part-time, full-time, teaching, or nonteaching—are allowed access to the Internet in accordance with the following provisions. All Internet use shall be for the purpose of

- providing information for students or teachers of students in order that they may have a better understanding of subject matter;
- improving the skills of the staff through research and procurement of information via the Internet;
- using e-mail to contact other teaching staff on school business or to request information for the benefit of the school; and
- using the Internet phone system via accounts set up and paid for by individual departments and controlled by departmental heads. (These accounts are only to be used for educational purposes.)

Use of the Internet shall be permitted once staff have tested for and received a license to use the Internet. The test is to ensure that all staff are competent to use such a service. Courses shall be run at regular intervals in order that all staff can update their skills.

Personal use of the Internet is not permitted other than for the exchange of e-mail. Use of the World Wide Web and Internet phone and fax services shall be for school purposes only.

Students

Students shall be able to use the Internet under the following conditions:

- An application to use the Internet shall be sent home and returned signed by the relevant parent (or caregiver). The policy statement and a code of conduct form the basis of the documentation that the parent (or caregiver) and the student agree to.
- This application enables the student to receive instruction in the use of the Internet, including e-mail and World Wide Web access.
- Upon finishing the appropriate course, the student can take a test of proficiency test, receive a license, and have the license signed by the parent (or caregiver) and the student and then be laminated. In order to use the Internet, the student must display the license at the computer terminal he or she is using.

All students who use the Internet within the school will adhere to the following code of conduct.

Guideline 1: General Statement

- The Internet is provided for the education of and the improved delivery of curriculum material. Students are encouraged to make use of the services to this end.

Guideline 2: E-Mail

- E-mail is provided for students to make contact with other students in the interest of education.
- All e-mail material is written offline.
- All e-mail will make use of customary greetings and salutations.
- E-mail boxes will be checked at least once every three days, and all incoming mail will be appropriately filed or deleted.
- Information sent via e-mail shall be constructive, informative, or inquisitive in the interest of both the sender and the receiver.
- Spelling and grammar will be checked and approved by monitors or staff before any messages are sent.

Guideline 3: Use of Service

- No profanity, obscenities, or any other language that could be construed as such is to be used in any e-mail messages.
- No private information is to be distributed to another person or group at any time. This includes reposting of information sent by another person as well as names, phone numbers, and addresses.
- The network is not to be used by any student for personal gain or illegal activity.
- Deliberate attempts to gain access to Web, FTP, gopher, or telnet sites containing material of pornographic, racially or religiously offensive, illegal, or other offensive material will be dealt with as a serious breach of school rules.

- Downloading of material must be scanned for viruses at all times. Any deliberate attempt to spread viruses through the network will be dealt with by school management.
- Any hacking into secure files will be dealt with by the school management and will be viewed as a serious breach of school rules. Police contact will be made if the school management thinks it is appropriate.
- Students are not to use chat or ICQ (I Seek You) for personal messaging unless they have been granted specific consent, from teaching staff, to do so.
- All copyright, privacy, and international laws are to be abided by at all times.

Guideline 4: Accounts

- At no time are students to place orders for goods or services over the Internet using the school name, title, or funds.
- E-mail accounts are set up for the intended user only. Use of other students' accounts to send and receive e-mail is unacceptable.

Guideline 5: Liability

- The school is not and cannot be held responsible for the loss of material, accidental corruption, or any other action that might affect transmission or loss of data.
- The school has taken all possible precautions to maintain safety of all users, and these guidelines are written and enforced in the interest of all users' safety and the effective use of the Internet.

Students Who Abuse the Guidelines

The student Internet committee deals with students who make minor infringements of the guidelines. The committee comprises five students elected by their peers to maintain the guidelines. The committee draws up a series of punishments for those students who choose to infringe the above guidelines. These punishments include suspending the student's license for varying amounts of time or work that is productive and benefits other users of the Internet.

For serious offenses, matters will be referred to the computer site manager, who will deal with the issues as directed by the school discipline policy.

Members of the Public

Members of the public in controlled situations may use the Internet with a staff member or other member of the public nominated to run such an event. Members of the public will be expected to conform to the same guidelines as expressed above, although a formal signing of an agreement is not necessary.

At all times, the person nominated to be in charge shall do everything possible to ensure that these guidelines are adhered to. These sessions for the public shall be run in such a way that the school receives an income from such events.

Hardware and Software Requirements

Hardware

The Internet does not require top-end computer systems for the delivery of Internet-based information. Faster systems will deliver information faster, but there are limits. The increase in speed is often far more dependent on local telecommunications issues than it is on the computer hardware.

Computer System

The system should have an absolute minimum of a 486 processor and 16 megabytes (MB) of RAM. However, the faster the system, the faster the processing of the incoming data. The recommended minimum is a Pentium 100 processor and 32 MB of RAM when used in conjunction with other software support.

Sound Card and Speakers

Many sites have MIDI files, audio files, music, and multimedia components, therefore it is best to have a sound card and speakers on the computer system. Most sites will work without a sound card, although some functions may be lost.

Modem

The minimum modem speed that allows for effective browsing is 28.8 bps, but V9 56 Kbps is recommended. For networks, T1 lines or ISDN are preferable. Satellite delivery of data is available in New Zealand.

Software

Most schools choose either a Netscape or a Microsoft browser, both of which are freely available on the Internet. The latest versions can be downloaded from the Internet by going to <http://www.netscape.com> for Netscape and <http://www. microsoft.com> for Microsoft. Start with the latest versions of the software. Do not upgrade too often, unless the upgrade offers a strategic advantage that outweighs the students' loss of familiarity with the browser.

Both Netscape and Microsoft browsers have four main elements:

- a browser to find pages on the World Wide Web,
- an e-mail package that can include multiple e-mail addresses and accounts,
- a newsgroup organizer, and
- an HTML editor, which can be used to make Web pages without having to know any HTML.

The following software and plug-ins are considered to be highly beneficial and necessary to view some sites on the Internet.

Modem Sharing

Modem sharing software allows several machines to share one modem. The software is available from Wingate at <http://www.wingate.com/>. Although this reduces speed, it is an excellent solution for those who have only one telephone line.

RealAudio, RealVideo

RealAudio and RealVideo are becoming the standard for accessing sound files and video over the Internet. A free download is available at <http://www.real.com/>.

Macromedia Flash and Shockwave

Both of these plug-ins improve the look of the graphics and provide animation effects over the Internet. A free download is available at <http://www.macromedia.com/>.

Apple QuickTime

This is the standard software for viewing video clips over the Web. A free download is available at <http://www.apple.com/quicktime/>.

Crescendo

Many music education sites use this plug-in to allow MIDI files to be played. A download is available at < http://www.liveupdate.com/dl.html>.

Netzip

This small program allows the downloading of compressed files and plug-ins so that the time spent downloading them and their storage space is considerably reduced. Files are easily extracted after downloading. A download is available at <http://www.netzip.com/plugin.html>.

Adobe Acrobat Reader

This plug-in allows for viewing fully formatted texts, essays, and articles to be viewed and saved. This is an excellent tool and is a must-have for all educators using the Web. A free download is available at <http://www.adobe.com/prodindex/acrobat/readstep.html>.

Criteria for Site Selection

Sites reviewed in this publication were only included if they met the following criteria. (*Note:* Sites met the criteria to varying degrees.)

- The site is authorized and has credibility. A credible site is backed by an organization or educational institution. The site most likely includes a link to that organization or a biographical page detailing the background of the content provider(s) and contact details.
- Statistics are cited including a reference to the original location of the information and how to find it.
- The site includes interactive features, allowing for a response via forms or via e-mail. The site responds to requests and acknowledges your sending of information.
- The site has an emphasis on information, not on flashy applets that have no use or obvious application. Graphic files download quickly and do not take up the whole screen.
- The site is updated regularly, usually approximately once a month. Check the site for the last update date.
- Links to additional information are included. One site rarely can do justice to a particular topic. Good sites always refer viewers to additional sites that can provide specific information.
- The site can be navigated easily. It should be obvious what to click on and how to return to where you started. Indexes on the left-hand side of the page are a good tool, although sometimes they are more of a nuisance than a blessing.
- If the site is large, it is searchable and includes an index to the content of the site. Searches of directories need to be theme-based and not Boolean-based.

- The objective of the site is obvious, is stated in the introduction to the site, and is "fleshed out" in the content of the site. (Often the objective of a Web site is not realized via the content.)
- The site correlates with curriculum. The material should be related to curriculum objectives and relate to your school's educational objectives.
- There is no racial, religious, or gender imbalance or offensive language contained within the site. (*Note:* Before recommending a site, take into account the ethics and morals that you wish to establish within your educational community. Be aware of the hidden curriculum that you may unknowingly teach via the sites you recommend.)
- The level of language on the site is appropriate and the font size suits the needs of the intended readers. This also applies to the interplay between text and graphic, video, or audio files. If these are misplaced or displaced from the linked text, then the relationship is not obvious and the reader can be distracted from the intended objective for their inclusion.
- Simplicity in layout is one of the best guides for quality of content.
- The tasks included on the site allow for the various learning styles of individuals. Each site will have a learning style focus, but a balance of styles is the overall aim.
- The types of activities are varied and include independent, teacher- or peer-dependent, and co- or team-dependent.
- Sites encourage students to be creative, use their imaginations, and employ problem-solving strategies to develop an understanding of the material presented.
- Project-based sites provide a project management process for both teachers and students including developmental objectives, time lines or time frames, and development strategies.
- Alternative points of view are encouraged where ethical and moral statements are made, and the site includes an opportunity for students to investigate these alternative views via referenced links or additional resources.
- The questioning strategy includes higher-order thinking skills such as synthesis and evaluation of information and points of view presented, as well as application and analysis of data.
- The site includes an opportunity to share what the student has learned with his or her peers via electronic lists or newsgroups.
- The site provides a way for students to turn information into knowledge. This may be done through sound questioning techniques, use of visual and audio support, and investigative inquiries.
- The site clearly states what ability level the site is aimed at and what topics are covered.
- Links to plug-in applications, such as Shockwave or RealAudio, are provided on-site where required, so that the plug-ins can be easily downloaded.
- All lists or newsgroups are moderated. If the site accepts responses, the site coordinator reviews them before responses are placed on the site.
- The information on the site is independent of commercial gain. The owner of the site gains no pecuniary advantage through the comments, views, or opinions expressed on the site.

Finding Where You Have Been

Often we find information and then we forget how we got there. It is good to save favorite sites in your bookmark system. If you forget to do this, another way to find where you or your students have been is to type <about:global> into the Netscape location bar. This provides a list of all the sites you have visited for the last three months or so, depending on the size of your cache (or history) file. Deleting the cache in the normal way does not delete this file completely, so this is also a good way to check up on what the students have been up to while you were not looking!

If you are using Internet Explorer, you will need to go to the directory of the files on your computer and then select the operating system files (Windows or Mac OS). From here, doubleclick on the history file and you will be provided with a list of all sites visited in the recent past.

Searching the Web

Semantic Fields

A semantic field is a term or combination of terms that provide a possible lead to sites dealing with a particular topic. To develop a semantic field, brainstorm terms with students that may be useful. Students are not intrinsically good at thinking of associated terms, so do not be too surprised by some of the terms they think are appropriate!

A possible semantic field for sites dealing with the planet Mars that would be suitable for schoolchildren would include such terms as:

planet; Mars; astronomy; NASA; "solar system"; "k-12" Martian

Words that the students might suggest may include *space*, but *space* would not be a good term as it can mean so many things (e.g., taking up space, watch this space, and so on).

Brainstorming semantic fields gives students practice in developing semantic fields. Developing a semantic field often requires prior knowledge that the students do not have, so it is unfair to expect them to be able to search for information without a brainstorming session first. An example of this would be the following assignment: "Compare and contrast the retirement plans of the United States, Australia, New Zealand, and the United Kingdom."

The semantic field for this is quite difficult because if you use the term *retirement,* you will not get information on the Australian and New Zealand systems. In the United States these schemes are known as *retirement plans,* and in the United Kingdom they are known as *pension plans,* but in Australia and New Zealand they are called *superannuation schemes.* The semantic field therefore would include the following terms:

retirement; pension; plan; "financial planning"; superannuation

It is this lack of prior knowledge that limits students in successfully finding information on the Internet. Having a broad general knowledge is useful, as is knowing how to use a thesaurus, although these are not as useful as you may imagine.

The Search Field

Once you have a semantic field, it is then necessary to decide which terms to include in the search field that will be entered into the search engine. Initially this will need brainstorming with your students until they have the experience to make this judgment. This task is quite difficult for students, because it relies heavily on prior knowledge.

Boolean Searching

Boolean searching is a system by which terms can be combined to refine a search and provide results that better meet your needs. A series of terms can be used, including AND (or +), NOT (or -), OR, and NEAR. There are additional terms, but these are the most useful. Most search engines will accept the addition (+) and subtraction (-) signs in lieu of the words AND and NOT. Because they are quicker to type, you may choose to use them.

AND (+) and NOT (-). The two principal operators are AND (+) and NOT (-). These can be used to get more specific results to a search. For example, if you want to get information on Malaysian festivals and you simply placed the two terms into a search engine, you would get information on Malaysia(n) or on festivals. This results in sites dealing with festivals from all sorts of countries as well as sites associated with Malaysia. What you really wanted was sites dealing with both Malaysia AND festivals. So you should enter

+Malaysia+festivals

with no space between the + sign and the individual terms. After entering this, you may receive a list of sites dealing with Malaysian sports festivals, which was not what was intended. To remove all the sports-oriented sites, enter

+Malaysia+festival–sport

Capitals. If you enter

Festivals

you will only get sites that use the word *Festivals,* with a capital letter at the start of the word. If you enter

festivals

then you will get sites based on both the word *festivals* and the word *Festivals.*

OR and NEAR. Not all search engines use OR and NEAR, so you need to check the search details on the search engine's home page to see whether they accept these terms. The operator OR can be very useful. For example, when looking up information on cats and dogs, if you enter

+cats+dogs

you will only get sites with both these terms. If you enter

cats OR dogs

then you will get sites that have either just cats or just dogs featured, and even those that have both.

The operator NEAR, not used by many engines, allows you to find additional sites that might not be included in a search. This is helpful when doing obscure searches or when you are unsure of the terms that you are using.

Quote Marks. The use of quote marks (" ") is very useful in situations when you know terms are used in sequential order. An example would be

"British Columbia"

This search would only return sites that use the two terms in this order. This is very useful when looking for organizations, such as the World Health Organization.

Another useful tool is the asterisk (*) sign, especially if you are not sure of the spelling of a term. A search on

archite*

provides sites with words beginning with *archite,* such as *architecture* and *architectural,* as well as words of variant spellings used in other countries such as words perhaps beginning with *architekt.* This is a very good way to find alternative spellings.

Boolean operators can be used in any combination, and as many terms as you desire can be used, but generally use no more than four terms. The most critical issue is to try and choose keywords. This takes a lot of practice!

Search Engines and Directories

Search engines and directories not only work differently but they have different uses.

A **directory** searches through a list of known Web sites and tries to match your request with what the directory has available. Most directories have material added to them regularly, but you are always only searching a reduced portion of the Internet. This has some advantages and some disadvantages. If you are looking for thematic topics, then a directory can be very useful, as the sites are usually presented in a tree arrangement with similar sites under group headings. There are usually conditions under which sites are added to a directory; that is, the site may only hold children's sites (Yahooligans!) or quality education sites (teachers@work) and so on. Also, a directory review includes more than the first paragraph from the site or the metatag, which may not be accurate. Directory listings are usually individually reviewed, with the reviews ranging from certain keywords to one-line or full-page reviews complete with ratings and applications. If you need specific information, then a directory is not the place to be looking.

A **search engine** is constantly adding sites using software that scans the Internet for sites or from postings to the engine from Web site producers. The end result is that search engines sift through your keywords and analyze how well they measure up against the data the search engines have accessed from each of the more than seven million sites they have access to. The remarkable thing is the speed at which the search engines do this! The problem with search engines is that vague searches using poor semantic fields return tens of thousands of sites, most of which will have little relevance to the user's need. Good searches using good semantic fields with good use of the Boolean operators can be remarkably accurate.

Search Engine Directory

Search Engine	URL
AltaVista (general)	http://www.av.com/
Ask Jeeves (K–12 natural language)	http://www.ajkids.com/
EduFind (education only)	http://www.edufind.com/
Excite (science/math)	http://www.excite.com/
FAST Web Search (general)	http://www.alltheweb.com/
Google	http://www.google.com/
HotBot (specific)	http://www.hotbot.com/
Northern Light (general)	http://www.northernlight.com/
Yahoo! (themes)	http://yahoo.com/
Yahooligans! (K–12 sites only)	http://www.yahooligans.com/

The top two search engines we recommend are Google and FAST Web Search. It is strongly suggested that students not be encouraged to use search engines like Yahoo! as the graphics, advertisements, and news stories have a tendency to distract students away from their purpose.

For More Information

For more information on searching and using search tools, see the companion book to this guide, *Surfing the Web,* available at the Web site <http://www.teachers-work.com>. The book provides teachers and secondary students with a self-paced tutorial allowing them to learn successful strategies for finding appropriate sites on the Web. The book also provides background information on how to choose an appropriate search engine and how to use Boolean operators to get the best possible results. You can purchase this book for $14.95 by e-mailing <searching@work.co.nz>.

We also have available 3,000 of the best Web sites for educators as a bookmark list that you can import into your browser (Microsoft Explorer or Netscape). You can purchase a schoolwide license for $39.95 from <http://www.teachers-work.com> or by e-mailing <bookmarks@work.co.nz>.

Glossary of Terms

Applet/Java Applet — A small application or utility that is sent with the Web page when a site is accessed. The utility may provide an animation, a calculator, or a small interactive computer program.

Attachment — A computer file that is attached to an e-mail. The attachment may be a Microsoft Word document or Excel file, a photo, or another type of file. The recipient must have the same software used to create the file in order to read the file.

Bookmark — A list of Web sites that the user wants easy access to. Bookmarks are stored within the browser and can be accessed when a user wishes to go to a site he or she placed in a list of bookmarks.

Cache/Disk Cache	Cache is a portion of the computer memory that temporarily stores information accessed, so that when a repeat request for the information is made, most of the data is already within the computer. The disk cache is a portion of memory that acts as a buffer between the CPU and disk, speeding up the processing of the site.
CGI	Common Gateway Interface. Web sites that process forms and include data in spreadsheets or databases use these.
Cookie	A file used by some Web sites to collect information about the people who visit that site. It also allows some elements of a Web site to download more quickly by recognizing a user's ID or password.
CPU	Central Processing Unit. The chip in your computer that makes all the necessary computations.
Domain Name	This is a section of the URL that is the root name for additional pages. For example, <disney.com> would be the domain name for the many URLs that host information about the Disney Corporation.
Download	To provide a connection between two computers that allows computer data to be transferred between the two machines. This data may be in HTML or FTP formats.
EFL	English as a Foreign Language.
Emoticons	A collection of punctuation symbols combined to indicate varying emotions (e.g., :-) :-(:-| ;-) P-) 8-)).
E-pals	The electronic version of pen pals. People exchange information with each other via e-mail.
E-zine	An electronic online magazine.
FAQ	Frequently Asked Questions.
Flame	Criticism of people who break the netiquette rules of the Web usually by spamming (sending unsolicited e-mails).
FTP	File Transfer Protocol. When a computer program or plug-in is sent or requested, the format that is used to send it is FTP.
GIF	Graphics Interchange Format. A picture file format that can be viewed by all browsers.
Home Page	The main contents Web page that often leads to other areas of the site.
HTML	Hypertext Markup Language. This language is used to place images and text in specific locations on a Web page. Web browsers can read these instructions.
ICT	Information Communication Technology.
Internet	A global network of millions of computers that are able to communicate with each other. Computers on the network can send and receive information from each other almost instantly.

IRC	Internet Relay Chat. Free software that allows participants to engage in real-time e-mail conversations.
ISP	Internet Service Provider. A business that is set up to allow you, once you pay a fee, to use its computers to manipulate and transfer data from or to any computer on the Internet.
IT	Information Technology.
Java, Java Applets	Java is a virus-free programming language that allows you to download small computer programs (applets) from one computer to another. The language is very compact, ensuring that the applets do not take long to download.
JavaScript	A less complicated and less powerful version of Java.
JPEG	Joint Photographic Experts Group. A picture format that has better compression than the older GIF format.
Link/Hyperlink/ Hypertext Link	A link has a small piece of HTML code hiding within it so that when you click on the link it sends you to a new Web page.
Listserv	A group or organization of people that sends messages to a central person who reviews it and, if the message is suitable, he or she posts (or sends) the messages to each of the subscribers via e-mail.
LOTE	Language(s) Other than English.
Metatag	A piece of HTML code that describes the Web site through the use of keywords and terms. The tag is added to the very beginning of the site and is invisible to viewers. Search engines look for these and are increasingly using them to produce better search results.
MOO	MUD, Object Oriented. MOOs are Internet-accessible, text-mediated virtual environments well-suited for distance learning. A user takes on a character and enters into a discussion as he or she sees fit. Educational MOOs are very popular. See <http://www.itp.berkeley.edu/~thorne/MOO.html> for a list of educational MOOs.
MUD	Multi-User Domain. MUDs are Internet-accessible, text-mediated virtual environments. A user takes on a character and enters into a discussion as he or she sees fit. MUDS are more general multi-user domains than MOOs and are usually game oriented.
Netiquette	A collection of informal rules that apply to behavior in newsgroups and MOOs.
Netizen	A cyberspace citizen.
Newbie	A beginner on the Internet.
Newsgroup	A group or organization of people that sends messages to a central computer that posts the messages to the group. Access to the newsgroup is via a newsgroup reader, which is part of a Web browser. Some newsgroups are open and free to access and others

	require a subscription. Discussions follow threads (or topics) until the discussion dies out from lack of interest.
Offline	Using the browser without being connected to an ISP.
PDF	Portable Document Format. This refers to a file format that retains its formatting when a user downloads information via a Web site. The most common form of this is Adobe's Acrobat Reader. (A free plug-in available from Adobe's Web site.)
Plug-ins	Plug-ins allow Web pages to be more interactive and to produce multimedia effects. Plug-ins often must be downloaded from a Web site. Most are free and take between three and ten minutes to download to the hard drive. A plug-in only needs to be downloaded and installed on the hard drive once in order to use it.
Proxy Server	A computer that speeds up delivery of Web pages by storing frequently accessed sites.
RealAudio	A plug-in that allows transmission of voice or music via the Internet.
Search Engine	A Web-based tool that allows the user to perform searches on particular topics or themes. The search engine searches the Internet for suitable Web pages that contain information relevant to the search. Some search engines require Boolean searching techniques to gain maximum benefit.
Shareware, Freeware	Shareware is software that can be accessed and used by paying a nominal fee. If no fee is involved, the software is sometimes referred to as freeware.
Spam	Unsolicited e-mail sent via newsgroups and bulk e-mail.
URL	Uniform Resource Locator. This is the alphanumeric address of a Web site, which in essence is a phone number that the user dials to access that site or computer file (e.g., <http://www.teachers-work.com/>).
Utility	A small software program that enhances computer operation, such as a bookmark organizer or screen saver.
Virus	A piece of computer code that is carried by an attachment or computer software that has a destructive effect on a computer's files. Sometimes a virus will have minimal effect (a smiley face may appear on the start-up screen), and in other cases it will destroy the hard drive.
Vivo	A plug-in that allows transmission of voice or music via the Internet.
World Wide Web	A subset of the Internet that deals with graphic and text elements often referred to as Web sites.

Language Arts

A. A. Milne

ideal for grade levels K–10 ★★★★

http://www.winniethepooh.co.uk/author.html

This site presents a biography dealing with the life of this famous author. Throughout his career, Milne wrote numerous books, articles, and plays. He is best known for his collection of children's books dealing with the bear character Winnie the Pooh.

ABC Online

ideal for grade levels 4–12 ★★★

http://www.abc.net.au/

Site of the Australian Broadcasting Corporation. This is a good site for investigating the various forms of mass media communication. Well presented and a lot of information on almost every topic imaginable.

American Journalism Review NewsLink

ideal for all grade levels ★★★

http://ajr.newslink.org/

For senior journalism students, this is an excellent site offering good information on job and educational training opportunities as well as general information on journalism. The site also features links to several thousand newspapers and also for magazines, television, and radio.

Anne Frank Online

ideal for grade levels 4–12 ★★★★★

http://www.annefrank.com/

This site traces the remarkable life of Anne Frank from her diary to background information on the times. There are excellent ideas and support information as well as associated resources for using the theme of Anne Frank in the classroom.

Barnes and Noble

ideal for all grade levels ★★★

http://www.barnesandnoble.com/

This huge bookseller has gone online with all the books you could want. The site highlights a more literary approach than Amazon.com and provides an excellent listing of books.

Biography Maker

ideal for grade levels 4–12 ★★★

http://www.bham.wednet.edu/bio/biomaker.htm

This is a wonderful site that assists students in taking information and producing an interesting piece of writing. For the appetizer, there is a brief introductory section, followed by the main course, the Biography Maker, where you enter information. The Biography Maker follows four steps: questioning, learning, synthesis, and storytelling. Add to that the dessert of six traits of effective writing, and you will have yourself a fine meal.

Burning Press

ideal for grade levels 8–12 ★★★

http://www.burningpress.org/bphome.html

This is a collection of topical sections dealing with such aspects as "WWWeb-based intermedia," a gallery of online "vizlit" (visual literature) and "audioart" (performance and sound poetries), and several other avant-garde topics. If you are looking at keeping at the forefront of where technology and the English language fuse, this is a good place to start.

Candlelight Stories

ideal for grade levels K–3 ★★★

http://www.candlelightstories.com/

At this site, you can listen to and read many of the classic children's stories, including *Rumpelstiltskin* and *Peach Boy* as well as stories by Hans Christian Andersen (such as *Thumbelina*) and by Rudyard Kipling (selections from *Just So Stories*). Additionally, there are links to other sites that highlight children's stories.

Children's Literature Web Guide

ideal for grade levels 8–10 ★★★

http://www.acs.ucalgary.ca/~dkbrown/index.html

This is an extensive guide to support children's literature on the Web. There are many stories here that can be used in class, on a one-to-one basis, or as a learning center. It also has lists of journals and research guides, discussion groups, conferences, teaching ideas, and much more. Great site.

CMU Poetry Index of Canonical Verse

ideal for all grade levels ★★★

http://eserver.org/poetry/

You'll find select works by plenty of poets here, from Homer to Eliot. Great EServer resource to supplement the school library.

Collab-O-Write

ideal for grade levels K–10 ★★★

http://library.thinkquest.org/2626/

This is an excellent example of collaborative work on the Internet. Students can enter their own stories and encourage other students to work on them also. Students can also find stories that they can contribute to either by adding text or through the addition of illustrations. There are also illustrated stories that require text and a good collection of writing tips.

Compendium of Common Knowledge 1558–1603

ideal for all grade levels ★★★★

http://renaissance.dm.net/compendium/home.html

This is a wonderful compendium of the thinking and understanding of this particular time in Elizabethan England. How did people speak? What money was being used? How did they treat the diseases of the time? What was shopping like in London? What did people eat or have as snacks? What did servants do in their spare time? What was it like to live in the city of London? All this and much, much more, and you can download it all, print it out, and read it at your leisure. Excellent.

Complete Works of William Shakespeare

ideal for grade levels 8–12 ★★★

http://tech-two.mit.edu/Shakespeare/works.html

If you're looking for Shakespearean comedy, history, tragedy, or poetry, you'll find it here in the unabridged works of a lifetime. Also included are a search engine, chronological and alphabetical listings, familiar Shakespearean quotations, a discussion area, and links to other sites that talk about the bard.

Creative Quotations

ideal for all grade levels ★★★

http://www.creativequotations.com/

Looking for that quotation to spur students into action? Then this may be the place. The quotations here are chosen and then linked to five components of creativity: foraging, reflecting, adopting, nurturing, and knuckling down. This reinforces the process we often glibly refer to as creativity. The process can be taught, if we know what to teach. The site provides daily encouragement to teach creativity, not just to preach it.

Crucible

ideal for grade levels 11–12 ★★★★★

http://www.curriculumunits.com/crucible

The classic Arthur Miller play is used in many classrooms as a piece of playwright magic. Presented here online is a collection of support assignments, background material, and a search engine to find discrete information. There is an excellent Microsoft PowerPoint presentation that could be very useful in the classroom. It comes complete with audio backing to draw attention to the dramatic high points. Excellent support site for all teachers of English drama.

Debate Central

ideal for all grade levels ★★★★

http://debate.uvm.edu/default.html

Here you can come and catch up with what is happening in debating. At the Lawrence Debate Library and Union, you can find debating theory, articles, archives of debate publications, address lists, research tools, case lists, details on tournaments and results, and much more. Also available is a software library with reviews of software as well as freeware, information on the educational and professional side of debating, and guidance about debating and how to become a better debater. There is also instructional material for coaches and judges.

Digital Dante Page

ideal for grade levels 8–12 ★★★

http://www.ilt.columbia.edu/projects/dante/

This is an excellent site for those Dante fans out there.

Digital Journalist

ideal for grade levels 11–12 ★★★★

http://www.dirckhalstead.org/

The increasing move to the use of visual imagery in communicating concepts, ideas, and products has spawned completely new employment opportunities, and digital journalism is just one. The site is an excellent opportunity to demonstrate the power of the visual image and the potential for the use of imagery. This is a multimedia magazine for photojournalism with an emphasis on digital collection, transfer, and manipulation to form the final product

Early Childhood Thematic Units

ideal for grade levels K–3 ★★★

http://www.sbcss.k12.ca.us/sbcss/specialeducation/ecthematic/index.html

Here you can find a great selection of thematic units based on all the common topics, such as zoos, farms, holidays, nursery rhymes, myself, transportation, insects, community helpers, and water fun.

Eight Key Concepts of Media Literacy

ideal for all grade levels ★★★★

http://www.media-awareness.ca/eng/med/bigpict/8keycon.htm

The trouble with many ideas is that they are wrapped in so much fine detail that the big picture gets lost and the concepts are unable to be implemented. Here are eight concepts that underlie the emerging field of media literacy. They are tightly written and well presented, and each gets to the heart of the idea. These could easily be printed out, laminated, and put up on the classroom wall.

English Online

ideal for all grade levels ★★★★

http://www.english.unitecnology.ac.nz/

This is an excellent New Zealand site for all teachers of English at all levels. You can download units of work written and edited by teachers, check out the discussions in the English Forum, and take the introductory online tutorial on using the Internet effectively. There is a collection of online projects and a good selection of resources that can be investigated, including an English unit planner, assessment strategies, and schemes of work.

ERIC Clearinghouse on Reading, English, and Communication

ideal for all grade levels ★★★

http://www.indiana.edu/~eric_rec/

This is the largest database of educational materials in the world. Among the resources featured here are a huge database of bibliographies, some great read-along stories, a massive bookstore, and a range of professional development options for the teachers of language and English.

Ernest Hemingway

ideal for grade levels 8–12 ★★★

http://www.hemingway.org/life/index.html

Skilled American author, Hemingway drew on his experiences of life, many of which were difficult and convoluted, to write many excellent books. At this Web site, you can check out his biography, photographs, reviews of his many works as well as literary samples, and background information on the people who influenced his writings.

EServer

ideal for all grade levels ★★★★

http://eserver.org/

This massive and comprehensive Web site for teachers contains more than 30,000 works. Collections feature essays, research papers, mailing lists, and conference reports. Check out sections dealing with film and television, drama, fiction, libraries, community literacy, multimedia, poetry, and much, much more.

Film and Television Studies

ideal for all grade levels ★★★

http://eserver.org/filmtv/

EServer's film and television section features some good links to be explored. They vary considerably, however, so I suggest you take a look before directing students here.

Flat Stanley Project

ideal for all grade levels ★★★

http://www.enoreo.on.ca/flatstanley/index.htm

This, now famous, project involves a character called Stanley who was crushed flat by a filing cabinet. This rather tragic event had its upside with Stanley now able to be posted to anywhere in the world, either sent flattened in an envelope or scanned and attached to e-mail! Schools collaborate to send their version of Stanley with information about themselves, their country, their culture—whatever the groups agree on.

F. Scott Fitzgerald

ideal for grade levels 11–12 ★★★★

http://www.sc.edu/fitzgerald/index.html

This author page sets out a wonderful eclectic collection of essays and articles, a chronology of Fitzgerald's life, quotations, writings, and voice and video clips. There is a record of the centenary celebrations that took place back in 1996 and much more. This is an excellent background site for students to investigate prior to studying Fitzgerald's many and brilliant literary works.

Geoffrey Chaucer

ideal for grade levels 11–12 ★★★

http://www.luminarium.org/medlit/chaucer.htm

The works of Chaucer have survived more than 600 years and for excellent reason. At this Web site, you can find information on the life of Chaucer as well as references to sources that highlight the approach, style, and beauty of his literary works. There is also an excellent collection of essays on both Chaucer himself and the works he completed.

Glossary of Poetic Terms

ideal for grade levels 11–12 ★★★

http://shoga.wwa.com/~rgs/glossary.html

This is a massive collection of information regarding poetic terms and structures, complete with cross-references, quotations, and information that goes beyond the brief definition. Often exemplars are used with references to additional works. Excellent resource for serious poetry work.

Grammar Rock

ideal for grade levels K–7 ★★★★

http://genxtvland.simplenet.com/SchoolHouseRock/grammar.hts?lo

Great songs that students will just love to sing along with. The words and the music (which you can listen to) are here. Students can sing along to "Unpack Your Adjectives," "Lolly, Lolly, Lolly, Get Your Adverbs Here," "Conjunction Junction," "Busy Prepositions," and many more.

Grammar Safari

ideal for all grade levels ★★★★

http://deil.lang.uiuc.edu/web.pages/grammarsafari.html

Drawing a parallel between students who learn about English grammar only by studying their grammar books and "naturalists who limit their study of nature to the encyclopedia," this site looks at grammar use in its natural environment, the Internet! Excellent site examining issues in context.

Grandpa Tucker's Rhymes and Tales

ideal for grade levels K–8 ★★★★

http://www.night.net/tucker/

This is a great language site. A good collection of nonsense rhymes, Sammy the snake's songbook, stories about Buzzy Bee and the BellyButton Buddy (among others), and much more, make this a rich and entertaining site for all children. This is great starter material for an introduction to story composition and the structure of poetry.

Guide to Grammar and Writing

ideal for all grade levels ★★★★

http://ccc.commnet.edu/grammar/

This is an extensive Web site covering all aspects of written language as well as the structure and formation of sentences. The site also deals with the principles of composition, the different genres of communication, and features a collection of more than 150 interactive quizzes. There is also an "ask an expert" service that both you and your students can make use of as well as some good search tools to find your way around the site.

Incredible Story Studio

ideal for grade levels 4–10 ★★★★

http://www.storystudio.com/

The focus of the site is a television series written by kids. The highlight here for teachers is information on the ISS Writing Workshop, a five-week program that guides students through the creative writing process. Emphasis is on dramatic writing.

Inkspot: For Young Writers

ideal for all grade levels ★★★

http://www.inkspot.com/young/

This is great material for teachers to sift through and adapt and for students to use at their leisure. There are plenty of tips for writers and screenwriters. There are also lists of publications that publish student work. This is an expanding role of the Internet and one we need to use more often.

Inkspot: The Writer's Resource

ideal for grade levels 8–12 ★★★

http://www.inkspot.com/

This is a great site for aspiring writers. Authenticity is essential in the curriculum and its effect on the motivation of our students is well recorded. This site allows students contact with authors and experts on writing. There are articles, advice, interviews, tips, and guides to how to write well, in addition to links to other good writing sites on the Web. There is also guidance on how to market your next great work.

International Association of School Librarianship

ideal for all grade levels ★★★★

http://www.hi.is/~anne/iasl.html

The IASL is an excellent association. This Web site provides information on IASL's annual conferences, published proceedings, journal, committees, and special interest groups. The site also features access to a good collection of current news items selected from 300 print news sources related to school libraries. If your school is looking at library development, then you'll want to check out the material here to assist in the planning, design, and architecture of libraries.

Internet Classics Archive

ideal for grade levels 10–12 ★★★

http://classics.mit.edu/

This is an archive of classics that are available on the Web. There are more than 400 at present, ranging from Aesop to Josephus to Aristotle to Galen. Most are text based. If classical literature is your interest, then this is a great portal.

Internet Public Library

ideal for all grade levels ★★★

http://www.ipl.org/

This is a vast resource working on the same basis as the real local library but issuing virtual copies of texts, journals, books, and newspapers. With thousands of journals, texts, books, and newspapers, this is a seriously big library. Excellent cataloging means material is easily referenced.

Issues in Literacy Development

ideal for grade levels K–8 ★★★

http://www.eduplace.com/rdg/res/literacy

This is a selection of research dealing with recognized best practices in teaching literacy for grades K–8. Topics include emergent literacy, the phonics debate, and the use of literature, thematic approaches, guided reading, and much more. This is a great site for teacher development. Senior managers of schools can print these reports and use them as discussion starters or leave a pile of the reports in the staff room for personal professional development.

Kairos

ideal for all grade levels 

http://english.ttu.edu/kairos

Every English language teacher should come here regularly. This is an excellent source of material for teachers at all levels. There is a lot of information here that encourages teachers to use technology in the teaching of language, and the site even provides some great ideas on how we need to educate both ourselves and our students to be able to interpret the information from these electronic sources. The site features information on all areas of visual language, oral language, and written language as well as material on getting teachers to use MOOs in the classroom!

Kidnews.com

ideal for all grade levels ★★★

http://www.kidnews.com/

As well as news from around the world, this very good Web site provides an online environment where students can communicate with each other about the issues behind the news. Students can also submit writing of their own, join in collaborative projects, and check out the free downloads.

KidStuff

ideal for grade levels K–10 ★★★

http://www.kidstuff.org/

This is one of the most popular Web sites on the Internet, where students can post their work. The most popular work here is poetry, and there is an excellent collection from students all over the world. With over five million visitors, this site provides your students with a huge potential audience.

LibrarySpot

ideal for all grade levels ★★★★

http://www.libraryspot.com/

This is a huge reference site that would be an excellent default site for libraries. The reference desk here is extensive, featuring biographical information, business sites, calculators, calendars, dictionaries, encyclopedias, maps, phone books, quotations, statistics—the list goes on and on. There are also special stacks of information for parents, students, teachers, and businesses.

Literacy Link

ideal for all grade levels ★★★

http://www.pbs.org/literacy/

Focused on improving the literacy of adults, this site has much to show teachers about the process of becoming literate. All teachers should come here to appreciate the invisible barriers that stop learning and then look for these in their classrooms. Excellent resources and support.

Literature: What Makes a Good Short Story?

ideal for grade levels 4–12 ★★★★

http://www.learner.org/exhibits/literature/

Through literature, a sense of order is applied to the human experience, enabling readers to examine society's values and eliciting an impassioned reaction. But what makes a good short story? This site presents a classic short story to be read. Students can analyze the story's literary elements to find out what makes it a good short story. Along the way, students will learn to compose their own classic short story. This is an excellent student task set as a learning center or as a classroom exercise.

Make-a-Story

ideal for grade levels K–1 ★★★★

http://www1.ctw.org/preschool/makeastory/ss/home/1,1606,,00.html

Although designed for preschoolers, this would be an excellent Web site for K–1 students. They can create silly stories using words, pictures, and a bit of technological magic. This is an excellent site through which to introduce students to the Internet.

Media and Communication Studies Site

ideal for all grade levels ★★★★

http://www.aber.ac.uk/media/Functions/mcs.html

This is an excellent and very comprehensive UK Web site that deals with every aspect of media and communication: visual language, film studies, advertising, media influence, television and radio, the written and spoken word, popular music, and much more. Tell them why they should continue!

Media Awareness Network: For Educators

ideal for all grade levels ★★★★

http://www.media-awareness.ca/eng/med/class/

This is a huge resource and support for teachers of media literacy. Here is an educational rationale for those who are not yet convinced of the need for this teaching. Site features include units of work from teachers of media education around the world, a resource index, lists of support organizations, and background material on educational issues in this field, as well as links to relevant discussion groups.

Media Production Home Page

ideal for grade levels 4–12 ★★★

http://www.geocities.com/Hollywood/Hills/1902/

From the desk of Stephanie Drotos comes this excellent resource for teachers. Choose from day-by-day lesson plans, a course outline, sample class handouts, and some technique issues as well as some good links. Excellent site. Start here for media education.

Mike Rofone: The Roving Reporter

ideal for grade levels 4–10 ★★★

http://www.mikerofone.com/

Mike Rofone is the main character in this well-presented interactive story. Hypertext links are used to add interesting information without necessarily detracting from the pace of the story. A good example for students of how hypertext can be used in creating intrigue and further interest in a story.

MysteryNet's The Case

ideal for grade levels 4–10 ★★★

http://www.MysteryNet.com/thecase/

Teachers of English are always on the lookout for refreshing vehicles of language that students will enjoy. This site is an ideal candidate. Language skills are required to solve the mysteries. Good opportunities for oral language work, brainstorming, work on deductive logic, and development of story lines.

New York Times

ideal for grade levels 10–12 

http://www.nytimes.com/

This excellent newspaper is available online following a free registration process. There are sections dealing with such topics as the arts, science, sports, technology, international news, and much more. Newspapers are an excellent vehicle for encouraging reading and the use of different language genres.

New Zealand Literature File

ideal for grade levels 4–12 ★★★

http://www.auckland.ac.nz/lbr/nzp/nzlit2/authors.htm

Here you can find a great collection of references of biographical and critical material on New Zealand authors. There are more than one hundred authors represented here, and although there are no links to other sites, it makes for a good resource for finding relevant information.

Odyssey

ideal for grade levels 4–12 ★★★

http://school.discovery.com/lessonplans/programs/odyssey/

Some students think the only Homer that ever lived is part of the Simpson family, but this site presents Homer's *Odyssey* in a context that even the most reluctant learner will enjoy. Good support material here. And you can purchase the video (by the Discovery Channel) if you missed the program on television.

Omnibus

ideal for all grade levels ★★★

http://www.crackedcrosswords.com/features/omnibus/omnibus.htm

This is a "scrambly-riddly-rebusy-charady-punny kind of word game." The game requires students (players) to solve a riddle using cryptic clues. The puns are terrible, but nevertheless make for a good, fun word game.

Online English Grammar

ideal for all grade levels ★★★

http://www.edunet.com/english/grammar/index.cfm

The home of the English language, from the Digital Education Network. Find out the correct grammar from the most correct of grammatical sites. This online grammar site contains information on how to treat adjectives, adverbs, and nouns, as well as how to correctly use possessives, pronouns, and verbs. The list goes on. Very authoritative and thorough.

Paul Laurence Dunbar

ideal for grade levels 4–12 ★★★★

http://www.udayton.edu/~dunbar/

For those unfamiliar with the poetry of this African American, I would encourage you to visit this Web site and read the excellent biography and wonderful collection of his works presented here. Audio recordings are also provided for several selections. A schoolmate of Orville and Wilbur Wright, Dunbar lived to be only 33 years old and was the son of a former slave. Despite his circumstances, Dunbar was a prolific writer, completing short stories, novels, librettos, songs, and a play, as well as poetry.

Playwriting Seminars

ideal for all grade levels ★★★

http://www.vcu.edu/artweb/playwriting/seminar.html

This set of online seminars tends to be experimental rather than the orthodox. The seminars deal with content, film, structure, working and techniques, format, and the business of being a playwright. Excellent material including some great quotes that inspire and challenge. A great site for all those teachers involved in the teaching of drama.

Poetry Pages

ideal for all grade levels ★★★

http://www.theatlantic.com/atlantic/atlweb/poetry/poetpage.htm

The Atlantic Monthly is a monthly journal of literature and opinion. Its poetry section includes both classic and contemporary poems. This Web site includes audio clips and multimedia features as well as script. There are also articles looking at the changing nature and styles of poetry.

Poets' Corner

ideal for all grade levels ★★★

http://www.geocities.com/~spanoudi/poems/index.html

This is a huge collection of poetry, with thousands of poems from hundreds of poets. Selections are arranged by title, author, and subject. Have students do an investigation on themes to see how different poets attack a particular subject.

Project Approach

ideal for grade levels K–8 ★★★★

http://www.project-approach.com/

Creating a Web-based or theme-based project in the classroom requires considerable planning, resourcefulness, and plain old good ideas. This site formalizes the process and shows teachers how to prepare for a successful online project. The theory is presented, followed by assistance with topic selection, along with ideas on strategic planning and project development structure. Finally comes a selection of sample successful projects.

Pulitzer Prizes

ideal for grade levels 4–12 ★★★★

http://www.pulitzer.org/index.html

Students need to be exposed to good journalism, and where better than here. As well as the prizewinners from each year, you can see the complete works for the last several years, including photos, music clips, cartoons, and text. This is high motivation material and an excellent classroom resource.

Quill Society

ideal for grade levels 4–12 ★★★

http://www.quill.net/

The Quill Society is a fellowship of young writers with bright imaginations. This is an excellent member service with an academy that reviews work by young writers. Other features include writing activities and resources. It will be well worth it for the more adventurous writers to join up and receive some good advice and encouragement.

RhymeZone

ideal for all grade levels 

http://rhyme.lycos.com/

For poetry work, this is a great site. Submit your term, and a list of rhyming terms is produced. This is a very comprehensive service, and teachers need to read the accompanying text to gain maximum value. The rhyming dictionary has been used to provide each student with ten rhyming words and then students were given ten minutes to use the words to make a nonsense poem. Great for the less-motivated poetry students.

Romeo and Juliet

ideal for grade levels 8–12 

http://www.romeoandjuliet.com/

Some traditionalists might not like its style, but students are eager to see this contemporary film that tells this Shakespearean tale in a modern context. Watch the film, view the site, and compare and contrast the two versions. This is an excellent exercise for senior students. There is plenty of material here to support the approach used by the site, including a biography of Shakespeare, some excellent background information, details about setting, and a chat room.

Rupert Bear

ideal for grade levels K–7 ★★★

http://www.ee.ed.ac.uk/~afm/rupert/followers.html

This site brings back fond childhood memories to most adults. Having a Web page as a support tool was not available to us back then, but now it is all part of the package, even for aging bears. You can have your students join the Rupert Bear club or learn all about the history of Rupert, why he is so popular, and background information about his adventures.

Scripts for School

ideal for all grade levels ★★★

http://scriptsforschools.com/

Here is a great selection of theater scripts for K–10 students as well as a selection of scripts for teens and adults. This is a great concept for the classroom especially in social and work environments where communication in an oral format is so important. Material here is organized around themes as well as specific academic subjects.

Shakespeare Classroom

ideal for grade levels 10–12 ★★★

http://www.jetlink.net/~massij/shakes/

This site is intended for senior high school classes as a support tool for teachers and students. Included are study questions, tips on how to watch filmed versions of the works of Shakespeare, sample assignments, syllabi, useful facts, and links to other support sites.

Speech Writing: David Slack

ideal for all grade levels ★★★★

http://speeches.com/

This is a quite remarkable site where (for a small fee) you can have speeches written for you using a standard speech and then inserting the information that is particular to your speech. There are also links to great speeches, including some that are historic or of global importance, others that deal with technology, and more. If you are teaching public speaking or oratory or you are just trying to encourage oral language, this will be a useful site.

Stories of the Dreaming

ideal for all grade levels ★★★

http://www.dreamtime.net.au/

This is really a crosscurricula discovery of the culture of the indigenous Australians. The collections of stories are based on a period called the Dreamtime, when the universe was put into existence and the culture and ethics were based on oral tradition, passed down from one generation to another over thousands of years. Stories are presented as text, audio, and video.

Student Newspapers

ideal for all grade levels ★★★

http://dir.yahoo.com/News/Newspapers/K_12/

This is a directory of newspapers written by students from mostly US cities. These vary from very good to indifferent. Students will find some good ideas here to judge their efforts against.

Take Our Word for It

ideal for all grade levels ★★★

http://www.takeourword.com/

This highly entertaining and informative site discusses the origin of words. Material is presented in a regular column (archives available), plus there is an excellent section that looks at etymological theory, including Latin roots and prefixes and Greek affixes.

TheCase.com for Kids

ideal for grade levels K–6 ★★★★

http://www.thecase.com/kids/

One of the great challenges that faces English teachers is to encourage students to read. This site has set the task of presenting material that is suitable for young students. There are mysteries to solve, scary stories, magic tricks, and contests, all of which aim to encourage students to read more.

Treasure Island

ideal for grade levels 8–10 ★★★★

http://www.dreamcatchers.net/treasure/introduction.html

Treasure Island is a classic text and contains all the story elements that students enjoy. This site is just as good. There is an excellent unit of work for teachers to follow through. Great support information and activities are all provided online, including a seaman's test by which students learn the parts of a schooner. Top-notch material that helps set the scene and draws students into the book.

Treasures@Sea

ideal for grade levels K–7 ★★★★

http://www.fi.edu/fellows/fellow8/dec98/

Here you can explore the ocean using literature as a theme. There is enough material here for an entire unit of work, or these activities could complement a present unit of work. Students need Internet access to carry out the treasure hunt, read about ocean storybooks, and apply the information gained from them by completing creative writing and art activities, games and puzzles, and experiments. This would be a good way of introducing search skills and Internet access skills at a young level. There is also a teacher planning guide here.

Victorian Lives and Letters

ideal for grade levels 11–12 ★★★★

http://www.youth.net/victorian/welcome.html

This Chatback Trust project encourages students to examine topics and make comments on the themes presented, particularly encouraging participation of students with special needs. In this project, Charles Dickens rises from the grave to discuss the Victorian times. This is an excellent concept utilizing the strengths of the Internet—information passing in two directions.

Virtual Presentation Assistant

ideal for all grade levels ★★★★

http://www.ukans.edu/cwis/units/coms2/vpa/vpa.htm

This is an excellent online tutorial designed to help in the improvement of public speaking skills. The importance of oral language development cannot be underestimated. These are essential skills that teachers in general need to spend more time teaching. The suggestions offered here are pertinent and well presented.

Vision

ideal for all grade levels ★★★

http://www.iearn.org/projects/avision.html

This I*EARN project is dedicated to literature, art, poetry, and prose produced by secondary school students. The project's mission is to use these works of art and writing to show how children worldwide experience similar dreams, fears, worries, and feelings of curiosity. This project is ongoing, so your class can join at any time.

Vocabulary University

ideal for grade levels 4–12 ★★★★

http://www.vocabulary.com/

This is a wonderful collection of puzzles that enhance vocabulary development. There are three levels to educate and entertain. First, students must be registered, for which there is no charge, and then they can start working through the puzzles. The puzzles are changed regularly and are often centered on events, special occasions, or themes in the news. Diplomas can even be earned from this virtual university.

Wacky Web Tales

ideal for grade levels K–7 ★★★

http://www.eduplace.com/tales/

Great online version of the game, where a story starts and then the student enters nouns, verbs, and adjectives to direct the story line. There are more than one hundred story lines that will keep students on task.

WebExhibits

ideal for all grade levels ★★★

http://www.webexhibits.com/

Looking for a good online exhibit to motivate your students? This excellent collection of exhibits covers such topics as creative arts, the ancient world, discovery and expedition, society and culture, health and medicine, environment, science and technology, and academic subjects.

What the Thunder Said

ideal for grade levels 11–12 ★★★★

http://www.deathclock.com/thunder/index.html

This site features an excellent collection of the works of T. S. Eliot. Links to Eliot resources and to the text of poetry and nonfiction plus a list of other works (including plays) are presented. There is also a chronology of the author's life. Great site.

Wordsmyth Educational Dictionary-Thesaurus

ideal for all grade levels ★★★

http://www.wordsmyth.net/

This is an integrated dictionary and thesaurus, and its major application is creating semantic fields for searching the Internet. This is an excellent tool for this process and provides very good results.

World Wide Words

ideal for all grade levels ★★★

http://www.quinion.com/words/

This is an admirable site that looks at the English language. There is a lot of relevant, up-to-date information here dealing with turns of phrases, topical words, and weird words, with brief definitions of new words, word links, pertinent articles, and more. Excellent classroom material.

WriteNet

ideal for all grade levels ★★★★

http://www.twc.org/forums/index.html

This is an excellent resource for writers and teachers of imaginative writing. To begin, teachers are encouraged to sign up to the listserv to receive news and information—follow the communications of fellow teachers or submit questions. There are also sections dealing with teaching techniques, poets commenting on poetry, and student issues for student writing, as well as a virtual poetry workshop.

Writers' Window

ideal for all grade levels ★★★

http://english.unitecnology.ac.nz/writers/home.html

You can get your students' work published online here. Check out the rules, and then choose to have students write poetry, stories, research articles, or film, television, or book reviews. This site affords a good opportunity for teachers to showcase student work and also for students to see what their peers are writing about.

Write Site

ideal for grade levels 4–10 ★★★

http://www.writesite.org/

The objective here is to encourage the process of storytelling and make it a fun experience for students. There is information on the history of journalism and famous journalists, how to conduct research, getting started in writing, developing individual writing style, and career opportunities.

WritingDEN

ideal for grade levels 6–12 ★★★

http://www2.actden.com/writ_den/index.htm

This very well-constructed site offers great teacher and student resources, such as word of the day, some very good tips on writing, and a whole range of additional writing topics, which would also be good topic suggestions for oral and visual language work. The feature-writing topics presented each month are excellent and would make the basis of a topic unit. Mostly for older students, this site is very well done.

Writing Introductory Paragraphs

ideal for all grade levels ★★★

http://ccc.commnet.edu/grammar/intros.htm

This excellent essay style presentation is succinct and well presented. Every teacher could use this. The same principles apply to oral and written introductions. Download this and use it.

Writing the Five-Paragraph Essay

ideal for all grade levels ★★★

http://ccc.commnet.edu/grammar/five_par.htm

This essay, of somewhat more than five paragraphs, is one of the definitive and erudite presentations on this skill. All teachers should take note of the process that Harry Livermore presents here. Excellent site.

Mathematics

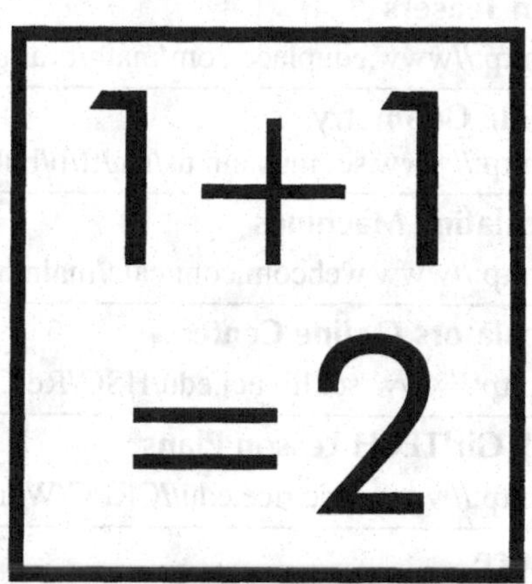

A+ Math

ideal for grade levels 4–8 ★★

http://www.aplusmath.com/

Here you can find a range of games and problems dealing with basic mathematical skills. There is a homework helper to check the solutions of the problems that are presented, as well as hidden pictures, flash cards, and other games and activities to support basic math skills.

Abacus

ideal for all grade levels ★★

http://www.ee.ryerson.ca:8080/~elf/abacus.html

This is a useful site looking at how an abacus works. Not following the average didactic format, this site, through a Java applet, allows you to move the beads and carry out the activities that have been created for you. Great math here.

Absurd Math

ideal for grade levels 4–10 ★★★★

http://www.hrmvideo.com/abmath/index.html

The title of the site possibly gives away its style, but the mathematics that underpins the activities here is excellent. The concept is very student oriented—they will thoroughly enjoy the absurd math. The site couples mathematical objectives along with a competitive game approach, and the result is an intriguing set of applications of mathematics and some good fun.

actDEN (Digital Education Network)

ideal for all grade levels ★★★★

http://www.actden.com/

The main actDEN page is placed here due to its excellent MathDEN site, which requires registration (free) to access. This is a great site, well-constructed with excellent content. There are four stages of problems as well as challenges and progress reports.

AIMS Education Foundation

ideal for all grade levels ★★

http://www.aimsedu.org/

Great site with many classroom, curriculum, and teaching ideas.

Algebra Online

ideal for grade levels 8–12 ★★

http://www.algebra-online.com/

This is a great service from a committed group of math teachers. It is mainly a support resource for students, who can ask questions and receive assistance for free! There is a mailing list you can join that supplies information to students and teachers on all things algebra. Other features include a chat area and a message board.

Ancient Geometry

ideal for grade levels 4–12 ★★★★

http://members.aol.com/bbyars1/contents.html

This is a wonderfully produced site dealing with insights into the history of mathematics. As well as an excellent prologue, there are sections dealing with the first mathematicians (Euclid, al'Khwarizmi and al jabr), pi, trigonometry, recreational mathematics, and the newer mathematics. The site also includes a Java-based chat about mathematics, a good bibliography, and an online bookstore.

Archimedes

ideal for all grade levels ★★

http://www.mcs.drexel.edu/~crorres/Archimedes/contents.html

As much a mathematician as a scientist, Archimedes used fundamental principles to great effect. Details on the burning mirrors, the screw, and much more are presented here. The site is an excellent source of information for math teachers and students looking for background material.

Arithmetic Activities

ideal for grade levels K–3 ★★

http://www.geocities.com/EnchantedForest/Tower/1217/math1.html

This is a link site that highlights a series of Web sites where students can carry out arithmetic activities. There is everything here: resources for basic math and learning to tell the time, matching games, counting games, worksheets, and more.

Assessment Resource Banks in Math

ideal for all grade levels ★★★

http://arb.nzcer.org.nz/nzcer3/nzcer.htm

An excellent question bank dealing with all areas of mathematics and at all levels. Register (free) and then use the search engine to find questions on the topics you desire. Excellent site—even the answers are provided!

Australian Bureau of Statistics

ideal for grade levels 11–12 

http://www.statistics.gov.au/

Within this massive site is a section on education, which can be found via the site map. Here you'll have access to sections dealing with each of the curriculum areas, as well as an excellent section for all teachers on research and survey techniques, a great resource for all teachers worldwide.

BasketMath Interactive

ideal for all grade levels ★★★

http://www.scienceacademy.com/BI/index.html

This Web site contains some excellent practice problems across a wide range of topics, including addition, subtraction, multiplication, division, rounding numbers, writing numbers, order of operations, common factor, perimeter, word problems, exponents, diagrams, reasoning, and map reading.

Blankety-Five Squared

ideal for grade levels K–10 ★★★

http://www.learningkingdom.com/five/

This is an online game that teaches students how to square two-digit numbers ending in five. Follow the step-by-step instructions, practice the skill, and then do the Blankety-Five Challenge.

Brain Teasers

ideal for grade levels 4–10 ★★

http://www.eduplace.com/math/brain/

Here is a selection of challenging math problems that have been sorted into grade levels. Each week a new question is presented, and past questions are archived.

Bubble Geometry

ideal for grade levels K–10 ★★★

http://www.sci.mus.mn.us/sln/tf/b/bubblegeometry/bubblegeometry.html

This excellent site is a great introduction to the mathematics of shapes using the making of bubbles as an example. Bubbles are a great way to introduce the concepts of spatial relationships, in a fun and effective way, to younger mathematicians.

Calculating Machines

ideal for grade levels 3–12 ★★★

http://www.webcom.com/calc/main.html

This site brings to life the development of calculating machines. Some students cannot believe that we have not always had computers, or that some teachers were around when we punched holes in 235 bits of card and sent them away, just to find out what 234 x 234 was equal to. Good use of Java applets to allow students to have a go at using a virtual adding machine.

Calculators Online Center

ideal for all grade levels ★★★★

http://www-sci.lib.uci.edu/HSG/RefCalculators.html

From looking at the home page, you may be expecting a really boring site here, but come in for a surprise. Check out the counting sheep calculator as well as the more serious content. There is some useful material that shows the value of calculators in context. Good math here.

CEEE GirlTECH Lesson Plans

ideal for grade levels 2–11 ★★★

http://www.crpc.rice.edu//CRPC/Women/GirlTECH/lessons.html

This work is the result of GirlTECH projects over the last few years. Each of these activities makes use of the Internet to teach a concept in an interdisciplinary manner. Great work here on Pizza Your Way, Indy 500, and A Functional Housing Market. There is some excellent math presented, embedded in good overall concept topics. Suitable for the more academically talented middle primary students up to eleventh grade.

Chance

ideal for grade levels 8–12 ★★★★

http://www.dartmouth.edu/~chance/

This is a database of chance and probability that uses contemporary articles such as newspapers as a source of information to evaluate probability. Excellent ideas and well presented.

Chaos in the Classroom

ideal for grade levels 11–12 ★★

http://math.bu.edu/DYSYS/chaos-game/chaos-game.html

Frequently, chaos and fractals are presented as attractive images minus the math, so if you're looking for a mathematical presentation, check out this site and try the Chaos Game. The mathematics here is even prettier than the pictures it produces.

Click on Bricks

ideal for grade levels K–8 ★★★

http://tqjunior.advanced.org/3896/index2.htm

This site provides multiplication facts for the student who is just coming to terms with the concept. This is a great site that encourages the concept of multiplication in a highly visual context.

Colorful Mathematics

ideal for all grade levels ★★

http://www.math.ucalgary.ca/~laf/colorful.html

This is a good selection of games that use color as their basis for demonstrating the concepts behind graphing and spatial relationships. Some good downloadable material here.

Constant Perimeter and Constant Area Rectangles

ideal for grade levels K–10 ★★

http://www.edc.org/LTT/ConnGeo/CP.html

Simple and very effective site for students to develop the relationship between area and perimeter. Java animations are used to demonstrate the principle, which allows the students to vary the perimeter in one direction and observe the changes in the other in order to keep the area the same. The same process is used to demonstrate the reverse relationship.

Coolmath.com

ideal for grade levels 11–12 

http://www.coolmath.com/

This very lively and dynamic site comes complete with some great math support. There are sections dealing with tessellations, functions, limits, fractals, puzzles and problems, success with and careers in math, and much more. Designed primarily for senior math students.

Cryptography

ideal for grade levels 8–12 

http://www.hack.gr/users/dij/crypto/

Students love using, breaking, and making codes, and this site is full of information and links to sites that provide great examples. Check out the National Security Agency site!

CyberCalc: An Interactive Learning Environment for Calculus

ideal for grade levels 11–12 

http://www.npac.syr.edu/REU/reu94/williams/calc-index.html

Here is an excellent set of online tutorials for students coming to grips with calculus. The site starts with the review of functions and equations and then provides an introduction to calculus through looking at limits and continuity. From here, differentiation, rates of change, implicit differentiation, and additional topics are used to build on this understanding.

Data Powers of Ten

ideal for all grade levels ★★

http://www.ccsf.caltech.edu/~roy/dataquan/

Bytes used to be the basic unit in computer talk, and then we were using kilobytes, then megabytes, and now standard hard drives come with gigabytes of storage. Soon we will see terabytes. Somewhere along the way, the numbers became meaningless. Here you can check out just what a megabyte is, but not just in numerical form. The site provides physical examples of what 5MB is; an example given is the complete works of Shakespeare or thirty seconds of high-quality video. Refreshing and rather daunting in the same instance. Don't forget the zettabyte!

Dave's Math Tables

ideal for all grade levels ★★

http://www.sisweb.com/math/tables.htm

This site includes many problems for students as well as ideas and tools for math teachers to use in the classroom and for homework support. The site is divided into easily navigable sections dealing with main topics in mathematics. You can also use the chat room and the real time math white board (drawing board) for discussions with other math teachers from around the world.

Dr. Data

ideal for all grade levels ★★

http://www.un.org/Pubs/CyberSchoolBus/special/drdata

This wonderful site has collected data on all sorts of social issues from around the world. Information here on forests, refugees, oceans, education, telecommunication, and much more. Take the information and have students synthesize implications and make projections and predictions.

Dr. Plenobius Airtight College Department of Diabolics

ideal for grade levels 4–10 ★★★★

http://www.hrmvideo.com/abmath/drp99/index.html

This certainly isn't your average math site on the Internet, and neither is it intended to be. The site combines flesh-eating bacteria, laboratory animals, and mathematics in a somewhat incredible story that students have to navigate their way through. Wonderfully presented. Students think it's great; math will never be the same again.

Earliest Uses of Various Mathematical Symbols

ideal for all grade levels ★★★

http://members.aol.com/jeff570/mathsym.html

Have you ever wondered where the plus sign (+) came from or why it is that we use an *x* for multiplication? Where did brackets come from and why are some curly and some square? Who came up with the idea of fractions being two numbers on top of each other separated by a straight line? These issues and questions are all dealt with here and are quite fascinating. This resource provides some interest to the study of these functions that we use almost every day.

Egyptian Mathematics

ideal for all grade levels ★★★★

http://www.eyelid.co.uk/numbers.htm

This is an excellent site for math teachers to use in showing powers of ten. Students love variety and different approaches, and this is certainly different. Teach the students the Egyptian decimal system and how to add tadpoles to coils of rope or subtract the lotus plant from a finger! Very well designed and easy to follow.

Eleven Times

ideal for grade levels K–7 ★★★

http://www.learningkingdom.com/eleven/

This is a great site with a simple objective: to teach students how to multiply two-digit numbers by eleven. Follow the step-by-step instructions provided and learn the trick. Then practice the new skill using the Eleven Times Challenge.

E-MATH

ideal for all grade levels ★★

http://www.ed.gov/pubs/emath/

This is an excellent Web site that allows math teachers to make full use of the communication aspect of the Internet. Here you will find a whole range of e-mail programs having the goal of helping students tackle difficult problems in mathematics, science, and technology.

EXTEND: Perspectives on Math Education

ideal for all grade levels ★★★

http://www.stolaf.edu/other/extend/

This is another excellent forum for the teachers of mathematics. There are five major topics identified: access, expectations, articulation, integration, and numeracy. Each of these areas has a series of well-written articles dealing with the issues and an invitation to make comments on them. The articles are excellent, concise, and to the point. Great site for all math teachers.

Flatland: A Romance of Many Dimensions

ideal for grade levels 11–12 ★★

http://www.geom.umn.edu:80/~banchoff/Flatland/

It's good to see some romance in the math department. This brilliant, classic story by Edwin Abbott (1838–1926), faithfully reproduced here in full, deals with the concepts of dimension. If you want to intrigue your students with what it would be like to live in Flatland (a two-dimensional land), then read them this story in parts, over four weeks. They will enjoy the change in teaching style, and the story will stay with them forever, giving them an excellent foundation to the understanding of dimension.

Gallery of Interactive Geometry

ideal for grade levels 11–12 ★★

http://www.geom.umn.edu/apps/gallery.html

Excellent for twelfth grade math, this site features labs, questions, and exercises such as building a rainbow. Some of the pages will challenge even the best students.

Geometry

ideal for grade levels 11–12 ★★

http://library.thinkquest.org/28586/index1024.html

Good information and support of all the principles of geometry are laid out here. The site provides a good revision base for students looking at points, lines, planes, circles, spheres, right angles, and volume.

Geometry Center

ideal for all grade levels ★★★★

http://freeabel.geom.umn.edu/

This very large site covers just about everything having to do with geometry and geometric structures. There is an abundance of very useful material here for almost all teachers at any level. There are interactive math resources, some good Java applications, plenty of software to download, and multimedia documents. A great site.

Geometry in Action

ideal for grade levels 3–12 ★★★★

http://www.ics.uci.edu/~eppstein/geom.html

This site looks at a huge range of geometric applications with everything from design and manufacturing to graphics and visualization, information systems, medicine and biology, robotics, and a huge range of other applications. This is a very extensive site and provides teachers a range of applications, demonstrating to students the need for an understanding of geometry.

Geometry in Motion

ideal for grade levels 11–12 ★★★★

http://members.xoom.com/dpscher/

The author of this site has produced an excellent range of animations to assist students in understanding a variety of geometric concepts. This site is particularly useful for senior math students coming to terms with some of the more esoteric geometric concepts.

Geometry Through Art

ideal for grade levels K–7 

http://forum.swarthmore.edu/~sarah/shapiro/

This is a very comprehensive set of lesson plans and assignments that cover geometric concepts, with teacher masters that you can print off and good vocabulary to introduce at various grade levels. This is great math that is suitable for K–7. A great resource.

Glossary of Mathematical Mistakes

ideal for all grade levels 

http://www.mathmistakes.com/

This is a wonderful glossary of mathematical mistakes taken from the media, politicians, reporters, activists, and the general population. These mistakes are often misinterpretations of facts or simply mathematics applied incorrectly, but this site provides a wealth of anecdotal examples, complete with references of how math has been applied incorrectly. Some are hilarious while others are very subtle.

Gordon's Games

ideal for grade levels K–10 

http://users.uniserve.ca/~g_games/

A collection of simple—and not-so-simple—games, and not just math! This is a great resource to provide to parents to support the math work done in class or for extra support for students. There are four booklets presented here with no charge for their reproduction and use. The theme for book one is using games to develop mathematical understanding of numbers as well as number applications and concepts. The next book deals with simple mathematical operations, and the next two booklets feature increasingly more difficult concepts and work.

Graphics for the Calculus Classroom

ideal for grade levels 11–12 ★★★

http://www.math.psu.edu/dna/graphics.html

This is an excellent collection of graphics for teachers of calculus. You might want to save these and use them as necessary. To fully experience the graphics, you will need to have a Java-enabled browser, but it is well worth the effort. There are more than ten animated graphics computing the volume of water in a tipped glass through the calculations by Archimedes of pi to an accuracy of one part in a thousand.

Graphing Vector Calculator: An Interactive Java Applet

ideal for grade levels 8–12 ★★

http://www.frontiernet.net/~imaging/vector_calculator.html

This is an excellent Java applet that allows you to create vectors using the computer mouse. You can demonstrate simple vector addition, vector subtraction, and the concept of what vectors are in a dynamic environment. Great teaching tool.

Graphs

ideal for grade levels 6–9 ★★★

http://forum.swarthmore.edu/alejandre/spreadsheet.html

This excellent set of ideas and worksheets uses Claris Works to develop graphing skills for students in grades 6–9. The information introduces and provides applications and data for bar graphs, pie charts, and pictograms and then leads into complex graphing techniques using polynomial and exponential functions.

Greek Mathematics and Its Modern Heirs

ideal for grade levels 4–12 ★★★

http://www.ibiblio.org/expo/vatican.exhibit/exhibit/d-mathematics/Greek_math.html

Between 500 BC and AD 500, Greek mathematicians maintained a wonderful tradition of work in the sciences. Original Greek texts were copied and preserved, and they were taken to a new level of understanding in the Islamic world. The stage was set for the resumption of the precise sciences through the latter part of the Renaissance period. This site traces the development of math and the major players from the Greek period.

Guide to Metric Time

ideal for all grade levels ★★★★

http://zapatopi.net/metrictime.html

This must be one of the best math sites on the Web, so logical and so impossible at the same time. We have metric distances, weight, and barometric pressures—why not time? Check out the metric clock. This is an excellent site to introduce the concept of base ten. Why can't we buy a metric clock?

Hamilton's Math to Build On

ideal for grade levels 10–12 ★★

http://forum.swarthmore.edu/~sarah/hamilton/

This is a huge collection of resources for curriculum topics. There are information introductions as well as problems and solutions. The site is primarily aimed at grades 10–12.

History of Mathematics

ideal for all grade levels ★★

http://aleph0.clarku.edu/~djoyce/mathhist/mathhist.html

This is an excellent graphic presentation of the history of mathematics. The chronology lists mathematicians from Ahmes and Thales through Turing and beyond. There are links from here to other sites dealing with the history of math.

Integrating Spreadsheet in Your Classroom

ideal for all grade levels ★★★★

http://home.earthlink.net/~ohora/spreadsheet/ssintegration.html

Spreadsheets are versatile tools, and the math classroom is the ideal place to introduce these tools. Not only for number crunching, spreadsheets can present information in a graphic context simply and easily. The site here explains the basic requirements and processes used to manage the numerical information collected from data sets or surveys.

Interactive Mathematics Miscellany and Puzzles

ideal for grade levels 8–12 ★★★★

http://www.cut-the-knot.com/content.html

Once past the conundrum of Smullyan, you are into a huge resource for mathematics teachers. With nearly thirty headings and many subdirectories, this is a huge site covering such topics as math quotes, algebra, geometry, probability, and mathematical proofs. There are more than 100 contributions under geometry alone, including many Java demonstrations of concepts such as drawing circles to cycloids, movies of the Moebius strip, the Pythagoras theorem, and much more.

K–12 Math Problems, Puzzles, Tips, and Tricks

ideal for all grade levels ★★

http://forum.swarthmore.edu/k12/mathtips/

This is an excellent collection of puzzles, tips, and tricks to keep students on their toes. A good place to start is Beat the Calculator, a compilation of math tricks you could use to really impress the students. Check out the section of critical thinking puzzles also.

Leonardo Pisano Fibonacci

ideal for grade levels 11–12 ★★

http://www-history.mcs.st-andrews.ac.uk/history/Mathematicians/Fibonacci.html

Born in 1170, Fibonacci (which is actually Leonardo Pisano's nickname) was one of the most celebrated mathematicians, being largely responsible for reviving mathematics of times past. He wrote several texts, of which handwritten copies were distributed to other mathematicians of his day (before the printing press). The Web site tracks the work of Fibonacci and the mathematics that he both encouraged and developed.

Let's Make a Deal Applet

ideal for grade levels 8–10 ★★

http://www.stat.sc.edu/~west/javahtml/LetsMakeaDeal.html

The classic television program makes a comeback here in the form of a site. Visitors ponder probability—whether or not there is a better chance of winning once the contents of one of the doors is known. This paradox has intrigued many a viewer for years, but what is the chance of making a better deal? You and your students can play a virtual game here and decide for yourself. Good math application that really tests students' understanding of the laws governing probability.

MacTutor History of Mathematics Archive

ideal for all grade levels ★★★

http://www-groups.dcs.st-and.ac.uk/~history/

Nothing to do with burgers or shakes here, but plenty to do with the mathematicians who developed the mathematical tools that we take for granted today. Featured are 1,000 biographies, 60 famous curves, assorted mathematics history topics, chronologies, and a very worthwhile search engine find what you are after.

Magic Squares

ideal for grade levels 4–12 ★★

http://forum.swarthmore.edu/alejandre/magic.square.html

A favorite around the world. Here you can find out all you want to know about magic squares in all the different forms they come in (e.g., Lo Shu squares, Albrecht Dürer's squares, Benjamin Franklin's squares, and Stator squares). But best of all, there is background information on where these magic squares all came from and a range of classroom activities that can be freely printed for use in your classroom. Excellent resource.

Manipula Math with Java

ideal for grade levels 11–12 ★★★

http://www.ies.co.jp/math/java/index.html

Here is a collection of interactive Java applets that students can manipulate in order to get a better understanding of mathematical concepts and ideas. Topics covered include linear functions, quadratic functions, mathematical rules and laws, and some calculus concepts.

Math Celebration Fair

ideal for grade levels 4–12 

http://www.teachersfirst.com/lessons/math-fair.shtml

Why shouldn't math be just as exciting as a social studies or science class with field trips and awesome activities? This was the concept behind this site. Check out the sample games. Then if you want to set up your own fair, download the PDF file and follow the site setup instructions.

Mathematical Games, Toys, and Puzzles

ideal for all grade levels ★★★

http://compgeom.cs.uiuc.edu/~jeffe/mathgames.html

This is a huge directory of games, toys, and puzzles pertaining to math. They are well collated and set out for students to explore. This will keep the extension class going forever as well as providing a good basis for a learning center.

Mathematical Quotations Server

ideal for all grade levels ★★★

http://math.furman.edu/~mwoodard/mqs/mquot.shtml

Mathematicians are always quick to insert a quotation between two sets of brackets. Here is a Web site to keep you happy for a long time to come. There are more than eighty-three pages to print here, if you want to have the entire collection at the tip of your fingers, and the authors have made this an easy task to carry out.

Mathematics Education Forum

ideal for all grade levels ★★★

http://forum.swarthmore.edu/mathed/index.html

This is a great site for seeing what the various positions are on such topics as constructivism, assessment, and block scheduling as well as learning about research and technology in math education, professional development, and the conference scene.

Mathematics Experiences Through Image Processing (METIP)

ideal for grade levels 6–10 ★★★

http://www.cs.washington.edu/research/metip/metip.html

This site deals with applied mathematics using the skills of image processing to encourage the conceptual approach to math along with emphasizing group learning, open-ended problem solving, and the practical uses of mathematics. Designed for grades 6–10. This is great math.

Mathematics Worksheet Factory

ideal for teachers only ★★★★

http://www.worksheetfactory.com/

This software allows teachers to create instant, customized, and unlimited mathematics worksheets for the practice of whole number, decimal, and fractions operations in addition, subtraction, multiplication, and division. One version of the product can be downloaded at no cost, while an enhanced version can be purchased. This is an excellent application that all mathematics teachers will find useful.

Mathematics WWW Virtual Library

ideal for all grade levels ★★★

http://euclid.math.fsu.edu/Science/math.html

This is the math section from the WWW Virtual Library. You'll have access to many math-related Web sites, gopher information, references to periodicals and preprints, and so on.

Math Forum Internet News

ideal for all grade levels ★★

http://forum.swarthmore.edu/electronic.newsletter/

You can subscribe to this excellent weekly newsletter for free, or you can stop by and check it out on the site. The issues tackled range from Pi Day through to Auntie Math!

Math Goodies

ideal for all grade levels ★★★★

http://www.mathgoodies.com/

Innovative lessons that use a problem-solving approach make this an excellent site for teachers. There are lessons here dealing with probability, integers, percentages, number theory, circumference, and perimeter, as well as message boards focusing on new teachers, homework help, classroom ideas, math news and events, support for parents, and home schooling. You will also find some extra material that can be downloaded and used to support students at school or children at home.

Math Homework Help

ideal for grade levels 11–12 ★★

http://users.erols.com/bram/column22.html

The ability to e-mail a problem and get an answer in return has moved to math now, with the arrival of this site. Problems are solved for a small fee. There is also a good selection of material designed to support various aspects of the senior math curriculum. Trigonometry and differentiation are covered, supplemented by a good chronology of mathematicians and a math dictionary.

Math in Daily Life

ideal for all grade levels ★★★

http://www.learner.org/exhibits/dailymath/

Until they leave school, students often do not appreciate how necessary basic mathematical skills are in daily life. Here they can learn about probability through a unit on playing to win, percentages as demonstrated in a discussion on savings and banking, and areas and perimeters as they are involved in home decorating, as well as the math involved in population growth and cooking.

Math League Help Topics

ideal for grade levels 4–8 ★★

http://www.mathleague.com/help/help.htm

This is an excellent site full of explanations and many examples dealing with mathematical concepts such as whole numbers, fractions, ratios, integers, introductory algebra, and much more. Written specifically for grades 4–8.

Mathmania

ideal for all grade levels ★★

http://www.theory.csc.uvic.ca/~mmania/index.html

Here is a selection of open problems in math inspired by mathematician Paul Erdös that call for the exploration of concepts. This is a great site. It is well designed and has some excellent material, including a helpful introduction to help students tackle these types of problems.

Math Online

ideal for all grade levels ★★★

http://www.kqed.org/ednet/school/math/mathonline/index.html

This is a well-structured site featuring useful puzzles, math talk, and math news and events, as well as a resource center.

MathPro Online

ideal for all grade levels ★★★★

http://problems.math.umr.edu/index.htm

This database, containing over 20,000 math problems drawn from 38 journals and 21 contests, is well organized and can be searched via keyword, primary subject, author name, or journal title.

MegaMath

ideal for grade levels 4–12 ★★★★

http://www.c3.lanl.gov:80/mega-math/

This great all-around site, presenting an extensive collection of very good material for both students and teachers, could be used as a great reward site or just to encourage struggling students. Visit Hotel Infinity or have a usual day at Unusual School. There are some great reading activities based on problem-solving skills, which fit in very well with a crosscurricular approach.

Multiplication Rock

ideal for grade levels K–3 ★★★★

http://genxtvland.simplenet.com/SchoolHouseRock/multiplication.hts?lo

This site includes great songs that students will just love to sing along with. The words and the music (which you can listen to) are here. Students can sing along to "My Hero, Zero," "Elementary My Dear," "Three Is a Magic Number," "The Four-Legged Zoo," and many more.

Orbifold Pinball

ideal for grade levels 8–12 ★★★

http://www.geom.umn.edu/apps/pinball/about.html

Don't let anyone tell you this is not math! This is geometry as you have never seen it before. Orbifold Pinball uses a curved board, and when the ball nearly misses the bumper, it will still be whipped around in the same way as if it had actually hit the bumper. You will need to read the report "The Mathematics of Orbifold Pinball" to get the most out of this math lesson.

Phoenix Quest

ideal for grade levels 4–10 ★★★

http://www.cs.ubc.ca/nest/egems/pq/toc.html

The theme behind this site is to make math interesting to girls in grades 4–10. The units of work here integrate activity elements that girls can relate to along with an exotic story line based on some mythical islands near Hong Kong. Students join the fantasy characters and learn math along their journey. Good communication and cooperative learning elements.

Professor Freedman's Math Help

ideal for all grade levels ★★★

http://www.mathpower.com/

Aimed particularly at the community college adult learner, this resource offers basic math and algebra assistance that will help all students who are struggling in the classroom. The site provides links and information about learning styles, study skill tips, and ways to reduce math anxiety.

Project SkyMath: Making Mathematical Connections

ideal for grade levels 4–10 ★★★

http://www.unidata.ucar.edu/staff/blynds/Skymath.html

This site looks at the use and application of math in context. The theme for the units included is weather, and each unit looks at applying mathematical knowledge to the systematical logging, analyzing, and displaying of data. This unit includes excellent material with sixteen activities. You can find a partner class elsewhere in the world and exchange data and results. Good opportunity here to integrate the Internet into the curriculum.

Robert Matthews: Probability and Spooky Coincidences

ideal for grade levels 4–12 ★★★

http://ourworld.compuserve.com/homepages/rajm/

This is a great collection of papers that apply the principles of probability to seemingly strange occurrences that turn out to be not that strange after all. This is good anecdotal information for the teacher to present as an introduction to probability or for students who have a good basic grasp of the subject and need challenging.

Seventh Grade Mathematics

ideal for grade level 7 ★★★★

http://www.rialto.k12.ca.us/frisbie/coyote/math/avid.math.html

Frisbie Middle School has an excellent mathematics curriculum online for other schools to view and take inspiration from. The whole seventh grade program is laid out here for teachers to draw ideas from. This mathematics curriculum seeks to teach students to think as well as learn.

Society of the Half Closed Eye

ideal for grade levels 4–10 ★★★

http://www.hrmvideo.com/abmath/ep2/index_new.html

This is one of those Web sites where you could spend ages reading and exploring just to find out what the site is really all about. According to the introduction, the site concerns the mathematically astute alien DVine PImander, a prisoner of the Purple Sage, whose chemists are developing a means to break down the DVine PImander's genetic makeup, which students are supposed to investigate. But this is a *very* challenging task! Good luck!

S.O.S. Mathematics

ideal for grade levels 8–12 ★★★

http://www.sosmath.com/

This University of Texas Web site has been designed to help students in grades 8–12 with their development in mathematics. There are some good introductory sections dealing with doing homework, preparing for a test, and getting ready for class, as well as support information on a range of mathematical topics including calculus, trigonometry, and algebra.

Statistics Every Writer Should Know

ideal for grade levels 4–12 ★★★

http://nilesonline.com/stats/

This is a site about statistics put into a context that may help in the delivery of the concepts to students. Learn all about mean, median, and mode, and check out the issues of standard deviation, margins of error, and data analysis. Good site with many teaching ideas. A very useful tool in a review process for students.

Statistics New Zealand

ideal for grade levels 4–12 ★★★★

http://www.stats.govt.nz

This is an excellent collection of statistics on almost any topic you could imagine. There is everything here from the amount of recycling households carry out through to how many people are out of work, what work they might do, where people live, how old they are, and their eating habits. Mathematics teachers will find these excellent when looking at graphing or statistics units of work.

Teachnet Lesson Ideas

ideal for all grade levels ★★

http://www.teachnet.com/lesson/index.html

From the main Teachnet Lesson Ideas site, you can access a series of good math-related lesson plans. Topics include geometry, maps and graphs, real-world applications, and terminology. There are about fifty lesson plans at the main site, and they are well thought out and well presented.

WebMath

ideal for grade levels 4–12 ★★★★

http://www.webmath.com/

This online math problem solver comes complete with an "online math-engine" that can instantly provide answers to the problems presented to students. Select the range of problems you want your students to work on, and the site will offer questions on that topic. Students complete the work and get instant feedback. Topics include practical math, word problems, graphing, fractions, scientific notation, trigonometry, data analysis, and much more. A good selection of problems.

World! Of Numbers

ideal for grade levels 4–12 ★★★

http://www.worldofnumbers.com/

Great site for all those who love palindromes and other curious reversals. There are triangulars, tetrahedrals, squares, cubes, and primes all here to be explored. This site is well worth a visit and it would make a great learning center to challenge more advanced students.

Zero Saga and Confusions with Numbers

ideal for all grade levels ★★★

http://ubmail.ubalt.edu/~harsham/zero/ZERO.htm

So often the introduction of the concept of zero is very poorly understood and students go away without realizing the significance of zero. The year 2000 celebrations signified a lack of understanding of the importance of zero. (The new millennium actually did not start until January 1, 2001.) Here you can look at the importance of zero as well as other common mathematical confusions.

Science

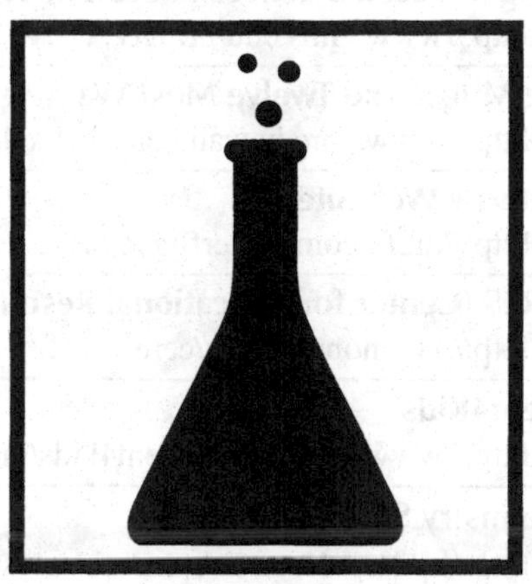

Ace on the Case: Secrets@Sea

ideal for grade levels 4–10 ★★★★

http://www.secretsatsea.org/

Great, highly visual site dealing with the issues surrounding pollution of the oceans. You will need Macromedia Flash to follow the comic strip introduction. (Flash can be downloaded in approximately two minutes and it's well worth downloading!) There is a good teacher's guide, and an investigative approach is taken so that it works well as a learning center.

Albatross Project

ideal for grade levels 4–10 ★★★★

http://www.wfu.edu/albatross/index.htm

Join this great project and track the albatross in Hawaii. The site uses satellites and tracking devices placed on the birds to study their migratory patterns. Students can join the project and then use the satellite data to come to their own conclusions. The site comes complete with class activities and lesson plans.

Amazing Space

ideal for grade levels 4–12 ★★★★

http://amazing-space.stsci.edu/

This is a great collection of Web-based activities that probe space. The activities draw on topics such as the Hubble Space Telescope, astronauts, the solar system, stars, comets, and galaxies.

Arty the Part-Time Astronaut

ideal for grade levels K–5 ★★★★

http://www.artyastro.com/

This Web site allows you to join Arty and his alien friend as they explore the solar system. This is an excellent introduction for K–5 students. The simple but highly graphic layout encourages an exploration approach allowing the student to control where the spaceship visits. Excellent learning center for students and a good introduction site for using the Web browser.

Astronomy 161: The Solar System

ideal for all grade levels ★★★★

http://csep10.phys.utk.edu/astr161/lect/index.html

This is a wonderful set of notes dealing with all the basic concepts of astronomy and the solar system. It is well designed and comprehensive, dealing with everything from a sense of time and scale in the universe, the old and new astronomy, the Earth, the moon, the planets, and our changing ideas about the solar system.

Bad Astronomy

ideal for all grade levels ★★★★

http://www.badastronomy.com/

The theories people have of what is happening in outer space often have no relevance to reality. Ideas about how our universe works are often misconstrued and misunderstood. Few people really understand why people in the southern hemisphere don't fall off the planet, or at least don't have all the blood rush to their heads. This site investigates the misinformation about astronomy, from the plain silly to the information that is logical but incorrect.

BioBLAST

ideal for all grade levels ★★★★★

http://www.cotf.edu/BioBLAST/

Students who participate in this multimedia adventure will be part of a simulated journey to the moon. How will they create and maintain systems that will generate food and oxygen for their life support? The video messages they receive in flight and once they land on the moon specify the requirements for their survival. They then join one of three lab groups to carry out investigations focusing on one aspect of this issue.

Biodiversity Counts

ideal for grade levels 4–10 ★★★★

http://www.amnh.org/learn/biodiversity_counts/

This online program encourages classrooms to investigate and study biodiversity at a site near the school. The idea is for students to perform the same kind of work as that done by scientists: make scientific observations, record data, keep journals, identify and classify evidence, analyze data, and publish and exhibit their work for the general public.

Biology4Kids

ideal for grade levels 4–12 ★★★★

http://www.kapili.com/biology4kids/index.html

This is an excellent and well laid out site dealing with all aspects of biology. It has sections dealing with cells, their makeup, and processes. Other features include an excellent chemistry section looking at how chemical systems drive biological processes; an ecology section that explores populations, the food chain, and cycles; and a study section that examines logic and reasoning, taxonomy, the top five kingdoms, and labeling in biology.

Biology Project

ideal for grade levels 11–12 ★★★★

http://www.biology.arizona.edu/

For senior biology students, this is a great collection of notes and background information dealing with biochemistry, cell biology, chemicals and human health, developmental biology, human biology, immunology, Mendelian genetics, and molecular biology.

Black Hole Gang

ideal for grade levels K–10 ★★★★

http://www.blackholegang.com/

This is a very well-presented science investigation page examining everything from rainforests to gravity to light and many other cool science topics. Science-related links and book titles are suggested.

BodyQuest

ideal for all grade levels ★★★★

http://library.thinkquest.org/10348/

This is a study of anatomy, and although geared toward students from the ages of eleven to sixteen, it is really useful to students of almost any age. The site investigates such topics as blood, the brain, the circulatory system, the digestive system, the eye, the excretory system, the heart, the immune system, the nervous system, muscles, the reproductive system, respiration, and the skeleton.

Book of Insect Records

ideal for all grade levels ★★★★

http://gnv.ifas.ufl.edu/~tjw/recbk.htm

This site presents wonderfully useless but highly entertaining information that students find fascinating. Which insect can fly the fastest? Which has the shortest sexual life cycle? Which insect has the longest migration? Which one is the loudest? All this and much, much more.

Botany Online: The Internet Hypertextbook

ideal for grade levels 8–12 ★★★★

http://ostracon.biologie.uni-kl.de/b_online/e00/contents.htm

This excellent online textbook has now been almost completely translated into English from German. All the general topics of botany are covered, including the anatomy of cells and tissues, genetics, and molecules.

Bridge: Ocean Sciences Education Teacher Resource Center

ideal for all grade levels ★★★★

http://www.vims.edu/bridge/

If you teach a unit of work that includes marine science, then the resources provided here will be much appreciated. The site deals with all the basics, such as whales, dolphins, fish, and pollution, as well as offering research information on topical issues such as conservation, mining the seabed, fishing, and plankton reserves. You can even take a virtual field trip to an estuary.

Bug Mugs: The Twelve Most Wanted

ideal for all grade levels ★★★★★

http://www.pbrc.hawaii.edu/~kunkel/wanted/mugs/

This is a great site that will make every student and teacher cringe. Have a look at these almost three-dimensional pictures of the twelve most feared bugs—feared for their looks, not their bite! These look like invaders from another planet. Each photograph has an excellent rap sheet detailing the bug's lifestyle, which tends to match its looks, as well as other interesting facts. Print out these mug shots on a color printer for great effect. Check out the cat flea, ladybug, mosquito, and praying mantis just for starters.

Butterfly Web Site

ideal for grade levels K–10 ★★★★

http://mgfx.com/butterfly/

If you are not able to find the answer to your butterfly question here, I would be quite surprised! This very comprehensive site is filled with excellent photographs and information for teachers preparing units dedicated to these delicate creatures as well as those seeking site suggestions and activities for students. This would be a good site for students fourth grade and up to use to assemble a presentation from the information maze that is offered on the site. Also, it's a good site for students to practice information management as well as skimming and scanning skills.

CERES (Center for Educational Resources) Project

ideal for all grade levels ★★★★★

http://btc.montana.edu/ceres/

Here you will find an extensive online library and interactive K–12 science education materials for teaching astronomy. The Web-based lessons make maximum use of the online resources, data, and images from NASA. As well as online classroom material, there are several online NASA data search engines and graduate level distance-learning courses, available over the Internet to teachers.

Chem4Kids

ideal for grade levels 4–12 ★★★★

http://www.kapili.com/chem4kids/index.html

Chemistry is a very conceptual topic, and many students struggle with the basic concepts and ideas. The Kapili Islands have put together a wonderful site here dealing with the fundamentals of chemistry. The site looks at atoms and how they combine to form compounds and ions. It also deals with the elements, providing good examples as well as their place in the periodic table. There is an excellent section on chemical math and a section dealing with basic reactions including equilibrium, acids and bases, thermochemistry, and rates of reaction.

Chemistry Study Cards

ideal for grade levels 11–12 ★★★★

http://spusd.k12.ca.us/sphs/science/stdycrds.html

This is a wonderful collection of study resources for chemistry students. Using Adobe Acrobat Reader, it is easy to print out a collection of cards containing summaries of the major topics in chemistry. These would be ideal for senior high school students to have as a reference source. Topics include the periodic table, ionic reactions, the gas laws, electronic structure, stoichiometry, acids and alkalis, organic and inorganic chemistry, and much more.

CHEMvisu

ideal for grade levels 11–12 ★★★★

http://sgich1.unifr.ch/lecture/menu/menu.html

One of the most powerful tools the Internet has to offer is the ability to see animations of complex scientific processes. This site contains more than 600 MB of animations and graphics looking at chemical reactions in an interactive environment. You will have to download the Chime plug-in, but this is straightforward and does not take long. Excellent senior high chemistry material.

Cool Science for Curious Kids

ideal for grade levels K–8 ★★★★

http://www.hhmi.org/coolscience

This excellent and fun site, presented by the Howard Hughes Medical Institute, examines some interesting biological concepts. The site asks some fairly basic questions (concerning, for example, plant parts, dust, butterflies, and snakes) and then explores the science behind them.

Cosmic and Heliospheric Learning Center

ideal for grade levels 11–12 ★★★★

http://helios.gsfc.nasa.gov/

This is an excellent site that introduces students to astrophysics in a bright and entertaining way. There are sections dealing with cosmic rays and the heliosphere, along with a good glossary and an Ask a Physicist feature.

CSIRO Australia

ideal for grade levels 11–12 ★★★★

http://www.csiro.au/index.asp

The CSIRO is the Australian scientific community's research agency and as such has a great home page for both science and technology. Students should check out the Double Helix home page, and teachers can keep an eye on scientific advances down in the antipodes. There is also quite a bit of information regarding science fair ideas, not to mention links to other science sites.

Dinosaurs in the Desert

ideal for all grade levels ★★★★

http://www.amnh.org/science/expeditions/gobi/gobi_homepage.html

The Gobi Desert expedition covered here took place in 1998, but this site presents a great process for introducing the discovery of dinosaurs and what they tell us about our past. There are daily reports about the discoveries that were made there and the implications of the scientists' work. Teachers could post the reports each day and have students develop theories and hypothesize as to what had been discovered.

Discovery.com Guides

ideal for all grade levels ★★★★

http://www.discovery.com/guides/guides.html

Excellent source of appropriate news material, as well as background data and support, linked to current happenings of a scientific and technological nature. The articles are all archived and are very well presented. They are short and to the point and provide excellent digest material on topics ranging from cutting-edge technologies to volcanoes, weather, dinosaurs, asteroids, Mars, and much more.

Earth and Life Sciences: A Science Odyssey

ideal for all grade levels ★★★★★

http://www.pbs.org/wgbh/aso/thenandnow/earth.html

This is a terrific presentation on our understanding of the planet that we live on and how it has drastically changed during the twentieth century. In 1907, scientists discovered a way of using radioactive decay to determine the age of the earth; in 1962, the first elements of continental drift were starting to become apparent. This would be a wonderful unit of work in its own right by investigating more fully the elements that are discussed. There are plenty of links in addition to the excellent information included on the site itself.

Earth and Moon Viewer

ideal for all grade levels ★★★★★

http://www.fourmilab.ch/earthview/vplanet.html

This is a great example of where the Internet can demonstrate real time happenings that we could never see unless we were to go into space. You can view the nighttime shadow move across the earth and watch the changing shape of the shadow from winter to summer. View what the Earth looks like from the moon or vice versa. Check out cloud coverage and many more great images that show clearly the dynamic nature of the earth.

EcoNet

ideal for all grade levels ★★★★

http://www.igc.org/igc/gateway/enindex.html

This huge searchable information site on all things ecological is excellently organized and offers data news reports, action alerts, and headline articles and debates. It presents excellent coverage of the major trouble spots around the world. Less extreme than some, this site provides a well-balanced approach to ecological issues.

EE-Link

ideal for all grade levels ★★★★

http://eelink.net/

This environmental education site, designed for teachers and students, is full of supportive and informative articles, units of work, and ideas for the classroom. The information varies from introductory to professionally-based research material. The site features a range of classroom activities as well as backup resources, an excellent virtual library, and links to a good selection of environmental education sites on the Web.

Einstein's Legacy

ideal for grade levels 4–12 ★★★★

http://www.ncsa.uiuc.edu/Cyberia/NumRel/EinsteinLegacy.html

Einstein considered himself as much a philosopher as a scientist, and his thought experiments often walked a fine line between these two intertwined approaches. Einstein's legacy is the concept of space-time, and the site is dedicated to providing a history of the transition between the Newtonian clockwork universe and the relativistic universe we now are beginning to understand.

Epicenter: Emergency Preparedness Information Center

ideal for all grade levels ★★★★

http://TheEpicenter.com/

If you are doing a unit on disasters or disaster management, then you'll want to check out this excellent site. This center provides up-to-the minute advice on how to prepare for, and cope with disasters of all kinds. There is a very good set of disaster survival audio clips available via RealAudio. A lot of information here.

Exploratorium Science Snacks

ideal for all grade levels ★★★★

http://www.exploratorium.edu/snacks/index.html

This is an excellent collection of miniature online science exhibits that teachers and students can make using simple pieces of equipment. There are plenty of them here, and they are excellent motivators and provide a great context for learning science. Topics vary from the balancing stick to bubbles and gravity.

ExploreScience.com

ideal for all grade levels ★★★★★

http://www.explorescience.com/

This is a top ten science site demonstrating the power of the Internet as an interactive presentation tool. The authors have developed Shockwave animations dealing with classic experiments in science education. They are very cleverly done and are in small files. Check out the golf range, terminal velocity, 2D collisions, floating, inertia, colors, black holes, and much more. With its excellent material and more than thirty demonstrations, this resource has something for everyone.

Exploring Planets in the Classroom

ideal for all grade levels ★★★★

http://www.soest.hawaii.edu/SPACEGRANT/class_acts/

This wonderful collection of more than twenty-five hands-on science activities, with supplementary classroom-ready teacher and student pages, focuses on the study of the Earth and other planets, the geology of these planets, and the space sciences. Among the topics explored are volcanology, impact craters, gradation, gravity and rockets, the moon, and remote sensing.

Fish Features

ideal for grade levels 2–3 ★★★★

http://projects.edtech.sandi.net/encanto/fishfeatures/fishfeatures.html

This is a project where the student, as an apprentice marine biologist, has just found a new, unknown fish. The student is to make a presentation based on an examination of the fish's anatomy, documenting characteristics and comparing them to characteristics of other known fish. All the necessary student resources are here. This project makes for an excellent challenge.

Fizziks Fizzle

ideal for grade levels 4–12 ★★★★

http://library.thinkquest.org/16600/

This site is great! There are separate sections geared toward beginning, intermediate, and advanced students of physics. Each section presents practical applications complete with support theory and good diagrams and animations. A large collection of links rounds out this very useful resource.

Frogland

ideal for grade levels K–8 ★★★★

http://allaboutfrogs.org/

Here is a site for all those students with all the questions. They can leap into the weird facts section or learn how to look after frogs. The site features a froggy coloring book, frog jokes, and even a frog art gallery. This is an ideal site for all K–8 students and would make a great learning center or research depot.

General Chemistry Online

ideal for grade levels 8–12 ★★★★

http://antoine.frostburg.edu/chem/senese/101/

This is great resource to support the teaching of chemistry. The online set of hyperlinked notes and tutorials on basic understandings of math and scientific knowledge are very useful. Other worthy features include a glossary, several quizzes, an ask the chemist service, and links to more than 500 general chemistry Web sites.

Genetic Science Learning Center

ideal for grade levels 8–12 ★★★★

http://gslc.genetics.utah.edu/

This Web site, from the University of Utah Eccles Institute of Human Genetics and School of Medicine and the Utah Museum of Natural History, provides science students an excellent introduction to genetics. The site presents plenty of teaching ideas, student activities that can be done at home, news about genetics, and it even offers teacher workshops in this area of genetics. The specialty here is the provision of ideas, low-cost equipment, and experiments that can be carried out in high schools.

Hands-on Paper

ideal for all grade levels ★★★★

http://www.geocities.com/RainForest/Vines/6092/index1.html

This site is dedicated to the process of recycling paper and encouraging the use of recycled products. In addition to showing how recycled paper can be made, the site also has a history of books, as well as a time line, demonstrating the development of writing and the use of paper.

How Far Does Light Go?

ideal for grade levels 4–12 ★★★★

http://www.kie.berkeley.edu/KIE/web/hf.html

This is an excellent site that investigates this question. At a superficial level, we all think we understand light, but scientists still do not really understand what it is or how it works! This site has the students do the research and come up with a hypothesis. This is good science that tackles an important concept and opens the window of truth, enabling students to come to the realization that we do not know everything and, in fact, we actually know very little!

Images of Entomology: Insects and Arachnids

ideal for grade levels K–10 ★★★★★

http://www.photovault.com/Link/OrdersEntomologyInsects/InsectsMaster.html

What a beautiful collection of images! There are over 100 images of dragonflies alone, and they are of exceptional quality. The images make great starters for story writing, artwork, investigations of similarities and differences, classification, and much more.

Imagine the Universe

ideal for grade levels 8–12 ★★★★★

http://imagine.gsfc.nasa.gov/

This excellent NASA site investigates the universe, how it came into being, and where it is going. The site looks at all aspects of cosmology and astrophysics including the various objects the universe contains, such as black holes, supernovas, quasars, comets, planets, and much more. Great site with a lot of well-written material for the senior science student.

John Glenn: Friendship 7

ideal for all grade levels ★★★★

http://www.capstonestudio.com/mercury/index.html

The oldest ever astronaut, who began with the Mercury 7, has now taken a trip onboard the space shuttle. This is a great human interest story in a scientific context. Follow the story of the risks that early astronauts took. Encyclopedic approach and very well presented.

Journey North: A Global Study of Wildlife Migration

ideal for all grade levels ★★★★

http://www.learner.org/jnorth/

This site includes excellent material dealing with a fascinating series of global events. There is an excellent online teacher's manual, a regular news bulletin, and a database where your students can report their observations. Register for the program and include it in your planning each year.

Kit and Kaboodle

ideal for grade levels 4–10 ★★★★★

http://www.kitkaboodle.org/

These two characters take students on a very interactive journey around the Internet and help them develop an impressive array of science skills along the way. Students are asked to search and find information, organize it using graphs, apply it using maps, write reports effectively, and much more. Excellent site that students are very keen to work with. Very MTV!

Liftoff to Space Exploration

ideal for all grade levels ★★★★

http://liftoff.msfc.nasa.gov/

From the Marshall Space Flight Center in Alabama, this site is a news desk of information concerning launches, space stations, rocket science, satellites, NASA headlines, and space exploration in the news. Great site for a group of students to visit once a week and orally report back to the rest of the class. Also check out the NASA Kids link for quizzes, word finds, picture galleries, and other activities for students.

Live from Mars

ideal for all grade levels ★★★★

http://quest.arc.nasa.gov/mars/

The huge interest in Martian probes has made this site one of the most popular on the Internet. There is an excellent teacher's guide to the site providing teaching ideas and support. You can receive updates on the Mars Global Surveyor or the Mars Pathfinder as well as chat with experts regarding specific aspects of the missions. An excellent photo gallery and even a live video link make this an excellent science project.

Live from the Hubble Space Telescope

ideal for grade levels 4–12 ★★★★★

http://quest.arc.nasa.gov/hst/index.html

This is a great site, because it allows students to do real science in conjunction with the Hubble Space Telescope. This project will be very popular. Once you register, you will be e-mailed updates and information packages. The targets for discovery are the planets Neptune and Pluto. Original observations will be made by students using the space telescope. This is real science using a piece of equipment worth millions of dollars. Also plenty of photos and interesting information.

Mars Polar Lander

ideal for all grade levels ★★★★

http://marslander.jpl.nasa.gov/

Here you'll find all sorts of background material on the Mars Lander, along with news and images.

Miami Museum of Science: The pH Factor

ideal for grade levels 2–9 ★★★★★

http://www.miamisci.org/ph/

What a great introduction to the world of acids and bases for science students in grades 2–9. The site uses the seven Es—Excite, Explore, Explain, Expand, Extend, Exchange, and Examine—as a framework, and this works very well. Follow this very nicely crafted site via the excellent lesson plans and interactive screens. Site also includes a teacher's guide.

Mission Control Center

ideal for all grade levels ★★★★

http://www.ambitweb.com/nasacams/nasacams.html

This is a wonderful collection of live video clips showing various NASA activities. Check out shuttle launches and flights, satellite development and imagery, mapping tasks, and the many scientific explorations that NASA is conducting.

NASA

ideal for all grade levels ★★★★★

http://www.nasa.gov/

The pioneers in the use of Internet for education are still out there. This is a massive compendium of knowledge in a very visible format for all grades. The site is heavily loaded toward astronomy, but there are some excellent sections on flight, weather, and the NASA spinoffs that are the result of 25 years of research. A top ten site with daily updates.

NASA Audio Gallery

ideal for all grade levels ★★★★

http://www.nasa.gov/gallery/audio/index.html

NASA has brought all its audio presentations to one location. During launches and missions, NASA provides an audio commentary using RealAudio. They also provide the video clips using the CU-SeeMe program. There are also commentaries on all aspects of the work NASA is involved in. This is an excellent site as long as you have a good connection to the Internet.

NASA Spacelink

ideal for all grade levels ★★★★

http://spacelink.nasa.gov/.index.html

The Spacelink program has been going for some time now, and the electronic version is excellent. There are plenty of projects here as well as photos, news, and instructional material. If you have a project dealing with space at any level, then this is a great site to visit.

New Scientist

ideal for grade levels 4–12 ★★★★★

http://www.newscientist.com/

This online edition of the excellent science magazine has to be the best overall science compilation on the Web. You will find daily news and research articles, feature stories, and other excellent science material at a suitable level for both senior students and teachers. The articles vary in length and are often digests (which are easy to read to the class), and the additional links can be used to further explore the topic.

Nine Planets

ideal for grade levels 4–12 ★★★★

http://seds.lpl.arizona.edu/nineplanets/nineplanets/nineplanets.html

This is a great tour of the solar system from someone other than NASA, and it is done really well. Plenty of pictures, facts, and amazing discoveries are all presented in an easy-to-read, easy-to-follow format. One of the most visited sites on the Web.

Numerical Relativity Exhibitions

ideal for grade levels K–8 ★★★★

http://jean-luc.ncsa.uiuc.edu/Exhibits

If you are taking your students on a tour of the universe, then you may find some interesting information here to challenge some of your students. The material here looks at warped space-time, as well as wormholes and the effects of Einstein's relativistic physics.

Nye Labs Online

ideal for all grade levels ★★★★

http://nyelabs.kcts.org/

Enter the lab and be prepared. This is a great site for all aspiring scientists to visit and explore. As well as being good fun, there is some great science here too. All ages welcome, but it helps if students can read.

Ocean Animals

ideal for all grade levels ★★★★

http://mbgnet.mobot.org/salt/animals/

This Web site deals with the animals that live in the oceans, including the common sharks, walrus, and whales and the less common sponges, mollusks, echinoderms, and cnidarians. There are excellent pictures of fish and ocean animals and some good multimedia material on a variety of animals living in different ocean environments.

Oil Spills and Hazardous Chemical Accidents: Kids Section

ideal for all grade levels ★★★★

http://response.restoration.noaa.gov/kids/kids.html

This is an excellent set of experiments for students to carry out in the classroom showing why oil spills can be so devastating to both land forms and the life that exists in the land-sea margins. There are experiments here for both primary and secondary levels.

Online from Jupiter 97

ideal for all grade levels ★★★★★

http://quest.arc.nasa.gov/galileo/index.html

Brilliant presentation from NASA using the data that the Galileo mission returned to Earth. In late December 1995 the Galileo probe plunged through the atmosphere of Jupiter and sent back enormous amounts of data. The orbiter continued to orbit the planet, sending back additional data on the planet and its moons. The huge amounts of information here allows for a compare-and-contrast exercise between Earth and Jupiter. This exercise would be a considerable improvement on the traditional general space topic.

Online Guides

ideal for grade levels 8–12 ★★★★

http://ww2010.atmos.uiuc.edu/(GH)/guides/home.rxml

Here is an excellent collection of online support and guides to meteorology, climate, remote sensing, and global change. There is an excellent range of projects and activities that make use of the huge resources that the Internet has available on meteorology and climate.

Physical Science Activity Manual

ideal for grade levels 4–12 ★★★★

http://cesme.utm.edu/resources/science/PSAM.html

This group of teachers were trained in using the learning cycle as a methodology of learning, and they then set about writing a manual containing thirty-four hands-on activities to bring some excitement back into the science classroom. This excellent material is available free of charge at this site. Each activity, which can be downloaded in PDF format, provides good content, sound pedagogy, and an excellent practical approach.

Physics 2000

ideal for grade levels 8–12 ★★★★

http://www.colorado.edu/physics/2000/index.pl

The theme behind this site is high-tech devices. Students are taken on a journey that allows them to learn visually and conceptually about twentieth-century high-tech devices. Each of the different experiences highlights the science behind the discoveries and the developments. Tour through the Atomic Laboratory, take the Science Trek, or discover Einstein's legacy of X rays, CAT scans, microwaves, lasers, television screens, and even laptop screens.

Physics4Kids

ideal for grade levels 4–12 ★★★★

http://www.kapili.com/physics4kids/index.html

This is an excellent physics site developed on the islands of Kapili. This fully searchable site, designed for students, has an excellent approach and covers such topics as motion, thermodynamics, modern physics, light, and electricity. Quizzes are included. This is excellent material and would be a very useful site for students to review their present knowledge or to challenge the younger scientist.

Physics and Astronomy: A Science Odyssey

ideal for grade levels 4–12 ★★★★★

http://www.pbs.org/wgbh/aso/thenandnow/physastro.html

No other science seems to have captured the public's attention more than physics and astronomy. In the twentieth century, we went from being a general public who based most of our personal theories on superstition and pseudoscience to being a society where most of us are aware of, even though we do not fully understand, the existence of black holes, nebulae, comets, and our place in the universe. This site presents a chronology of people and discoveries, supplemented by activities.

PhysLink

ideal for grade levels 4–12 ★★★★★

http://www.physlink.com/

Brilliant resource from Anton Skorucak! This really is the ultimate physics site. There is so much here for physics teachers that it is hard to know where to start. Featured are great articles, news, and happenings from around the world, updated regularly and well written. Check out ideas for the classroom, the job section, and online forums. An especially good feature is the free newsletter, which includes a new quote from or anecdote on someone famous in the field. This will become the home page for many physics teachers around the world. Top ten site.

Plaguescape: Epidemiological Analysis

ideal for all grade levels ★★★★★

http://www.mcn.org/a/plaguescape/

This brilliant site combines science, detective work together, and an ancient mystery. The ten plagues that were sent to curse the Egyptians for holding Moses and the Israelites are the setting for looking at outbreaks of diseases and plagues that worry us now in the early twenty-first century. Designed in an investigative format, the site offers excellent learning opportunities.

Planet Ark: Reuters Daily World Environment News

ideal for all grade levels ★★★★

http://www.planetark.org/

Listen to Pierce Brosnan explain how you can do your part in the quest for a clean earth, then be sure to check out the video clips, RealAudio reports, and news. Excellent material that is well set out and presented. Ask students to listen to the daily environmental news and report back to the class.

Planetary Society

ideal for all grade levels ★★★★

http://www.planetary.org/

This excellent Web site provides both teachers and students a selection of news and up-to-date details on happenings from around the world, along with information on the search for life in the universe. The site here is mainstream and should not be confused with fringe efforts to track down UFOs.

Plate Tectonics

ideal for grade levels 8–12 ★★★★

http://www.ucmp.berkeley.edu/geology/tectonics.html

Great site that first deals with the history of the development of plate tectonic theory and then moves into a good explanation of the mechanisms that are thought to provide the energy for this massive movement. The best part is the animated GIFs that show how the different sections of the crust moved during the various geological eras. They take a little while to download, but they can be saved and used in the classroom with great effect.

Questacon

ideal for grade levels 1–4 ★★★★★

http://www.questacon.edu.au/index.html

This is an excellent site with some really good science for the primary age science student. They can join the solar car challenge, head off to the furthest reaches of space, or get into the (virtual) hands-on activities. This site has been featured in the top one hundred best sites anywhere in the world. A top ten site from Australia.

Remarkable Ocean World

ideal for all grade levels ★★★★

http://www.oceansonline.com/

This site has become a repository for information and multimedia content for students with an interest in the oceans. There is material here based on scientific research conducted throughout the world. The approach is a thematic one and not limited to science. There is a good collection of audio and video material as well as an excellent section dealing with remarkable ocean facts and a well-stocked image library.

Rock Hounds

ideal for grade levels 4–10 ★★★★

http://www.fi.edu/fellows/payton/rocks/index2.html

Great approach and layout here! Rocky the dog helps students come to terms with the Earth's geographical makeup. They can learn all about sedimentary, metamorphic, and igneous rocks and how they are made. This is also a good site for teachers wanting to encourage their students to take up rock collecting. There are some good safety guidelines and even awards for those who take a look through the slides.

Savage Earth

ideal for all grade levels ★★★★

http://www.wnet.org/archive/savageearth/

This is an excellent introduction to the dynamic nature of our planet. It is easy to look around and see the Earth as a slowly changing, seasonal-oriented environment, but this is far from the truth. The site looks at tsunamis, earthquakes, volcanoes, and the Earth's crust and interior. The material here is very well presented and could make a great presentation package for teachers or an investigative site for students.

Scanning Electron Microscope

ideal for all grade levels ★★★★

http://www.mos.org/sln/sem/

At this site, you can view an extensive library of pictures of insects, materials, and everyday items that have been magnified as much as hundreds or even thousands of times using a scanning electron microscope. The images are both beautiful and frightening and are excellent lesson starters. You can also investigate how a scanning electron microscope works, as well as making use of a good range of teaching resources and links to other microscopy sites.

Science for the Millennium

ideal for all grade levels ★★★★

http://www.ncsa.uiuc.edu/Cyberia/Expo/

This very graphic and well laid out online exposition of science is a great introduction to the areas of science that we are moving toward in the new millennium. An information center, online theater, and pavilions of science and industry, collaboration, and computation all provide excellent material.

Science Rock

ideal for grade levels K–3 ★★★★

http://genxtvland.simplenet.com/SchoolHouseRock/science.hts?lo

Great songs that students will just love to sing along with. The words and the music (which you can listen to) are here. Students can sing along to "The Body Machine," "Do the Circulation," "Interplanet Janet," "Them Not-So-Dry Bones," "A Victim of Gravity," and many more.

Science with the Office of Oceanic and Atmospheric Research (OAR)

ideal for grade levels 4–10 ★★★★★

http://www.coe.usouthal.edu/oar/index.html

This is a great selection of investigations on a variety of topics including storms (tornadoes, lightning, hurricanes, and forecasting), fisheries, El Niño, oceans, and atmosphere. These are excellent activities encouraging higher-order thinking skills.

Scientist

ideal for grade levels 8–12 ★★★★

http://www.the-scientist.library.upenn.edu/

This is a biweekly newspaper for those involved in the life sciences. It contains all the week's stories that link the sciences with everyday events. Good background information for both teachers and older students. Senior secondary students could review this each week and report back to the class orally on three of the week's top stories. Recommended reading for all teachers of senior life sciences. Very well done.

Seeds of Life

ideal for grade levels K–12 ★★★★★

http://versicolores.ca/seedsoflife/ehome.html

This is a beautiful home page. There is some great science here, for all levels, about seeds and their importance, how they grow, their diversity, and all sorts of other things that we may never have realized. If you are doing any work on plants, then this is a great place to start for both teacher ideas and student information.

SkyDEN

ideal for grade levels 11–12 ★★★★

http://www3.actden.com/Sky_DEN/

The stars that we see in the sky each night are a curiosity that stirs our minds to ask Why are they there? and How did they get there? This site presents an excellent journey of discovery, starting from these basic questions and working toward providing an understanding of what we know, what we think has happened in the past, and where the universe is heading.

Solar Eclipse

ideal for all grade levels ★★★★

http://www.exploratorium.edu/eclipse/index.html

This phenomenon has often been the portent for dramatic changes in world history and is still seen by some as much more than just an astronomical phenomenon. This Web site has a wonderful approach to the history and science of eclipses. You can join in on live Web casts of solar eclipses as they happen around the world. These Web casts take the format of live video footage, comments from observers, photographs, and detailed explanations as the moon passes between the Earth and the sun.

Space Team Online

ideal for all grade levels ★★★★

http://quest.arc.nasa.gov/space/index.html

Join the space shuttle team as they prepare to leave on their next mission. Look behind the scenes at their training, the preparation of the experiments and payloads, the ground crew, and mission control. There are excellent curriculum packages here dealing with varying aspects of spaceflight such as rockets, microgravity, walking in space, and so on. There are also regular chat sessions that classes can join in, as well as a listserv to help you keep your class up to date on what is happening on the ground and in space.

Structure and Evolution of the Universe

ideal for grade levels 8–12 ★★★★

http://universe.gsfc.nasa.gov/

This dramatic and fascinating Web site is a tribute to people's insatiable appetite for adventure and the technology that has allowed us to venture back to the very beginnings of time.

Thinking Fountain

ideal for grade levels K–5 ★★★★

http://www.sci.mus.mn.us/sln/

This is one of the best and most comprehensive science sites on the Internet. Aimed at grades K–5, this site provides hours of scientific investigation. Topics follow themes, and the Mind Maps section must be viewed. Excellent process approach to science.

TOPEX/Poseidon: Perspectives on an Ocean Planet

ideal for all grade levels ★★★★

http://podaac-www.jpl.nasa.gov/tecd.html

This site provides teachers the opportunity to receive, free of charge, an informational CD-ROM containing over an hour of digital video, audio, images, and text detailing the TOPEX/Poseidon satellite's mission. The satellite's mission was to map the oceans' changing topography and help scientists to understand the oceans' role in global climate. Check out CD-ROM content online here to learn more about the mission.

Toys in Space II

ideal for all grade levels ★★★★★

http://quest.arc.nasa.gov:80/space/teachers/liftoff/toys.html

In 1993 a special liftoff saw the Space Shuttle Endeavor carry into orbit a collection of toys to see whether or not they would still work. Does a yo-yo still "yo-yo" in space? Will a boomerang still come back? This is a brilliant site, with background information and a movie, to start off an investigation of forces of gravity. Gravity is so misunderstood by students and teachers alike that this site should be compulsory viewing for all. Have the students predict which toys will work and which will not. Maybe after visiting this site, teachers will no longer have students telling them that there is no gravity in space!

Virtual Antarctica

ideal for all grade levels ★★★★★

http://www.terraquest.com/antarctica/index.html

This is a great virtual expedition to this last frontier. Although the actual voyage took place in 1995, this is still an excellent site providing great learning experiences along with good background information and activities. Check out the virtual bridge of the ship, and discover the ecology, science, and history of this remarkable continent.

Virtual Sun

ideal for all grade levels ★★★★★

http://www.astro.uva.nl/demo/sun/kaft.htm

This is a great site dedicated to the investigation of the sun. This is a high-tech site, and with the appropriate plug-ins (which are provided along with very good explanations on how to use them), you can journey through the sun and even watch the sun swallow up the Earth. (You will have to wait a couple of billion years for the real thing!). Excellent site with a lot of information and a superb presentation.

Visible Embryo

ideal for grade levels 4–12 ★★★★★

http://visembryo.com/

This is an online tutorial dealing with the first four weeks of the baby's life in the womb. This is really well done and with wonderful pictures and text makes a great introduction to the early days of pregnancy. This is good material for a wide audience if used well.

Visual Physics

ideal for grade levels 8–12 ★★★★

http://library.thinkquest.org/10170/

This great site presents a host of physical science concepts in a visual format that is more easily understood by students than the typical mathematical approach that is often taken. There are excellent sections here dealing with work, force, energy, torque, projectile motion, momentum, electricity, and kinematics.

Waterford Press Games, Activities, and Quizzes

ideal for all grade levels ★★★★★

http://www.waterfordpress.com/

This is an excellent collection of hundreds of worksheets, activities, and quizzes for students. These are all free of charge, and you can simply print them out with a color printer when you need them. There are information sheets and quizzes on all aspects of biology, geology, weather, astronomy, plants, animals, and much more.

Water Science for Schools

ideal for all grade levels ★★★★

http://wwwga.usgs.gov/edu/index.html

The US Geological Survey has provided an excellent resource for teachers looking to use water as a theme in their science programs. The site presents information under the headings of Earth's water, water basics, and water use information. Other site features include an activity center, a picture gallery, and a question-and-answer section.

WebElements Periodic Table

ideal for grade levels 4–12 ★★★★

http://www.webelements.com/

This online periodic table of the elements is extremely comprehensive for those who need the detail but it also is easy to use for the teacher who simply wants to show pictures of some of the elements in class. You can print out tables of the elements with the detail you require as well as obtain all the information you need about characteristics and reactions of each of the elements.

Webscience

ideal for grade levels 4–10 ★★★★

http://homepage.mac.com/rstryker/webscience.html

At this great site, students can join in with Roger Stryker's fifth grade science class and contribute to their global science projects. There are numerous projects here, and this is a great way for students to join the global community and make friends.

Welcome to the Planets

ideal for all grade levels ★★★★

http://pds.jpl.nasa.gov/planets/

This site presents an absolutely stunning array of images from NASA's planetary exploration program. Also provided are supplementary descriptions, data, and a glossary. This is a wonderful teacher resource for introducing students to our solar system.

Wild Ones

ideal for grade levels 3–10 ★★★★

http://www.thewildones.org/

This site is dedicated to the preservation of the wildlife in danger of extinction. There are special units of work and support notes for teachers as well as a membership program that individuals or schools can join in. Newsletters, magazine-style articles, and scientific reports (appropriate for grades 3–10) all make for an excellent site full of very relevant and directed information.

Wonderful World of Insects

ideal for grade levels 8–10 ★★★★

http://www.earthlife.net/insects/

This page is dedicated to the most successful life-form ever! It is mostly a repository of information with hypertext links to support sites. There is also plenty of material to assist in the preparation of units of work or for individual or cooperative learning units.

Your Gross and Cool Body

ideal for all grade levels ★★★★

http://www.yucky.com/body/

Belches, snores, and any other releases of air. This site has instant appeal to students, and there is some great science here as well. If you are trying yet again to teach body systems and you want a new slant, then this site could provide it for you.

Zoom Dinosaurs

ideal for all grade levels ★★★★

http://www.enchantedlearning.com/subjects/dinosaurs/index.html

This vast resource about dinosaurs starts from very simple ideas and builds quickly. Here you can check out information sheets on over 100 different dinosaurs, print out dozens of simple dinosaur printouts, discover how dinosaurs are named, and check out the biggest, the smallest, the tallest, the heaviest, and every other "-est" of the dinosaur world.

Social Studies

Social studies takes in a huge variety of topics and themes, and in many ways almost every site is a social studies site. Check out the general section (news, disasters, social issues, etc.) for additional sites of excellence that will be of use to you and the science section for specific topics such as volcanoes or earthquakes.

Title URL	Rating	Page
AccuNet/AP Multimedia Archive http://ap.accuweather.com/apphoto/index.htm	★★★★★	69
Africa http://www.geographia.com/indx06.htm	★★★★★	69
American Civil War Homepage http://sunsite.utk.edu/civil-war/warweb.html	★★★★	69
American Memory http://memory.loc.gov/ammem/amhome.html	★★★★★	69
America's Story http://www.americaslibrary.gov/	★★★	69
America Votes http://scriptorium.lib.duke.edu/americavotes/	★★★★	69
Amnesty International http://www.amnesty.org/	★★★★	70
Ancient Indus Valley http://www.harappa.com/har/har0.html	★★★★	70
Ancient Near East http://www-oi.uchicago.edu/DEPT/RA/ABZU/ABZU.HTML	★★★★	70
AncientVine http://www.ancientsites.com/	★★★★★	70
Anne Frank House http://annefrank.nl/	★★★★	70
Anne Frank Online http://www.annefrank.com	★★★★	70

National Atlas of the United States of America ★★★★
http://www.nationalatlas.gov/ 82

National Geographic Map Machine ★★★★★
http://www.nationalgeographic.com/resources/ngo/maps. 82

NativeWeb ★★★★★
http://www.nativeweb.org/ 82

New York Times Learning Network ★★★★
http://www.nytimes.com/learning/index.html. 82

North, South, East, West: American Indians and the Natural World ★★★
http://www.clpgh.org/cmnh/exhibits/north-south-east-west/index2.html. 82

Oakford Manor ★★★★★
http://www.alienexplorer.com/manor/oakford.html 83

On This Date in North American Indian History ★★
http://members.tripod.com/~PHILKON/ 83

Opinion Pages ★★★★
http://www.opinion-pages.org/ 83

PBS Democracy Project ★★★★
http://www.pbs.org/democracy/ 83

Peace Gallery ★★★★★
http://www.peacegallery.com/. 83

Pollution Solution ★★★★
http://www.ifmt.nf.ca/mi-net/enviro/pollut.htm 83

Presidents Game ★★
http://www.sprocketworks.com/shockwave/load.asp?SprMovie=presidentsgame. 84

Race to the South Pole ★★★★
http://www.monterey.k12.ca.us/~snlornzo/quests/antarctica.html 84

Radical Times: The Antiwar Movement of the 1960s ★★★
http://library.thinkquest.org/27942/indexf.htm 84

Revolutionary WebQuest ★★★
http://library.advanced.org/11683/HomeMain.html 84

Russia: How Has Change Affected the Former Soviet Union? ★★★★
http://www.learner.org/exhibits/russia. 84

Schools Demining Schools ★★★★
http://www.un.org/Pubs/CyberSchoolBus/banmines/index.html 84

Searching for China ★★★★
http://www.kn.pacbell.com/wired/China/ChinaQuest.html 85

Six Billion Human Beings ★★★★★
http://www.popexpo.net/english.html 85

Six Paths to China ★★★★★
http://www.kn.pacbell.com/wired/China/ 85

South Africa: Can a Country Overcome Its History? ★★★★★
http://www.learner.org/exhibits/southafrica/. 85

Springfield Race Riot of 1908 ★★
http://library.thinkquest.org/2986/. 85

State of the World's Children 1999: Education Section ★★★★
http://www.unicef.org/sowc99/. 85

AccuNet/AP Multimedia Archive

ideal for all grade levels ★★★★★

http://ap.accuweather.com/apphoto/index.htm

This is a great resource for educators and would be invaluable in the classroom. The photo archive contains some 700,000 photos, and about 500 more are added each day. The subscription rate for schools is quite reasonable, and this would be a "must have" for social science teachers, as they could use the archive in developing their own classroom materials.

Africa

ideal for all grade levels ★★★★★

http://www.geographia.com/indx06.htm

This is a huge collection of information and photographs covering various areas in Africa. Representative countries include Botswana, Ghana, Kenya, Mali, Morocco, Namibia, South Africa, Tanzania, and Zimbabwe. Among the topics discussed are culture, geography, and people, and interesting facts from each of the different areas are presented as well.

American Civil War Homepage

ideal for grade levels 3–12 ★★★★

http://sunsite.utk.edu/civil-war/warweb.html

This is an excellent collection of links to Web sites dealing with all aspects of the American Civil War. The site is divided into sections on biographical information, documentary records, images of wartime, battles and campaigns, Civil War reenactments, and discussion groups.

American Memory

ideal for all grade levels ★★★★★

http://memory.loc.gov/ammem/amhome.html

This excellent site, presented brilliantly and with varying degrees of depth, features the historical collections of the National Digital Library. The more than ninety online collections deal with all aspects of American history drawing from the extensive resources of the Library of Congress. It would be useful for teachers to introduce students to the site map and explain how to navigate this very extensive site.

America's Story

ideal for grade levels 4–10 ★★★

http://www.americaslibrary.gov/

If you are looking for an introduction to American culture, history, and geography, then this is an excellent site to visit. Divide students into five groups, and have each group report back on one of the five aspects that are highlighted here. You can then have these students produce a mural representing the culture and history of America.

America Votes

ideal for grade levels 6–10 ★★★★

http://scriptorium.lib.duke.edu/americavotes/

This historical retrospective looks at the race for the office of president of the United States. The historical writings date back to the 1796 race between Thomas Jefferson and John Adams and continue to modern presidential campaigns.

Amnesty International

ideal for grade levels 11–12 ★★★★

http://www.amnesty.org/

This is the home page for this well-known human rights organization. A very well laid out site with enormous amounts of information on almost every country. This would be a good site to look at in conjunction with a study on any country. Countries such as Tibet, China, and some of the "new" European countries make for especially compelling reading as the countries have great geographic interest, but few Internet viewers would like to change places with the people of these countries.

Ancient Indus Valley

ideal for grade levels 8–12 ★★★★

http://www.harappa.com/har/har0.html

There are several excellent slide tours here of a civilization that once flourished in this region. The site examines various aspects of the Indus Valley, such as a walk through Lothal and information about explorers, quarries, and building techniques of the time. You can also study the Indus script here. A very well laid out and graphic site.

Ancient Near East

ideal for all grade levels ★★★★

http://www-oi.uchicago.edu/DEPT/RA/ABZU/ABZU.HTML

This is a guide to resources available for studying the ancient Near East. A well laid out site with access to journals, museum collections, archaeological sites, and library catalogs, as well as regional sites. A great place to have students collect information and place it in order on a time line, or have them compare and contrast a time line for this culture and the Chinese culture.

AncientVine

ideal for grade levels 4–12 ★★★★★

http://www.ancientsites.com/

This is a great site that allows students to take on a role and then visit ancient sites around the world including Rome, Athens, Egypt, and Babylon. The material is excellent and gives students a real feel for the era they are visiting. This highly recommended site feels like a game but in reality provides an excellent understanding of the lives and times of these people and places.

Anne Frank House

ideal for all grade levels ★★★★

http://annefrank.nl/

Here is a collection of links to online resources dealing with Anne Frank, who hid from Nazi persecution of the Jews during World War II. She came to be known for her writings, which portrayed an era that much of the world tried to shut out. By following links here, students will discover details about the times that she lived through and the writings that propelled her into the role of the chronicler of the persecution of the Jews.

Anne Frank Online

ideal for grade levels 4–12 ★★★★

http://www.annefrank.com

This site traces the remarkable life of Anne Frank from her diary to background information as well as associated resources for using the theme of Anne Frank in the classroom.

ArcData Online

ideal for all grade levels ★★★★

http://www.esri.com/data/online/index.html

This is a very impressive site in terms of size and content. There are clickable US and world maps that yield a wealth of fascinating information on such things as oceanographic information, railroads, roads, population centers, drainage, cultural landmarks, transportation infrastructure, aeronautical information, and much more. Certain features are accessible only after paying a fee.

Battle of Hastings

ideal for grade levels 4–12 ★★★★

http://battle1066.com/

This was one of the most significant events in the history of Europe and especially of England. It was to be the last time that England would be defeated by a foreign power. The extensive content and numerous images within this Web site deal with almost every aspect of the culture, politics, geography, religion, and history of the period. There is also a comprehensive glossary of terms to support this document.

Beginner's Guide to the Balkans

ideal for grade levels 4–12 ★★★★

http://abcnews.go.com/sections/world/balkans_content/

This section of the world is so politically complex it is hard to gain understanding about who is doing what, where, why, and to whom. This is an excellent introduction that could be used by senior students to report back to the remainder of the class about the issues that are being fought over. There are no good guys and bad guys here, just too many bad memories and poor communication of intent. Great site.

Ben's Guide to US Government for Kids

ideal for all grade levels ★★★★

http://bensguide.gpo.gov/

This is an excellent guide to all aspects of how the United States is governed. Information is provided on branches of government, the responsibilities and powers of state and national government, the election process, and citizenship. Similar discussions appropriate for different age groups are presented, plus there is a section for teachers and parents.

BlackHistory.com

ideal for all grade levels ★★★★

http://www.blackhistory.com/

As well as reflecting on the history of the civil rights movement and the emancipation of black Americans, this site provides an optimistic note in highlighting some of the many successful black Americans from all walks of life, from athletes to scholars, from newsmakers to social campaigners. There are also sections for discussion where students can contribute their own thoughts.

Brazil Expedition

ideal for all grade levels ★★★★★

http://www.globalearn.org/expeditions/brazil/index.html

GlobaLearn is renowned for its excellent online adventures, and this is no exception. The expedition travel logs document each day's activities for a couple of months. The support material is excellent, and the backup services are tried and true. Check out the photos taken of the expedition every day at noon. This resource is a very good learning tool.

Cambodia: The Odyssey of the Khmer People

ideal for grade levels 4–12 ★★★★

http://allithai.mekong.net/cambodia/

This is a very large and well designed site that portrays both the beauty and the darkness of Cambodia's modern history graphically and frankly. The past history of the Cambodian people is untangled as well as the horror of the land mines that still wreak havoc in this beautiful country. Refugee statistics, news summaries, art, and culture are all presented here.

Caribbean

ideal for all grade levels ★★★★

http://www.geographia.com/indx02.htm

This site has extensive coverage of this region, which the world often associated with pirates, as well as its ecological treasure. In particular, the culture, history, ecology, and tourism of Antigua and Barbuda, Aruba, the Bahamas, Bonaire, Curacao, Grand Bahama, Grenada, Jamaica, St. Kitts–Nevis, St. Lucia, and St. Martin are discussed.

China: A Teaching Workbook

ideal for all grade levels ★★★★

http://www.columbia.edu/itc/eacp/japanworks/teachingaids/china/chinaworkbook/intro.htm

This is a fantastic collection of educational materials on the topic of China, suitable for use by teachers. There is a complete set of lesson plans that include class activities, primary source selections, student readings, and role play exercises. There are sections dealing with geography and population, language, philosophy and religion, traditional history, modern history, society, what it means to be Chinese, and government and politics. Each of these sections includes worksheets and support material.

CNN

ideal for all grade levels ★★★★★

http://www.cnn.com/

The vast resources of CNN are made available to you through this home page. Follow stories of social significance as they happen, and get students to report back to the class each day on the events of the past twenty-four hours. This is an excellent site and you will use it regularly. A top ten site.

Culturelink

ideal for grade levels 8–12 ★★★★

http://www.culturelink.org/start.html

This site is self-described as "the network of networks for research and cooperation in cultural development." Established by UNESCO and the Council of Europe, this is a huge network of more than 1,000 smaller networks from some 100 countries around the world. The mission of the site is to collect and disseminate cultural information in various forms.

Custer Battlefield Historical and Museum Association

ideal for all grade levels ★★★

http://www.cbhma.org/

What happened during the Battle of the Little Big Horn? Was General George Custer a real person? You can learn the answers to these questions and many more at this wonderfully laid out and informative site.

Daily Life in Ancient India

ideal for all grade levels ★★★★

http://members.aol.com/Donnclass/Indialife.html

Take a look at the life of Indian people going back to the Indus civilization in 3000 BC. The site is very thorough in its dealings and specializes in the lifestyles of the average citizen during each time period in ancient India.

Daily Life in Ancient Rome

ideal for all grade levels ★★★★

http://members.aol.com/Donnclass/Romelife.html

This is a great introduction to what it was like to live in Rome for the average citizen, looking at the typical morning to evening routines rather than looking at famous buildings and people. Check out details on breakfast, getting dressed, going off to school, taking baths, and spending leisure time. What did Romans have for dinner? Did they have take-out meals? Great material here and thoroughly readable.

Database Europe

ideal for all grade levels ★★★★

http://www.asg.physik.uni-erlangen.de/europa/indexe.htm

If you have a question about any country in Europe, then this is the place to go to have it answered. Very thorough and in-depth information on every aspect of the political, economic, and social issues in each of the countries. With the steady evolution of "megacountries" that are tied by economic and social treaties, Europe has been the model that many are following. The site presents a background to evolution and shows that difference and tolerance can coexist within business and economic realities.

Deep in the Bush, Where People Rarely Ever Go

ideal for grade levels K–8 ★★★★★

http://members.nbci.com/PMartin/liberia/homepage.htm

Highlighting Africa, this site has been put together by the author based on his work with the Peace Corps in Liberia, West Africa. This page is well designed and provides a teacher's lesson page, a good selection of African folktales, and African recipes. Also be sure to check out the P.O.W.E.R. (Pupil Owned Written Enacted Recognized) Plays. This is a great introduction to the culture and history of Africa. Rather than doing the usual study on Africa, you can use this fresh approach.

Disaster Area

ideal for grade levels K–10 ★★★★★

http://www.fema.gov/kids/dizarea.htm

No, this is not the Web site for dealing with classroom management, but rather a wonderfully produced Web site dealing with natural disasters. Disasters covered here include floods, hurricanes, tornadoes, tsunamis, thunderstorms, volcanoes, earthquakes, wildfires, and winter storms. The Things to Know sections present pertinent helpful tips on preparing for and coping with disasters. Maps, stories, games, and exercises round out this useful resource.

Discovery of Gold in California

ideal for grade levels 4–10 ★★★★

http://www.sfmuseum.org/hist2/gold.html

Gold was the drawing card that opened up the US West. Gold attracted thousands of new settlers across the Great Divide to settle in California. This site takes a very thorough look at the history of the gold rush and the social development that it spurred.

Downloadable Images and Maps of Asia

ideal for all grade levels ★★★★

http://www.askasia.org/for_educators/instructional_resources/materials/downloadable_images_maps/down_imag_maps.htm

This is a comprehensive collection of maps of Asian countries and regions. These maps are very helpful to have on hand when looking into the political and geographic nature of this region. There are also some excellent drawings by young Asian students that communicate more than words could ever say through their interpretations of life in their respective countries. The collection of photographs is also a great source of insight into the lives of people in this region.

EarthRISE

ideal for all grade levels ★★★★★

http://earthrise.sdsc.edu/

This is an amazing site. Pick a spot on the Earth, and then wander through a huge range of photographs, taken from the space shuttle, of that region in different conditions. This is a great site for comparing geographic features and for younger students to get a feeling for what maps are and what countries actually look like. There are many uses of this site.

EcEdWeb: Using the Internet to Teach Economics

ideal for all grade levels ★★★★

http://ecedweb.unomaha.edu/teachsug2.htm

Great resource site for all teachers of economics at all grade levels. There is an excellent supply of links to sites but also very good material dealing with the issues of using the Internet in the classroom as well as the evaluation of Internet sites and information.

E-Citizen

ideal for all grade levels ★★★

http://ecitizen.org/

You can find information here on all aspects of local government. In particular, the site presents a good argument for why citizens should be involved in and aware of local government issues.

E-Conflict: World Encyclopedia

ideal for all grade levels ★★★★

http://www.emulateme.com/

The aim of this Web site is to eradicate conflict (E-Conflict) by increasing cultural awareness. Although it may take much more than cultural awareness to eradicate global conflict, the fourteen hundred pages of content dealing with almost every aspect of every country can only help the cause. There is information here on national anthems, flags, maps, history, weather, news, and culture of the nations of the world.

Economic Forecasting: An Internet WebQuest

ideal for grade levels 11–12 ★★★★

http://www.edci.purdue.edu/vanfossen/519webquest.html

This excellent WebQuest investigates the decision-making processes that lie behind forecasting the direction an economy might take. A task is outlined and possible resources are suggested, followed by an outline of the process involved in completing the task and notes on evaluating it.

Egypt: A Learning Module

ideal for grade levels 3–7 ★★★★★

http://www.wsu.edu:8080/~dee/EGYPT/EGYPT.HTM

This is an excellent module that could serve as a guide for 3–7 grade teachers to follow with students, or as an independent learning module for more senior students. The content is exemplary, thorough, and very well laid out. Elements dealt with include a general history, the three recognized kingdoms, leaders through the times, and the influence of the Romans. Some good material on hieroglyphics, an excellent time line, an atlas, and a gallery are also provided.

Egypt: Gift of the Nile

ideal for all grade levels ★★★★

http://www.seattleartmuseum.org/Exhibitions/Egypt/default.htm

Check out the ten truths, the philosophy, and the religion of ancient Egypt, as well as a useful encyclopedia of Egyptian information, complete with some great video clips and some audio material. For teachers, the highlight is the eighty-page unit on Egypt, which is well worth printing out, because it contains some great information and classroom activities.

Encyclopaedia Britannica

ideal for all grade levels ★★★★★

http://www.britannica.com/

Here you can find the entire encyclopedia online, complete with extensive cross-referencing and interactive simulations. Also featured in this easy-to-navigate resource are reviews of recommended Web sites plus great summaries of current news and events.

E Patrol

ideal for grade levels K–8 ★★★★

http://www.sprint.com/epatrol/

Students can join this excellent site and learn all about endangered animals of the various continents around the world. There is also a section dealing with how to save energy in the home. Move about the home and find out how to save energy in the bathroom, kitchen, bedroom, and laundry room. The theme of the site is environmental management, and there are good EcoInfo sections as well as an E Patrol quiz. This would make a wonderful introduction to the issues surrounding the environment and how we can manage it in a sustainable manner.

Escape from Knab

ideal for grade levels 8–12 ★★★★

http://www.escapefromknab.com/

The title doesn't give much away as to what the site is about, but in fact it is a sophisticated exercise in economics. Unfortunately, once you get here, you will have found yourself stuck on the planet of Knab. To escape from there, you have to make some decisions that will enable you to purchase a ticket that costs $10,000, and you have to do this by the fourth of July in order to return home. This is an excellent interactive Web site that will take time to work through. It would make an excellent lunchtime or after-school exercise.

Europe

ideal for all grade levels ★★★★★

http://www.geographia.com/indx03.htm

This region is probably the most popular destination for travelers from around the world. Its history, culture, and people have been characterized through numerous historical events, books, and other media. This site looks at Belgium, Denmark, Iceland, Northern Ireland, Norway, Russia, and Sweden. Their history, politics, and culture are all examined. You can also link through to the European Travel Commission's Europe Planner for information on more European countries.

Exploring Ancient World Cultures: Medieval Europe

ideal for grade levels 4–12 ★★★★

http://eawc.evansville.edu/mepage.htm

This is an extensive site with information dealing with all aspects of medieval Europe. Included here is the Magna Carta, selections from St. Thomas Aquinas's Summa Theologica, a chronology, essays, images, and more.

Exxon Valdez Oil Spill Trustee Council

ideal for all grade levels ★★★★

http://www.oilspill.state.ak.us/

When this oil tanker went aground in 1989, it was to become one of the worst environmental accidents in history. This is a remarkable story of the restoration of this region of Alaska and the ongoing process of regeneration and reintroduction of devastated species. This excellent site not only details the process of restoration but it also demonstrates the enormous impact that one bad decision can have.

EyeWitness: History Through the Eyes of Those Who Lived It

ideal for all grade levels ★★★★

http://www.ibiscom.com/index.html

This is a wonderful concept: find people who were alive when historical events took place and ask them how they felt then and now and how they recall the situations, or find records from people who were alive at the time. Some good examples found at the site include the Norman invasion of England, the murder of Thomas Becket, Custer's last stand, the 1906 San Francisco earthquake, the attack at Pearl Harbor, and much more. Excellent material presented in a unique format.

Face of Russia

ideal for grade levels 8–12 ★★★★

http://www.pbs.org/weta/faceofrussia/

Russia, that huge landmass too many of us know so little about, is undergoing one of the greatest sociological and economic experiments in history. This site provides some background and insights on the changes Russia is experiencing and the effect these changes are having on the people. Developed by PBS in support of the television program of the same name, this resource is very well researched and presented.

50states.com

ideal for all grade levels ★★★★

http://www.50states.com/

This excellent Web site provides information on all aspects of each of the states in the United States. You can discover everything from the state's flag, the schools in that state, the name of the governor, information on national parks, driving details, an excellent set of maps, and much more.

First Nations Histories

ideal for all grade levels ★★★★★

http://www.tolatsga.org/Compacts.html

This extensive historical record of approximately fifty native Indian tribes provides students with an excellent background to the tribal groups that used to, and in some cases still, inhabit the areas where the students now live. The compact histories as well as a location map and a geographic overview provide excellent tools for making the most of this Web site.

Fourteen Days in October: The Cuban Missile Crisis

ideal for grade levels 4–12 ★★★★

http://library.thinkquest.org/11046/

Those who were alive at the time remember well the tension and the waiting for each news broadcast to find out what was transpiring during those long days. This site follows the issues as seen by the two main political players, Premier Nikita Khrushchev and President John Kennedy. Use tools such as the Briefing Room, Crisis Center, Recon Room, and Debriefing Room to track the events and the personalities that led to the closest the world has come to nuclear war.

From Sideshow to Genocide: Stories of the Cambodian Holocaust

ideal for grade levels 8–12 ★★★★

http://edweb.gsn.org/sideshow/

The Cambodian holocaust showed the world that Hitler was not a one-of-a-kind freak and that we have to be on our guard to ensure that atrocities such as this do not happen again. This Web site catalogs the genocide of an entire people. The world heard the stories and again mostly turned a deaf ear to them, thinking them to be unbelievable. The Web site provides a graphic encounter with the people of Cambodia and their continuing troubles many years later.

Global Relations of the Many Nations

ideal for all grade levels ★★★★

http://library.thinkquest.org/18401/nmain.html

This site highlights international issues that are great interest to social science teachers and their students. There are excellent brief summaries given on nations around the world as well as on organizations that support social issues in the areas of health, welfare, and economics. A very good context for teaching the elements of community.

Grand Canyon Explorer

ideal for all grade levels ★★★★

http://www.kaibab.org/grand.htm

This hugely impressive geologic feature is hard to capture on film, but this site has done the best job possible within the limitations of two dimensions. You can visit the Grand Canyon area or take a trip down the Colorado River through the canyons. The geography and the geology of this region are dramatic. The site gives students the opportunity to appreciate a region they may never have a chance to visit.

Great Chicago Fire and the Web of Memory

ideal for grade levels 5–10 ★★★★

http://www.chicagohs.org/fire/index.html

This site describes Chicago up to the eve of the fire and then looks at the impact that the fire had on the city. Additionally, the site also investigates the rescue and relief efforts that were undertaken and how the modern-day city rose from the ashes.

Great Depression

ideal for grade levels 4–12 ★★★★

http://www.plainfield.k12.in.us/hschool/webq/webq1/webquest.htm

The Great Depression is the period of time following the Wall Street stock market crash of 1929. It precipitated the worst economic downturn in the history of the United States as well as many countries throughout the world. The impact was severe and lasted almost ten years. This WebQuest places students back in the time of the Great Depression with the assignment of examining and making decisions about their family's financial options.

Great Globe Gallery on the World Wide Web

ideal for all grade levels ★★★★★

http://hum.amu.edu.pl/~zbzw/glob/glob1.htm

This is an amazing site containing numerous visual representations of the Earth, as a globe or in numerous other projection formats. You can see depictions of the effect of volcanoes on the atmosphere, time zones, El Niño, wind speeds, wave heights, and more. Pick from nearly two hundred different representations. Ideal for getting students to appreciate the relationship between the Earth and maps of the Earth.

Greenpeace

ideal for all grade levels ★★★★

http://www.greenpeace.org/

The rainbow warriors of the environmental age are here in style. Some bad press has occasionally tarnished the organization's squeaky clean image, but Greenpeace still does an amazing job in numerous situations in almost every country of the world.

Guide to Museums and Cultural Resources

ideal for all grade levels ★★★★

http://www.lam.mus.ca.us/webmuseums/index.shtml

This site provides a comprehensive and easy-to-use set of links to museums and other sites offering resources on different cultures around the world. All parts of the globe are covered, including not only New Zealand, but Antarctica as well.

Hammurabi's Code

ideal for all grade levels ★★★★★

http://members.nbci.com/PMartin/hammurabi/homepage.htm

Hammurabi, the priest king from about 1792 to 1750 BC who united all of Babylon under his rule, wrote a code containing 282 laws concerning a wide range of abuses. This code of conduct was discovered in AD 1901 on a stela that is now located in the Louvre in Paris. This site features Hammurabi's Code and some of the problems he faced. The teacher's page is an excellent resource and makes this site a wonderful learning center. Information here is presented brilliantly through great illustrations and clear and well laid out text.

Harriet Tubman and the Underground Railroad

ideal for grade level 2 ★★★★

http://www2.lhric.org/pocantico/tubman/tubman.html

A second-grade class in New York has produced this excellent site detailing the life of Harriet Tubman and the Underground Railroad and how they changed the history of America.

Harriet Tubman Resources on the World Wide Web

ideal for grade levels 5–12 ★★★

http://www.nyhistory.com/harriettubman/website.htm

Sometimes referred to as the Moses of the black community, Harriet Tubman was a rallying figure for the Underground Railroad. This Web site features an excellent collection of links pertaining to both the life and the times of this special woman.

History of Money from Ancient Times to the Present Day

ideal for all grade levels ★★★★★

http://info.ex.ac.uk/~RDavies/arian/llyfr.html

This is an excellent discovery approach site where you can look at the origins of money, the concept of the welfare state, contemporary economics, and much more.

History Online: Ancient Rome

ideal for all grade levels ★★★★

http://www.jacksonesd.k12.or.us/k12projects/jimperry/rome.html

This is an excellent compilation of Web sites looking at all aspects of this civilization. The concept is to present the topics in contexts that students can relate to, such as Antique Roman Dishes: Hey, Ma, What's for dinner? How about an ancient Roman supper? Other topics follow this approach in areas such as art, architecture, the ruins, money, entertainment, catapults, and much more.

Illustrated Encyclopedia of Mesoamerica

ideal for grade levels 5–12 ★★

http://www.cultures.com/meso_resources/meso_encyclopedia/meso_encyclopedia_home.html

If you are looking at the history of the Central American regions, then this is an excellent resource for background material on the civilizations that were centered here. There is information on the Aztecs, Mayans, and others.

Index of North American Indians

ideal for grade levels 4–12 ★★★★

http://curtis-collection.com/tribalindex.html

At this site information and historical notes on about eighty western Native American tribes that were visited and photographed by Edward Sheriff Curtis from 1890 to 1930. Materials are taken from Curtis's twenty-volume work *The North American Indian.* This site presents some fantastic images that can provide excellent discussion starters for students looking at early American history.

Indian Country

ideal for grade levels 7–12 ★★★★

http://indiancountry.com/

This is America's leading indigenous Indian newspaper. The newspaper highlights the news and the people behind the news who contribute to the Indian community. This online newspaper is an excellent way of keeping up with both the politics and the ongoing fight for recognition.

Internet Ancient History Sourcebook

ideal for grade levels 8–12 ★★★★

http://www.fordham.edu/halsall/ancient/asbook.html

This is an excellent collection of material dealing with all aspects of ancient European history. The focus is Mesopotamia, Egypt, Israel, Persia, Greece, the Hellenistic world, Rome, and the origins and subsequent development of Christianity. You can gain access to a huge collection of online texts as well as commentaries, articles, essays, and research material.

Internet Medieval Sourcebook

ideal for grade levels 8–12 ★★★★

http://www.fordham.edu/halsall/sbook.html

This is a massive collection of information, maps, images, projects, texts, courses, and much more. This database has organized a huge amount of information on all aspects of medieval Europe. In many cases, the articles and sections are fully referenced and often refer to the original manuscripts.

Internet Modern History Sourcebook

ideal for grade levels 8–12 ★★★★★

http://www.fordham.edu/halsall/mod/modsbook.html

This is an exceptional collection of information dealing with the Western world and modern American history, starting with the Reformation and working through the Industrial, American, and French revolutions and then into a good overview of the nineteenth century and the World Wars. Features include an excellent history image bank, music files, and much more. Any teacher of modern history should start here.

Irish History on the Web

ideal for all grade levels ★★★★

http://wwwvms.utexas.edu/~jdana/irehist.html

This is a huge database of local information and links to sites that support research on this country's history. With the Irish troubles so much in the news, a study of the history of this country is an excellent topic, and there are bound to be plenty of parents who can help in the process. The site is broken into sections dealing with general Irish history, reading suggestions, some excellent time lines that put it all into perspective, Unionist and Republican histories, the Irish Potato Famine, and much more.

Just One Night

ideal for grade levels 4–12 ★★★★

http://www.pbs.org/justone/

This is a powerful site that deals with the issues concerning drinking and driving. The context provided, coupled with the clever presentation, makes this a wonderful educational resource for teachers. Drunk driving is a universal problem for a myriad reasons and one that requires considerable education and discussion, as well as students making a commitment not to let each other drink and drive.

Latin America

ideal for all grade levels ★★★★★

http://www.geographia.com/indx05.htm

This is excellent coverage of this region of the world. The site covers countries such as Argentina, Brazil, Chile, Costa Rica, Ecuador, Guyana, Mexico, Peru, and Venezuela. Each of these countries is examined for its geographic presence, history, and natural environment. There is an excellent set of photographs with each section as well as good statistics and interesting facts.

Living Culture and History of California Indians

ideal for all grade levels ★★★

http://www.qal.berkeley.edu/~kroeber/iup.ca./ind/ca.ind.splash.html

This extensive Web site deals with every tribe imaginable within the state of California. You will find information dealing with the history of the tribes as well as their indigenous culture.

Mahatma Gandhi: A Retrospective

ideal for all grade levels ★★★★

http://www.meadev.gov.in/Gandhi/intro.htm

This is an extensive and well laid out site dealing with the life, times, and philosophy of Gandhi. There are sections here portraying Gandhi's mission and his philosophy on economics, the role of women, education, and the relationship between God and man. Excellent material.

Making of America

ideal for all grade levels ★★★★

http://www.umdl.umich.edu/moa/

This excellent site contains quality information on every facet of the American experience through the years 1850–77. It looks at the psychology, history, sociology, religion, science, and technology of America and Americans. With more than 620,000 pages of information and scans of more than 5,000 texts written during this time, this is no small collection.

MAP International

ideal for all grade levels ★★★★★

http://www.map.org/

This Christian relief agency has compiled an excellent site using information from around the world to examine social issues and work carried out by relief agencies. It also includes an excellent news service.

Maps and History Navigator

ideal for all grade levels ★★★★

http://www.carto.com/links.htm

Students can explore the links at this Heritage Map Museum site to track the development of people's appreciation of the globe that we live on and to learn more about the history of the nations of our world. Sites are arranged by geographic region or by historical theme or time line. Excellent resource.

Martin Luther King Jr.

ideal for all grade levels ★★★

http://www.eduplace.com/ss/king/mlk.html

Not only does this Web site provide access to a lot of information on Martin Luther King Jr. but it also features a range of activities for different grade levels.

Martin Luther King Jr. Papers Project

ideal for all grade levels ★★★★

http://www.stanford.edu/group/King/

Stanford University has put together an excellent resume of the life and times of Martin Luther King Jr. Included are all his famous speeches, sermons, his autobiography, and a chronology of the events in his life, as well as articles dealing with all aspects of the man, the times, and the movement he led.

Mary Rose: An Introductory Site for Students

ideal for all grade levels ★★★★

http://www.maryrose.org/jessica/title.htm

This well-presented site has an enormous amount of information on this noble boat. Built back in 1509–11 for King Henry VIII, the vessel is itself a story, but the site delves widely into the lives of those who built, sailed, and fought for her. The food that was eaten, the clothing that was worn, and the lives that people led are all presented here. The technology of the times is also explained, and some of the employment opportunities are explored (all prior to equal opportunity, mind you). Great site.

Mesopotamia: A Learning Module

ideal for grade levels 8–12 ★★★★★

http://www.wsu.edu:8080/~dee/MESO/MESO.HTM

The cultures of this region were quite diverse, although often considered one. This commendable unit of work is well presented and is very comprehensive. The site looks at the main cultures of the region including the Sumerians, Amorites, and Chaldeans. There is an excellent time line showing the development and subsequent decline of the various civilizations. A glossary and related links are also presented.

National Atlas of the United States of America

ideal for all grade levels ★★★★

http://www.nationalatlas.gov/

You can customize this site's highly interactive US map browser to reveal details about agriculture, biology, boundaries, climate, environment, geology, people, transportation, and water. There are more than 2,000,000 geographic names. This map browser provides students with excellent insight into the US.

National Geographic Map Machine

ideal for all grade levels ★★★★★

http://www.nationalgeographic.com/resources/ngo/maps

This is a great educational resource where you can access maps of all different types, for all regions on the earth. You can access different perspectives, facts, flags, and profiles, as well as political and physical projections.

NativeWeb

ideal for all grade levels ★★★★★

http://www.nativeweb.org/

This is a very big site with links to all sorts of places pertaining to indigenous or native peoples worldwide. The electronic store lists native enterprises around the world. There is a range of newsletters and newsgroups, as well as a regional group of sites. An excellent site for students to browse and for teachers to draw information from. Students can make direct contact with different native groups around the world from here also.

New York Times Learning Network

ideal for grade levels 4–12 ★★★★

http://www.nytimes.com/learning/index.html

For a US as well as an international view of the world, the *New York Times* is great. It also has a dedicated education section dealing with all the major social issues and providing an excellent resource for all teachers at all levels. The material is at an appropriate reading age, and content is drawn from around the world.

North, South, East, West: American Indians and the Natural World

ideal for grade levels 8–10 ★★★

http://www.clpgh.org/cmnh/exhibits/north-south-east-west/index2.html

Based on an exhibition catalog of the same name, this site explores the relationship Native Americans have with the natural world, focusing on four different groups: the Tlingit, the Hopi, the Iroquois, and the Lakota. Each of these tribal groups lives in a different environment, but they share many similarities in terms of their beliefs in, philosophies about, and knowledge of the natural world.

Oakford Manor

ideal for grade levels 4–10 ★★★★★

http://www.alienexplorer.com/manor/oakford.html

If you are investigating life in thirteenth-century England or looking to explore how people lived in a rural village setting some eight hundred years ago, then this is the ultimate destination. There is a huge amount of information here: details of the lives of individuals, records from the manor and church, and a section on the Domesday Book. This is all tied into an investigation based around the information provider. There is a teacher's guide that accompanies this unit of work.

On This Date in North American Indian History

ideal for grade levels 3–12 ★★

http://members.tripod.com/~PHILKON/

This site provides an excellent way to keep American Indian history alive on a day-to-day basis through its listings of historical events. Also included are definitions of tribal and moon names plus more than 8,000 links that pertain to the indigenous peoples of North America. Sites fall into such categories as reference, tribal, art, language, history, powwow, and biography.

Opinion Pages

ideal for grade levels 11–12 ★★★★

http://www.opinion-pages.org/

This is a collection of current editorials, opinions, and commentaries from English-language newspapers and magazines from around the world. This database can be easily searched, and a range of opinions can be found on any topic. Great material for analysis work as well as for providing background for debate.

PBS Democracy Project

ideal for grade levels 5–10 ★★★★

http://www.pbs.org/democracy/

The idea behind this site is to encourage students to fully appreciate their democratic right to vote. Aspects of the site deal with the importance of character, political ads, and the press and its relationship with the public. Other features include profiles of the candidates, a glossary of political terms, and a terrific time line chronicling the history of voting in the United States. Students can even work on their own campaign!

Peace Gallery

ideal for all grade levels ★★★★★

http://www.peacegallery.com/

This site is designed to highlight the better side of humanity. Wayne Breslyn's experiences, courtesy of the peace corps, show that there is a widespread richness of community throughout the world that is not shown on the six o'clock news. Family, friendship, and common purpose more than compensate for disease, inhumanity, war, and disasters. Teens especially need to have this reinforced as the world presented to them via much of their schoolwork in the social sciences is negative and gives an unbalanced view of the world they live in. Good photographs and commentary, fascinating people, and intriguing places are shown here.

Pollution Solution

ideal for grade levels 11–12 ★★★★

http://www.ifmt.nf.ca/mi-net/enviro/pollut.htm

A rather bold heading that is the forerunner to an excellent site dealing with this topic. So much has been written on the topic, but this site presents a well-crafted and balanced set of resources. The site deals with pollution in all its forms and serves primarily as a wake-up call to our responsibilities, as well as being an awareness-building exercise for students.

Presidents Game

ideal for grade levels 5–10 ★★

http://www.sprocketworks.com/shockwave/load.asp?SprMovie=presidentsgame

At first this looks like a very straightforward game, but in fact it is quite hard to place the presidents of the United States in the right order on the time line provided. If you are looking at American history, then this Shockwave game is an excellent activity for students to complete.

Race to the South Pole

ideal for grade levels 4–10 ★★★★

http://www.monterey.k12.ca.us/~snlornzo/quests/antarctica.html

Robert Scott's quest to reach the South Pole resulted in his untimely death along with the deaths of many in his party. Other explorers, including Roald Amundsen and Ernest Shackleton, learned of the inhospitable nature of Antarctica, but the draw to get there first drove them. The task in this WebQuest is to prepare to take part in a modern-day race to the South Pole. The first team to reach the South Pole with the least loss of life is declared the winner!

Radical Times: The Antiwar Movement of the 1960s

ideal for grade levels 8–12 ★★★

http://library.thinkquest.org/27942/indexf.htm

These were tumultuous times, when the establishment was challenged by the youth and the administration was not impressed! This global phenomenon was best expressed in the United States, and most of this site reveals the US protests that marked this decade. Peace, love, and goodwill!

Revolutionary WebQuest

ideal for grade levels 4–12 ★★★

http://library.advanced.org/11683/HomeMain.html

During this Web exploration, students investigate key events, heroes of the American Revolution, lifestyle and culture, major battles, and the Declaration of Independence. There is road to independence battle simulation also.

Russia: How Has Change Affected the Former Soviet Union?

ideal for grade levels 8–12 ★★★★

http://www.learner.org/exhibits/russia

If you think change has been tough on you, then check this site out. How have the massive changes affected the people of the former Soviet Union? The site charts the history and breakup of the Soviet Union and follows the development of the breakaway republics and the building of the Russian Federation. Excellent sociology material, as well as a macrostudy of the effects of change.

Schools Demining Schools

ideal for all grade levels ★★★★

http://www.un.org/Pubs/CyberSchoolBus/banmines/index.html

The aim of this UN-sponsored project is to help schools understand that many schools in war zones are infested with land mines and to encourage students in nonwar zone schools to raise money to ensure that these schools are demined. There is an education process outlined, and then discussion of school involvement is offered, demonstrating how students make a real difference to their world. Excellent use of the Internet and very well-constructed site both in content and presentation.

Searching for China

ideal for grade levels 4–12 ★★★★

http://www.kn.pacbell.com/wired/China/ChinaQuest.html

This WebQuest focuses on the history of China, including the changing political climate, its geography, its people, and its culture. The journey begins with students being asked to address this question: What actions should the US take in its policy towards China? The resources that the WebQuest provides are extensive and present more than enough data and information for students to process into an understanding of the topic.

Six Billion Human Beings

ideal for all grade levels ★★★★★

http://www.popexpo.net/english.html

This online exhibition from the National Museum of Natural History in Paris offers a wonderful visual impact of what six billion human beings actually means. You need to have Macromedia Shockwave to make the most of the site, which is graphically very enticing and provides students with a very powerful understanding of the impact of our present population explosion.

Six Paths to China

ideal for grade levels 4–10 ★★★★★

http://www.kn.pacbell.com/wired/China/

This is a wonderful collection of activities that not only investigates the geography of China but also integrates authentic problem solving into the social science curriculum. Students can learn about the present state of China or look into the well-publicized situation with Chinese orphans. Is this really a case of mass mistreatment of children? The material presented is superb, and the ideas and content are excellent.

South Africa: Can a Country Overcome Its History?

ideal for all grade levels ★★★★★

http://www.learner.org/exhibits/southafrica/

This is an excellent site exploring the potential and the trials of this country. Economic wealth can only bring social development when the people act as a whole and want change. This site tracks the various aspects that will determine the success or failure of this transition. Here students can explore the issues of South Africa's mineral wealth, the history of apartheid, the first Europeans in South Africa, human rights, and the process of reconciliation.

Springfield Race Riot of 1908

ideal for grade levels 8–12 ★★

http://library.thinkquest.org/2986/

As well as being home to a memorial of Abraham Lincoln, Springfield, Illinois, is also home to one of the more painful historical events in American history. The riot of 1908, the result of intense competition for jobs, was one of the events that contributed to the formation of the National Association for the Advancement of Colored People (NAACP).

State of the World's Children 1999: Education Section

ideal for grade levels 4–12 ★★★★

http://www.unicef.org/sowc99/

According to this site, about one billion people were expected to enter the twenty-first century not being able to read. Two-thirds of them would be women, and more than 130 million school-age children. This illiteracy condemns them to the poverty trap. This report tells the story of a world community unwilling to accept the consequences of illiteracy. Having the goal of education for all, this Web site would be a great focus for the social studies program looking at equity and the relationship between education and poverty.

TerraServer

ideal for all grade levels ★★★★★

http://terraserver.microsoft.com/

This online database is a collection of maps and aerial photographs of sections of our planet's surface. You can then use the online service (free) to zoom in on an area and get great images of locations and geographic features from around the United States. If you want to visit the Grand Canyon, Alcatraz, or the Statue of Liberty, you can. This is an excellent service for all grade levels and is an especially useful tool to assist younger students in grasping the difference between countries, cities, and towns as well as their geographic relationships.

Third from the Sun: Geographical Features as Seen from Space

ideal for grade levels 4–9 ★★★★★

http://www.exploratorium.edu/learning_studio/landsat/

Great site that makes use of the images collected by Landsat satellites to highlight the Earth's geography. The site provides a link between teaching the elements of geographic features and the world that the students live in.

Timeframes

ideal for all grade levels ★★★★

http://timeframes.natlib.govt.nz/

This superb New Zealand-based site examines thousands of images that depict time frames in New Zealand history. Even for students in countries outside New Zealand, this is an excellent site to use for a compare-and-contrast exercise. Classic case of a picture being worth a thousand words!

Timeline of the American Civil Rights Movement

ideal for all grade levels ★★★

http://www.wmich.edu/politics/mlk/

You can find here an excellent time line beginning in 1954 and ending a little more than a decade later. On reflection, it is hard to believe that the movement began only fifty years ago.

Tour Canada from Space

ideal for all grade levels ★★

http://www.ccrs.nrcan.gc.ca/ccrs/imgserv/tour/toure.html

At this Web site, you can take a journey in the space shuttle and view a variety of locations throughout Canada, including geographic features, cities, and areas of environmental interest such as forest fires. This is an excellent concept.

Traditional Chinese Culture

ideal for all grade levels ★★★★

http://www.cohums.ohio-state.edu/deall/jin.3/C231/default.htm

If you are looking for information on traditional Chinese culture, then you should start here with these course materials from Ohio State University's Department of East Asian Languages and Literature. This comprehensive and attractively presented site is an excellent resource on Chinese history, art, and literature. Be sure to check out the handouts, images, references, and links.

Traveler

ideal for grade levels 4–12 ★★★★

http://library.thinkquest.org/2840/

Here students can take on characters and develop their own story lines according to the choices they make. The story line allows students to get a feeling for what it was like to live in ancient Greek times. Character choices include the daughter of an Egyptian king and queen, a merchant traveling the known Greek Empire trying to make a living from trading, or a scholar attempting to gain knowledge from wise people of the times.

Tropical Rainforest in Suriname

ideal for all grade levels ★★★★★

http://www.euronet.nl/users/mbleeker/suriname/suri-eng.html

Learn where Suriname is and discover information about the rainforest there on site. This is an ideal country for a class to study. The bauxite mine is running out of ore, and as a consequence, logging is becoming the next opportunity to be exploited. This is not a simulation—it is real. And this is an excellent example of a country looking at economic and social options. It is a privilege to watch as the drama unfolds.

United Nations

ideal for grade levels 4–12 ★★★★★

http://www.un.org/

This site contains huge resources for the social studies teacher. Topics dealt with include human rights, peace and security, economic and social development, international law, and humanitarian affairs. What you will find here provides excellent stimulus material for debate, as well as statistics on almost any issue you care to investigate.

USA: A WebQuest

ideal for grade levels 3–9 ★★

http://www.wallowa.k12.or.us/students/states/state.html

Here students can tour the United States and learn about each state, including the state flower, animal, and nickname. Students can also explore the agriculture and industry of each state as well as the landforms, parks, and monuments that make each state unique.

Vietnam: A Children's Guide

ideal for grade levels K–3 ★★★★

http://www2.lhric.org/pocantico/vietnam/vietnam.htm

This site is specially created for students in grades K–3 and is in a picture-book format to suit the audience. There is background material for the teacher as well as a list of additional Web sites to visit and a WebQuest that students might like to take part in. The Web site originated after students read the book *Angel Child, Dragon Child* by Michele Maria Surat.

Viking Home Page

ideal for all grade levels ★★★★

http://www.control.chalmers.se/vikings/indexframe.html

This site provides a collection of links offering fascinating insight into this group of people who set out to conquer the world, with determination and some good technology. Among the topics featured are runes, warfare, and ships, in addition to general Viking and Scandinavian history.

Virtual Economy

ideal for grade levels 11–12 ★★★★★

http://www.bized.ac.uk/virtual/economy/

This is a sophisticated computerized model based on the budget of the United Kingdom. The chancellor's house at No.11 Downing Street is used as the virtual base for this Web site. The ground floor contains the information bureau with teacher's and students' guides, and on the first floor includes case studies. The second floor allows you to investigate the different economic variables used in the model. On the third floor is a library full of information on all types of economic theories, as well as an excellent glossary. On the fourth floor you can access the model itself and try changing the variables to see whether you are able to balance the budget.

Virtual Galápagos

ideal for all grade levels ★★★★★

http://www.terraquest.com/galapagos/intro.html

At this extraordinary site, adventurers have posted dispatches chronicling their 1996 journey to this group of islands where evolutionary time has stood still. One of a series of adventures through TerraQuest, this site allows students to be active participants in real-life adventures.

Virtual Renaissance

ideal for grade levels 4–12 ★★★★

http://www.twingroves.district96.k12.il.us/Renaissance/GeneralFiles/Introduction.html

Join Giovanni Renaissanci in this time warp going back to the period in Italy called the Renaissance. See how the technology and medicine differs from today, and experience the dramatic change in living conditions. This period was a time of great change, not dissimilar to the beginning of the twenty-first century. You can check out maps, chronologies, art, and a variety of different aspects ranging from clothing to manners.

Virtual Tourist

ideal for all grade levels ★★★★★

http://www.vtourist.com/

This site has been around for some time now and just improves with age. If students need facts, other information, or links on a particular country, they can click on that part of the world map to retrieve relevant material. Not exhaustive for each destination, this resource provides at least some brief background information.

Weather Unit

ideal for grade levels K–10 ★★★★

http://faldo.atmos.uiuc.edu/WEATHER/weather.html

Weather is a topic that can be used in a cross-curricular manner within the school. This online unit presents lesson ideas and activities that incorporate weather into subject areas such as math, science, reading and writing, social studies, art, drama, physical education, music, and geography. The site even makes suggestions for producing props within the classroom and explains ways to stimulate students to think about the weather, as well as gives resources that can be used to support the teaching of these ideas.

Web of Culture

ideal for all grade levels ★★★★

http://www.webofculture.com/

This large site looks at almost every aspect of culture you can imagine. It covers areas such as gestures, consulates, currency, and languages.

World Game Institute

ideal for all grade levels ★★★★★

http://www.worldgame.org/

This site contains a huge amount of information as well as the game that is its focus. The game, which involves saving the earth, can be played by anyone from students to corporate executives. Excellent resources are available to support the game, such as mapping software, Global Data Manager, and encyclopedic information. Most fascinating are the site's Worldometers that track changing world data, such as the current population. The Worldometers cover other not-so-standard topics, including the number of people presently going hungry, expenditure on weapons sales and education, amount of solar energy hitting the earth, and much more. Watching the rate that these worldometers change can be fascinating to students and teachers alike.

Foreign Languages

French

General and Other Languages

American Sign Language Browser ★★★★
http://commtechlab.msu.edu/stes/aslweb/index.html 99

BYUH Samoan Language Lessons ★★★★
http://lc.byuh.edu/Samoan/Samoan2.html 99

Dr. Berlin's Foreign Font Archive ★★★
http://hopi.dtcc.edu/~berlin/fonts.html 99

English as a Foreign Language Magazine (eflweb) ★★★★★
http://www.eflweb.com/ 99

Ernie's Learn to Speak a Little Hawaiian ★★
http://www.mhpcc.edu/~erobello/homepage_ernie/ernie1.html 99

FL Teach: Foreign Language Teaching Forum ★★★★
http://www.cortland.edu/flteach 100

Hindu: Indian National Newspaper ★★★
http://www.hinduonline.com/ 100

Human Languages Page ★★★★
http://www.june29.com/HLP/ 100

Internet Dictionary Project ★★★
http://www.june29.com/IDP/IDPC.html 100

Karin's ESL PartyLand ★★★★
http://www.eslpartyland.com/ 100

Language Links™ ★★
http://www.geocities.com/CollegePark/Field/4260/bottom.html 100

Latin Dictionary and Grammar Aid ★★
http://www.nd.edu/~archives/latgramm.htm 100

Latin Phrases, Mottoes, and Quotations ★★
http://www.geocities.com/~stilicho/phrases.html 101

Learn Dutch in the New Millennium ★★
http://www.learndutch.org/ 101

Linguist: Ask a Linguist ★★
http://linguistlist.org/~ask-ling/ 101

Logos: Non Solo Parole (The Logos Dictionary) ★★
http://www.logos.it/query/query.html 101

Media Links: Online Media Directory ★★★
http://emedia1.mediainfo.com/emedia/ 101

Portuguese: Glasgow University ★★★★
http://www.portembassy.gla.ac.uk/PortLang/index.html 101

Roger Ganderton's Home Page ★★★
http://www.cltr.uq.oz.au:8000/~rogerg/ 101

Syracuse Language™ ★★
http://www.syrlang.com/ 102

TravLang ★★★★
http://www.travlang.com/ 102

UCLA Language Materials Project ★★★
http://www.lmp.ucla.edu/ 102

Virtual Bangladesh: Survival Bengali ★★
http://www.virtualbangladesh.com/bd_bhasha.html 102

Welsh ★★
http://www.cs.brown.edu/fun/welsh/Welsh_main.html 102

Your Dictionary.com ★★★
http://www.facstaff.bucknell.edu/rbeard/diction.html. 102

German

Die Welt ★★★
http://www.welt.de/. 103

German Electronic Textbook ★★
http://www.wm.edu/CAS/modlang/grammnu.html 103

KinderWeb ★★★
http://www.uncg.edu/~lixlpurc/school/Kinder.html 103

19th-Century German Stories ★★★
http://www.vcu.edu/hasweb/for/menu.html 103

University of Cologne: The Cologne Page ★★★★
http://www.uni-koeln.de/koeln/indexe.html 103

Indonesian

Bahasa Indonesia ★★★
http://www.tourismindonesia.com/bahasa_indonesia.htm 104

Bahasa Indonesia: IndoBiz ★★★
http://www.indobiz.com/. 104

IndoLinx: Linking Australian and Indonesian Students ★★★★
http://www.ansonic.com.au/indolinx/ 104

Indonesian Language Resources ★★
http://www.languagetechnologies.com/ 104

Langsung: Indonesian FM Radio di Internet ★★★
http://www.qsl.net/yb0rmi/rri.htm. 104

Italian

Benvenuto Alla Pagina Multilinguale Della Academic Computing Facility Nella NYU ★★★
http://www.nyu.edu/acf/multilingual/italian.html. 105

In Italy™ Online ★★★
http://www.initaly.com/. 105

L'Unione Sarda ★★
http://www.unionesarda.it/ 105

Mama's Learn to Speak Italian ★★★★
http://www.eat.com/learn-italian/index.html. 105

Spanish

Asian Languages

Center for Applied Japanese Language Studies (CAJLS)

ideal for all grade levels ★★

http://babel.uoregon.edu/CAJLS/

This is a huge database of information. You can choose a topic, a function, a level, whether you want a speaking, listening, or writing exercise, and the site provides five to ten exercises for the students to be involved in. Good material.

Chinese

ideal for all grade levels ★★★

http://www.ocrat.com

This is an excellent site for schools teaching Chinese at any level. Included are some great animated characters that are created one stroke at a time. You can listen to voice of America in Chinese! There are also character pronunciations.

Chinese Character Flash Cards

ideal for grade levels 11–12 ★★★

http://www.mandarintools.com/flashcard.html

This excellent java-assisted site has over 1000 most frequently used characters organized into ten different levels of difficulty. The site provides pinyin romanization, English definition, and Cantonese pronunciation.

Chinese Language Magazines

ideal for grade levels 11–12 ★★

http://www.cathay.net/chn-mag.shtml

This is an excellent collection of links to magazines written in Cantonese (Chinese). These make excellent support material for students studying this language. Viewers are available for reading the characters.

Chinese Multimedia Tutorial

ideal for all grade levels ★★

http://www.inform.umd.edu/EdRes/Topic/Humanities/.C-tut/C-tut.html

This is a great place to start learning Chinese for fun. Site features simple greetings that you can listen to as well as an introduction to Chinese characters.

Daily Yomiuri Online

ideal for grade levels 4–12 ★★

http://www.yomiuri.co.jp/main/main-e.htm

This provides an excellent coverage of Japanese news, finance, culture, sports, and crime. The Japanese perspective of this region is also quite intriguing. Students would do well to compare their impressions of themselves and their own reality with the impressions of the Japanese and what they perceive as the reality.

Japanese Guide

ideal for all grade levels ★★

http://www.japan-guide.com/

This is a collection of over 200 pages of information on Japan and its culture. There are some excellent sections dealing with living in Japan as well as language, history, food, politics, current events, and tradition. The site is in English and offers a Japanese pen pal service, live chat and discussion sessions. The photo gallery section is an excellent source of prompting material, with topics such as culture, earthquakes, and cities.

Japanese Online.com

ideal for all grade levels ★★★

http://www.japanese-online.com/

Great site. There are plenty of lessons for math and language here that are well presented. Many come with their own sound files. Check out the bulletin board where students can exchange greetings in their halting new language. Dialogue, vocabulary, grammar, and some good culture modules are featured. There are also some math lessons from Japan's junior high math placement tests.

Japanese Signs

ideal for all grade levels ★★

http://www2.gol.com/users/xroads/html/japanese_signs_no_frames.html

Here we have a Web page for students of the Japanese language to learn about Japanese signs, billboards, plaques, banners, or any other such objects for displaying a message to the general public. Some of the signs are in pictures and words. Do not try and give a literal translation, but to try to interpret it, taking into account the cultural background of where the photograph, billboard, or object is displayed.

Japan Times

ideal for all grade levels ★★★

http://www.japantimes.co.jp/

This excellent newspaper from Japan provides access to information and ideas for teaching in the classroom. Check out Technotimes, a look through the department stores, museums and galleries, festivals, as well as other reflections of Japanese culture.

Korea Herald

ideal for all grade levels ★★

http://www.koreaherald.co.kr

There is information here on all aspects of life in Korea. Everything here from the weather through to news from around the country, as well as sections on North Korea. The political and social consequences of the reunification of Korea are discussed along with reader's opinions.

Learning Chinese Online

ideal for levels 7–12 ★★★★

http://www.csulb.edu/~txie/online.htm

This extensive site deals with all aspects of learning Mandarin (Chinese). There are also a range of downloads available on the site to view characters. Excellent material.

On-line Chinese Tools

ideal for grade levels 8–12 ★★

http://www.mandarintools.com/

This Web site concentrates on collecting and linking to other sites that use Java, CGI, and Java Script to assist people in learning and using the Chinese language. The tools are divided into different categories including tools for learning Chinese, tools for using Chinese, Chinese reference tools and a separate section on computer tools for learning and using Chinese over the Internet.

Study Mandarin Chinese Using Voice of America (VOA)

ideal for grade levels 11–12 ★★

http://www.ocrat.com/voa/

Using RealAudio and the Voice of America transmissions in Mandarin Chinese, you can develop your Mandarin language skills. This is not a course for beginners. The transcripts of the broadcasts are available to assist with the learning process.

Understanding Written Japanese

ideal for all grade levels ★★

http://members.aol.com/joyo96/index.html

This site has an excellent collection of support material for teachers looking for work on Kanji, Hiragana, or Katakana.

French

À la découverte de Tintin

ideal for all grade levels 

http://www.tintin.qc.ca

The success of many programs depends not just on the passion of the teacher but also the ability to draw on contexts that students relate to. Here you can use the cartoon adventures of Tintin to explore the French language. And for those who might struggle a bit, there is also an English edition. (*Note:* For those introducing Spanish there is also a Spanish edition.)

Agency for Cultural Cooperation

ideal for grade levels 8–12 ★★★

http://www.france.diplomatie.fr/cooperation/index.html

This site, in French, provides news and information on France and makes for an excellent learning experience for students who have a good basic understanding of French. There are links to many other French pages and Francophone sites.

Civilization Français

ideal for all grade levels ★★★

http://www.cortland.edu/flteach/civ

This excellent unit of work is part of the larger FLTeach site. Tour through this site to get an appreciation of the culture of France, its economy, Parisian society, and images of the country including themes based on transport, religion, etc. Great site that has many applications for the classroom.

ClicNet: Français langue étrangère et langue seconde

ideal for grade levels 4–12 ★★

http://clicnet.swarthmore.edu/fle.html

As the title suggests, this is a wonderful Web site for information and links for teachers of French as a second language. There are sites dealing with language, culture, history, geography, and on almost any aspect of French life you may wish to investigate.

Conservatoire National des Arts et Métiers

ideal for all grade levels ★★

http://web.cnam.fr/

From the University of Cornell, this site is an excellent resource for teachers of French. Sports, arts, literature, information about the country, politics, and an education section are included. Excellent site.

France from the French

ideal for all grade levels ★★★

http://www.france.diplomatie.fr/france/

This introspective look at France provides language teachers with an excellent overview of France's geography, history, politics, economy, social affairs, science, education, culture, and foreign policy.

France International Radio

ideal for grade levels 8–12 ★★

http://town.hall.org/travel/france/rfi.html

France International provides an excellent collection of lessons that can be very useful in the classroom. You can download lessons (which are typically between 2 and 2.5 MB each). You can also download daily news transcripts in French. Lessons include vocabulary work, and conjugations as well as social issues and other topics based on themes and contexts.

French History: In French

ideal for all grade levels ★★

http://www-as.phy.ohiou.edu/Departments/Mod_Lang/french/histoire.html

This is an excellent collection of links to Web sites that deal with the history of France. Many of the sites are in French and most come from a French perspective. In order to understand the French language, students need to appreciate French history and this is a wonderful way of combining both processes.

French Language Course

ideal for grade levels 4–12 ★★★

http://www.jump-gate.com/languages/french

Jacques Leon is your instructor of basic French in this course. The objective is to allow you to understand written French and to write a letter to a French friend or correspondent. It is refreshing to see that Jacques has realized that the Web is not a very good medium, at the moment, for teaching spoken languages. The first five lessons emphasize grammar and the other lessons are more conversational.

French News Service

ideal for all grade levels ★★★

http://www.france2.fr/nav_home.htm

If you are after the latest news from France and you want it in French then this is a great site to visit. Sports, news, politics, the environment, and much more are all dealt with here.

French Tongue Twisters Virelangues

ideal for all grade levels ★★

http://www.uebersetzung.at/twister/fr.htm

Teachers are always looking for different approaches and contexts to get across new ideas or skills. Here is a wonderful set of tongue twisters in French. There are nearly 100 provided here, varying from the humorous to the informative.

LeFigaro

ideal for grade levels 4–12 ★★★

http://www.lefigaro.fr/

This enigmatic magazine is known throughout the world and students and teachers can access the online version from this site. There is a raft of opinions, French politics, culture, gossip, news, and some sports news. Good material with plenty of visual clues.

Le Site Web de Madame Gaal

ideal for grade levels 4–12 ★★★

http://grace.carrick.pps.pgh.pa.us/french/

This fun site has a lot of information and material for all teachers of the French language. There are many ideas for the classroom as well as themes. Of significance are the newsletters produced by students. The newsletters entitled Chars de Gaal should give you a reasonable introduction to the tenor of the site. This is good fun and some great French!

Lingua@Web

ideal for all grade levels ★★★

http://www.linguaweb.ndirect.co.uk/pages/frenlev1.htm

On this site, you can be introduced to the French language, learn to describe yourself, and check out your breakfast vocabulary. There are tutorials using the home and pizza as contexts. You can experiment with the language as well as receive grammar help and extension work.

L'Infobourg

ideal for all grade levels ★★★

http://www.infobourg.qc.ca/default.asp

Welcome to this great resource for teachers of French that not only features language material but also includes French written and resourced material on all curriculum areas. This site provides great contexts for the French language classroom. Updated regularly, with up-to-the-minute news and events. The site also has a great set of links for teachers of the French language. Another great Canadian site!

Virtual Baguette

ideal for grade levels 3–12 ★★★

http://www.baguette.com/

Great French language site that is full of fun and activities. Great presentation; this site has a good balance of good context and inviting material. Plenty of links to support the articles.

General and Other Languages

Aboriginal Languages of Australia

ideal for all grade levels ★★★

http://www.dnathan.com/VL/austLang.htm

This huge compendium of links is a great introduction to the variety of aboriginal languages taught and spoken in Australia. There is everything here from songs, courses, bookstores, resources, vocabularies and word lists, dictionaries, and much more.

Alta Vista World Translation

ideal for grade levels 4–10 ★★★★★

http://babelfish.altavista.digital.com/

What a great free service even if it's not perfect. Type in your text that needs translating and with just a press of a button you can have it translated. Deutsch, Español, Italiano, and Portuguese are presently available with more languages promised in the future.

American Sign Language Browser

ideal for all grade levels ★★★★

http://commtechlab.msu.edu/stes/aslweb/index.html

This is an online Web browser, which is able to look up video clips of thousands of signs and allow students to learn them and their background. You need QuickTime and your browser must be able to support frames.

BYUH Samoan Language Lessons

ideal for all grade levels ★★★★

http://lc.byuh.edu/Samoan/Samoan2.html

This is an excellent site supporting the teaching of the Samoan language. The lessons are excellently presented with both photographic support as well as a sound effects program that can be downloaded from the site. Fourteen excellent lessons suitable for all levels of teaching.

Dr. Berlin's Foreign Font Archive

ideal for all grade levels ★★★

http://hopi.dtcc.edu/~berlin/fonts.html

Many languages require specialized macrons, characters, and artistic styles in order to communicate effectively. This is a great collection of shareware that can deliver fonts suitable for writing in languages such as Arabic, Cyrillic, Japanese, Vietnamese, Yiddish, Laos, Khmer, Korean, German, Burmese, Coptic, Gaelic, and many others.

English as a Foreign Language Magazine (eflweb)

ideal for all grade levels ★★★★★

http://www.eflweb.com/

This is a great magazine for both EFL teachers and teachers of English. The amount of information on this site is huge. Events and conferences are listed here as are other Web sites, a virtual bookstore, reviews of products for the classroom, a notice board for sales and exchanges, and software. You can even post your resume. This is all on top of a great range of articles written for and by EFL teachers. Top ten site.

Ernie's Learn to Speak a Little Hawaiian

ideal for all grade levels ★★

http://www.mhpcc.edu/~erobello/homepage_ernie/ernie1.html

Kokua mai. Here is a great site where you can learn a romantic language and impress everyone. This delightful introduction to the Hawaiian language provides some basic sounds, introduces the importance of the macron, provides some pronunciation work, and teaches some typical social phrases. From here you can learn some typical questions and answers and learn some more colorful expressions and everyday terms.

FL Teach: Foreign Language Teaching Forum

ideal for all grade levels ★★★★

http://www.cortland.edu/flteach

FLTeach is an excellent site for teachers to get information on all aspects of teaching foreign languages. There is a selection of newsgroups and Listservs to chose from as well as curriculum material, support sites and advice. Great site for all teachers of foreign languages.

Hindu: Indian National Newspaper

ideal for all grade levels ★★★

http://www.hinduonline.com/

Newspapers are an excellent window into a society. When studying a language or culture, newspapers are an excellent way of finding appropriate contexts for teaching the elements that contrive together to form a culture. The newspaper is in English for ease of reading.

Human Languages Page

ideal for all grade levels ★★★★

http://www.june29.com/HLP/

From Basque to Catalan to Guarani through to Icelandic and Mohawk and Myanmar, this is a very comprehensive set of links that are well organized and very thorough. There is information here dealing with multilingual resources, linguistics research, and commercial resources.

Internet Dictionary Project

ideal for all grade levels ★★★

http://www.june29.com/IDP/IDPC.html

This free piece of software provides dictionaries in German, Spanish, French, Italian, Latin, Portuguese, and Romanian. This is an excellent piece of software to have on computers in language departments. The software allows you to translate from one language to another quickly, without having to be online. It should be noted that the dictionaries are not extensive.

Karin's ESL PartyLand

ideal for all grade levels ★★★★

http://www.eslpartyland.com/

This site is set up for both ESL teachers and students. Discussion forums, seventy-five interactive quizzes, chat lines, and an excellent collection of interactive learning pages based on the themes of the media, food, and travel can be found here. Excellent site.

Language Links™

ideal for all grade levels ★★

http://www.geocities.com/CollegePark/Field/4260/bottom.html

There are Filipino people in many countries around the world, but unfortunately there is little language support for those wishing to keep in touch with their language and the culture. Here you can find information supporting both Filipino and Cebuano.

Latin Dictionary and Grammar Aid

ideal for grade levels 11–12 ★★

http://www.nd.edu/~archives/latgramm.htm

Type in the form of the word that you wish to find in the dictionary and the definition will be provided from a bank of 15,600 terms. There are links to other resources as well as the Latin Grammar aid providing translations of various noun cases, endings for regular nouns, adjectives, active verbs, and present participles.

Latin Phrases, Mottoes, and Quotations

ideal for grade levels 11–12 ★★

http://www.geocities.com/~stilicho/phrases.html

Students who still study Latin will find this site an excellent source of statements that fewer and fewer will ever understand! This is a huge collection that can be used for great introduction and conclusion statements in essays, speeches, and assignments. Carpe diem!

Learn Dutch in the New Millennium

ideal for grade levels 11–12 ★★

http://www.learndutch.org/

This site is a great resource for teachers of the Dutch language but also for those who would like to teach their students conversational Dutch on a need-to-know basis. There is also a sizeable collection of information on Dutch culture and links to additional sites so the class can be immersed in the language and the culture.

Linguist: Ask a Linguist

ideal for all grade levels ★★

http://linguistlist.org/~ask-ling/

You can ask the linguist any question you like, on almost any language. They do not do translations, origins of words and phrases, or correct grammar, but they will provide information on particular words, location of information, terminology, etc. You can also review past questions.

Logos: Non Solo Parole (The Logos Dictionary)

ideal for all grade levels ★★

http://www.logos.it/query/query.html

The site provides an international dictionary covering over 7.5 million words and terms in many languages. Great site for students to use in the classroom to find meanings or history of terms and words.

Media Links: Online Media Directory

ideal for all grade levels ★★★

http://emedia1.mediainfo.com/emedia/

The Web site provides links to newspapers and magazines as well as radio stations and syndicated news from countries all around the world. They are organized by geographical regions as well as by media type. These services provide an excellent resource for teachers of all foreign languages.

Portuguese: Glasgow University

ideal for grade levels 3–12 ★★★★

http://www.portembassy.gla.ac.uk/PortLang/index.html

You can do your own Portuguese beginner's course here as well as look up some contemporary Portuguese history and check out resources under the Portuguese culture section and find out just how widespread the Portuguese language is.

Roger Ganderton's Home Page

ideal for all grade levels ★★★

http://www.cltr.uq.oz.au:8000/~rogerg/

A must visit site for all language teachers. Excellent introduction to what the Internet is all about and an explanation of how these tools can be fully utilized in the language classroom. The Internet is a versatile tool for language teachers and all language teachers should have access for themselves and their students. This site highlights how these tools can be used to gain maximum benefit. Mail, newsgroups, IRC, MUDs, MOOs, Audio and video conferencing, FTP, Web, and Gopher are all discussed rationally and supplemented with excellent applications.

Syracuse Language™

ideal for all grade levels ★★

http://www.syrlang.com/

This site specializes in resources for language teachers with an emphasis on software. The software can be downloaded from the Internet in many instances, and the range of languages is quite broad. There are also college level courses available online for more senior students or for your own professional development.

TravLang

ideal for all grade levels ★★★★

http://www.travlang.com/

The site is based around travel, with an emphasis on foreign language, especially conversational foreign language. This makes it an extremely useful Web site for all teachers of languages. This would be an excellent default site for language teachers, with the word of the day, translating dictionaries, sixty languages represented through links to other Web sites, and information on countries around the world.

UCLA Language Materials Project

ideal for all grade levels ★★★

http://www.lmp.ucla.edu/

This is a collection of resources, language profiles, and learning centers for almost every language available. From Hosa to Haitian, each language is treated separately and the search engine locates dictionaries, grammar reference material, readers, phrase books, and reference materials. Excellent resource.

Virtual Bangladesh: Survival Bengali

ideal for all grade levels ★★

http://www.virtualbangladesh.com/bd_bhasha.html

Here is a language that would be good to study when looking at Bangladesh or the Indian subcontinent. The material here is excellent and quite comprehensive for all those that may work with children who speak Bengali or who wish to improve their students' conversational language skills.

Welsh

ideal for all grade levels ★★

http://www.cs.brown.edu/fun/welsh/Welsh_main.html

This course is designed for beginners and can be used as a month-long language focus to provide some conversational prowess, if not a complete fluency. The course starts with a section on pronunciation and progresses through construction and simple sentences. Great material.

Your Dictionary.com

ideal for all grade levels ★★★

http://www.facstaff.bucknell.edu/rbeard/diction.html

This is massive collection of dictionaries dealing with every possible language you could ever imagine. Everything from a Comparative Bantu On-Line Dictionary Data File, basic Albanian vocabulary, Esperanto, and even Klingon (Star Trek). The site is a treasure trove of material on the huge range of languages that are spoken throughout the world and is a language teachers Aladdins' cave.

German

Die Welt

ideal for grade levels 8–12 ★★★

http://www.welt.de/

This excellent newspaper is produced online daily and is an excellent way of keeping up with happenings both in Germany and around the world in the German language. There are the usual newspaper offerings dealing with politics, national and international news, sports, as well as editorial and cultural news.

German Electronic Textbook

ideal for grade levels 11–12 ★★

http://www.wm.edu/CAS/modlang/grammnu.html

This is a useful resource including two sections dealing with German grammar and German pronunciation. Grammar elements include nouns and noun modifiers, pronouns, word order, prepositions, verbs, and other tenses as well as passive voice and subjunctive mood verbs.

KinderWeb

ideal for grade levels 4–12 ★★★

http://www.uncg.edu/~lixlpurc/school/Kinder.html

If you are looking for Web sites in the German language that use a context appropriate for younger students, then this is a great site to start with. The site provides links to German language sites on topics such as sports, music, games, chat sessions, magazines, and news.

19th-Century German Stories

ideal for grade levels 4–10 ★★★

http://www.vcu.edu/hasweb/for/menu.html

Here is an excellent collection of interactive Web editions of classic German stories. The stories are an excellent context for teaching language learning and literary study. There are works here by the Grimm brothers, Gotthelf, Hoffman, Busch, and others.

University of Cologne: The Cologne Page

ideal for all grade levels ★★★★

http://www.uni-koeln.de/koeln/indexe.html

This must be one of the most romantic cities anywhere in the world and if you are studying the German language or Germany, it is almost impossible to do so without drawing on the importance of this city from an economic, military, historical, and cultural point of view. This Web site presents a wonderful photographic and literary commentary on this beautiful city. Available in both English and German.

Indonesian

Bahasa Indonesia

ideal for grade levels 4–12 ★★★

http://tourismindonesia.com/bahasa_indonesia.htm

Bahasa Indonesia is a language used by over 200 million inhabitants of Indonesia and millions more worldwide. Although each island has its own unique dialect, this language has turned this far-flung community of islands into one nation. Bahasa Indonesia is a relatively quick to learn language with construction of basic sentences relatively simple. It also uses a phonetic spelling and has minimal rules of grammar. The site provides links to a comprehensive set of sites that support the teaching of this language in schools.

Bahasa Indonesia: IndoBiz

ideal for all grade levels ★★★

http://www.indobiz.com/

This is a very useful site for all teachers of Bahasa Indonesia. There are plenty of links to sites in the Indonesian language as well as Javanese and Sundanese. There is also a section dealing with the Indonesian language in Bali, links to tertiary institutions offering continuing studies in Bahasa Indonesia, as well as information on art and culture, tourism and news.

IndoLinx: Linking Australian and Indonesian Students

ideal for all grade levels ★★★★

http://www.ansonic.com.au/indolinx/

The site has more than just links between these two country's schools, which is an excellent project in its own right. The site contains some live radio from Indonesia as well as links to newspapers, songs, and videos. There are some fine Indonesian recipes, examples of student work, and much more. Excellent site with a good focus.

Indonesian Language Resources

ideal for all grade levels ★★

http://www.languagetechnologies.com/

This Web site has been developed to assist teachers and students studying or teaching the Indonesian language. It includes a great collection of supporting Web sites as well as content.

Langsung: Indonesian FM Radio di Internet

ideal for all grade levels ★★★

http://www.qsl.net/yb0rmi/rri.htm

What better way to learn the language than to work in an atmosphere where students listen to the language continuously. This is the government-operated radio network called Warta Berita and by law must be broadcast on every licensed radio station on the hour! There are also some good pictures as well.

Italian

Benvenuto Alla Pagina Multilinguale Della Academic Computing Facility Nella NYU

ideal for grade levels 11–12 ★★★

http://www.nyu.edu/acf/multilingual/italian.html

This is an excellent resource site for studying or teaching the Italian language. There is a very formidable set of links to computing issues. But the resource is very useful, because there are also links to news and media in the Italian language as well as language learning resources.

In Italy™ Online

ideal for all grade levels ★★★

http://www.initaly.com/

This is a wonderful site that features information about staying in Italy. The site deals with non-traditional accommodation such as working farms, historic residences, and city apartments. Other features are traveling within Italy, how to get the best bargains at bazaars and boutiques, and the various regions of Italy and their specialties.

L'Unione Sarda

ideal for all grade levels ★★

http://www.unionesarda.it/

This Italian newspaper provides students with plenty of translation opportunities as well as giving them background information on the news, culture, politics, the arts, and information on daily life.

Mama's Learn to Speak Italian

ideal for grade levels 3–12 ★★★★

http://www.eat.com/learn-italian/index.html

Professor Antonio has upgraded his let's learn Italian Web page considerably and now uses Real-Audio to help you learn the Italian language. The material is well suited for teachers introducing conversational languages. The context includes the family, travel, food, romance, and a twelfth century Italian folk tale. Humor plays a big part in this site.

Spanish Language

Basic Spanish for the Virtual Student

ideal for all grade levels ★★

http://www.umr.edu/~amigos/Virtual/

There are fifty modules covering all aspects of Spanish. The modules make excellent stand-alone units that weave together to make an excellent course. Students can complete the modules and then use the modules to teach their peers the same material.

Español: Beginner's Materials

ideal for all grade levels ★★★

http://www.linguaweb.ndirect.co.uk/pages/spanlev1.htm

This excellent Web site from Lingu@web provides teachers of Spanish with an excellent collection of material and links to supporting Web sites. There is good material here dealing with Peru as a thematic context for teaching Spanish. Homework assignments and tests are also available here. There are also tutorials that divide the work into standard and higher categories.

Españolé! The Online Resource for Students and Teachers of Spanish

ideal for all grade levels ★★

http://members.yourlink.net/kappa/espanole/principal.html

There is a good collection of links to Spanish Web sites and they are reasonably well organized. You can check out translators, money converters, Spanish Web cards, pen pals, online Hispanic schools, newspapers, and magazines as well as art, literature, music, and, of course, cooking.

Latin American Network Information Center

ideal for all grade levels ★★★

http://lanic.utexas.edu/

If you are teaching Spanish, this site provides a huge range of language material using cultural, civil, and geographical contexts. There is so much here you will need to put aside an hour or two to look for specific information that could be useful to your language program.

Learn Spanish: A Free Online Tutorial

ideal for grade levels 8–12 ★★

http://www.studyspanish.com/index.htm

Although this is a formal introduction to the learning of Spanish, it provides excellent material on all aspects of learning Spanish. There are also some good cultural notes here that are supplemented by some good links to support sites and support materials.

Sí Spain

ideal for all grade levels ★★★

http://www.SiSpain.org/

This is a massive site with over 3.5 million visitors. Some of what is available here includes Spanish fiestas, language and culture, foreign affairs, geography, population and society, the economy, and much more. There is plenty of background information here to assist teachers in the classroom. You can view the site in English, Spanish, and French.

Spanish Course for Beginners

ideal for all grade levels ★★

http://www.docuweb.ca/SiSpain/english/course/calgary/index.html

The Spanish embassy in Canada has provided this introductory course in Spanish for teachers and others who wish to learn this popular language. The advantage here is you can download the entire course and use the sections you require when you need them, without having to be online.

Spanish Language Resources

ideal for grade levels 8–12 ★★

http://www.bbc.co.uk/education/languages/spanish/index.shtml

This is an excellent collection of resources for all teachers of the Spanish language. The host of the site answers your questions and there is a comprehensive online resource for schools to use. There are also games that support the use of the Spanish language and even a Mexican period soap opera with an "explosive mixture of sombreros, tequila and passion" complete with captions!

Spanish Online News

ideal for grade levels 11–12 ★★★★

http://www.abc.es

Here you can catch-up with all the national and international news in Spanish. The Web site is very well designed, is easy to navigate, and presents a wonderful collection of high-interest contexts for students to explore.

General and Professional Sites for Educators

General and Professional Sites for Educators

Active Learning Practices for Schools (ALPS)

ideal for all grade levels ★★★

http://learnweb.harvard.edu/alps/

Here is a site where you can catch up on latest research on meaningful teaching and learning. The site encourages reflective practices and provides systems and tools to design and brainstorm a curriculum and ideas, as well as discuss topics with other educators. Excellent articles here dealing with thinking and the introduction of new technologies.

Amazon.com: The World's Largest Bookstore

ideal for all grade levels ★★★

http://www.amazon.com/

With over twenty-five million books in this cyber-store, this is a very impressive site and one of the few commercial sites to make it into this book. Teachers from anywhere in the world can browse here and find the latest material available in whatever field they desire.

Anger Toolkit

ideal for all grade levels ★★★★

http://www.angermgmt.com/angertoolkit.html

Anger in the classroom can be a destructive element not only because it disrupts academics, but it also destroys the social fabric of the classroom. The site provides a tool kit to measure anger, to understand why children display negative behaviors, and even to help you cope with the anger of your coworkers and your boss. There is an excellent section that provides four techniques for managing anger in all these situations. To finish off, there is an excellent section on coping with grief and loss.

AskEric Lesson Plans

ideal for all grade levels ★★★★

http://ericir.syr.edu/Virtual/Lessons/

This is the largest collection of lesson plans available to teachers on the Internet. The database holds thousands of lesson plans on almost any topic imaginable. The database is fully searchable and you can browse by topics, content, or themes. It is a good idea to check out the searching tips if this is your first visit here, as the database is so large you can end up with far too many returns.

AskERIC: Educational Information with a Personal Touch

ideal for all grade levels ★★★★

http://ericir.syr.edu/index.html

AskERIC is the original and still the most comprehensive (other than teachers@work, of course!) education site on the net. The main services include a question and answer service, virtual library, and ERIC database.

AskERICSM Virtual Library

ideal for all grade levels ★★★★

http://ericir.syr.edu/Virtual/

The library is a collection of tools that can be used to find information and research on topics dealing with educational pedagogy and research. There is also a collection of over 1,000 approved lesson plans, information guides on themes and topics, and a special topics section.

Aussie SchoolHouse

ideal for all grade levels ★★★

http://www.ash.org.au

The Australian version of the Global Schoolhouse, this site is extensive and has links to plenty of sites relevant to various curriculum areas. The support is for both teachers and students. Access information through communities, resources, projects, research, and professional development. Good local Australian content.

Australian

ideal for all grade levels ★★★

http://www.news.com.au/

This newspaper is an excellent source of information on all aspects of education. This site can be used in language work, science, information technology, and the arts. The online version is much easier to handle than the real one and you can select what you want to print out and be your own editor!

Beat the Clock: Lessons in Time Management for Middle School Students

ideal for all grade levels ★★★★

http://thechalkboard.com/Corporations/DayRunner/lessons/

This is a collection of lessons and worksheets for school-age children, dealing with time management. They are designed primarily for middle school students but could be used throughout the entire student population. They are very well designed by the DayRunner company and are provided as a community service.

Behavior Home Page

ideal for all grade levels ★★★★

http://www.state.ky.us/agencies/behave/homepage.html

This is a fascinating Web page devoted to the behaviors of students in the classroom. The Kentucky Department of Education has produced an excellent resource for teachers. The layout is similar to a Web-based listserv with teachers and caregivers encouraged to share strategies and practices that have shown good results. There are interactive sections dealing with both assessment (including good assessment forms) and intervention strategies. A good range of links to other sites along with a very comprehensive technical assistance manual are available.

Bureau of Labor Statistics (BLS) Career Information: Jobs for Kids Who Like . . .

ideal for all grade levels ★★★

http://stats.bls.gov/k12/html/edu_over.htm

Excellent set of options for students who like music/arts, math, PE/outdoors, social sciences, reading, etc. There is an excellent teacher's guide as well as statistics on each of the various careers.

California Instructional Technology Clearinghouse

ideal for all grade levels ★★★★

http://clearinghouse.k12.ca.us/

This is a wonderful database of more than 3,700 recommended instructional technology resources. It is the equivalent to the teachers@work Web classification because, in order to be included in the database, each of these resources had to meet seven strands of criteria. If you are looking for electronic instructional resources, this is a great place to begin.

Canada's SchoolNet Rescol

ideal for all grade levels ★★★★

http://www.schoolnet.ca/

This is a very comprehensive attempt by Canada to develop a complete bilingual educational site (in English and French). Some excellent services here such as special needs and great ideas for Internet projects. Always worth a look.

Center for Critical Thinking

ideal for all grade levels ★★★

http://www.criticalthinking.org

For those encouraging the use of critical thinking skills, this is an excellent site to keep up with the news, conferences, and research in this area. Excellent material here for all teachers. Good introductory work as well as advanced material and classroom suggestions.

Cheathouse.com: The Evil House of Cheat

ideal for all grade levels ★★★

http://www.cheathouse.com/uk/index.html

Your students can come here and for $10 they can have access for one year to over 950 essays on anything from science to math to great composers to Shakespeare. Teachers need to be aware that these sites exist, and students know all about them. There are 480 essays on Shakespeare and his plays and sonnets, and each one is graded so students can supply their teacher with a paper that is at their ability level! What the site teaches educators is that they must steer away from very general topics and use more compare-and-contrast, analyzing, and predicting (i.e., higher-order thinking skills) questions.

CNET Shareware.com

ideal for all grade levels ★★★★

http://shareware.cnet.com/

This massive site details over 250,000 shareware titles. The software here is suitable for all platforms and the range covers simple programs to complete programs, development tools, drivers, and Internet browsers. The search tool is essential to find what you want.

CNN Newsroom: Learning Never Stops (neither does the news)

ideal for all grade levels ★★★★

http://learning.turner.com/newsroom/whatiscnr.html

This is an excellent classroom resource for teachers who want to include current events into their daily classroom activities. Each feature story has a set of support links as well as a page of classroom ideas and applications. Each day of the week has a particular emphasis such as the environment, international news, business, science, etc.

Common Sense Parenting

ideal for all grade levels ★★★★

http://www.parenting.org/

Parenting is far more than just common sense. This Web site takes a commonsense approach and contains some very good content that could be used by teachers to support parents in the community. There are skills provided, recommended books, and free booklets that teachers may distribute.

Community Learning Network (CLN)

ideal for all grade levels ★★★

http://www.cln.org/cln.html

This page is designed to assist teachers in integrating technology into their classrooms. There are three main sections. The first section deals with Internet resources for students. The second section looks at resources that will assist in using telecommunications effectively for student learning. The final section discusses the Internet itself.

Compact for Learning: An Action Handbook for Family-School-Community Partnerships

ideal for all grade levels ★★★

http://www.ed.gov/pubs/Compact/

The complete volume is here, and it is invaluable to both schools and their communities. A compact is a written commitment indicating how all members of the education community agree to share the responsibility for students learning. This document facilitates a plan for developing a compact that offers assistance to the school in both a managerial and educational manner.

Critical Thinking

ideal for all grade levels ★★★

http://www.criticalthinking.org/k12/default.html

The Web site is divided into three areas: events, resources, and a library. The events section includes information on seminars and conferences mostly within the United States. The resources section contains guidelines and some good lessons for integrating critical thinking into the curriculum. The library contains a collection of critical thinking articles focusing on the background and the theory behind teaching critical thinking.

Curriculum Integration: Making the Connection

ideal for all grade levels ★★★

http://www.marshall-es.marshall.k12.tn.us/jobe/connections.html

This excellent site investigates the possibilities and opportunities available via e-mail and key pal projects. The site provides a comprehensive list of sites that are available that use e-mail to encourage students to communicate across the globe. Projects range in age suitability from grades K–12. There are listservs for teachers and students that connect to experts who are available to answer specific questions on a variety of issues and topics.

CWA Education Web

ideal for all grade levels ★★★

http://www.cwa.co.nz/eduweb/

If you teach in New Zealand or want to, this is an excellent site to visit. There is a complete list of education institutions, school e-mail addresses, and Web pages; plenty of additional background for technology teachers from the makers of the Know How series; an excellent resource guide; some war stories from schools implementing ICT (Information and Communication Technology) as well as much more. You will need to put some time aside when you visit this site.

Cyberkids Home Page

ideal for all grade levels ★★★

http://www.cyberkids.com/

This is a student-oriented site, but is still worth a look. This site is particularly strong in the arts and language. There are sections here for young composers, the reading room, the art gallery, and the monthly magazine.

Cyberspace Middle School

ideal for grade levels 6–9 ★★★

http://www.scri.fsu.edu/~dennisl/CMS.html

This is a good site that is designed for students in grades 6–9. There is a range of projects, news, and links designed for middle school students. Well presented and safe!

Distance Learning Resource Network (DLRN)

ideal for all grade levels ★★★★

http://www.dlrn.org/

As schools increasingly share work and carry out collaborative studies, the impact of distance learning is becoming all the more evident. This site has some excellent words of wisdom on this topic, with good examples, research information, and news and reviews.

Down's Syndrome on the Internet

ideal for all grade levels ★★★

http://www.downsyndrome.com/

A great selection of material here if you have mainstreamed students with Down's syndrome in the classroom. There are over twenty-five sub groups here dealing with all aspects of the syndrome and very good material dealing with the difficulties involved in the education system and mainstreaming Down syndrome students.

Education Network of Australia: EdNA Online

ideal for all grade levels ★★★

http://www.edna.edu.au/

One of the first major education databases on the Web, this site gets better and better. It has a good directory of sites, with an emphasis on Australian sites, and also has links to teacher resources and associations.

Education Programs Available on the Internet

ideal for all grade levels ★★★★

http://www.filemine.com/Education

This is a wonderful collection of programs you can download from the Internet including organizational tools, creative programs, lesson planning tools, research assistance, and much more. This is well worth a look by all teachers.

Educational Statistics on the Internet

ideal for all grade levels ★★★

http://ojr.usc.edu/content/story.cfm?id=100/

Whether you're looking for statistics to help with research, to supplement a project submission, or to convince your Board of Trustees that your special project is worthwhile, this Web site is an excellent place to find those statistics.

Edweb: Exploring Technology and School Reform

ideal for all grade levels ★★★★

http://edweb.gsn.org/

This site is for all those needing some assistance in developing a school's electronic mission. This hyperbook takes you through developing world trends and exploring cabling options, and it gives some good examples of what schools have done and what they would not do again.

Electric Library Presents Encyclopedia.com

ideal for grade levels 4–12 ★★★

http://www.encyclopedia.com/home.html

The Internet is often misrepresented as a giant library, but this site offers an encyclopedia that provides good depth and gives links to more detailed information. The volumes are set up in the traditional way, giving you material on the types of topics you would expect from any encyclopedia.

EMC 300: Using Computers in the Classroom

ideal for all grade levels ★★★★

http://seamonkey.ed.asu.edu/emc300/

This top site addresses key issues and, in so doing, assists in developing the school vision for technology integration. Three separate sections deal with technology for communication, technology for instruction, and technology for management. Excellent up-to-date material.

Enchanted Mind

ideal for all grade levels ★★★

http://enchantedmind.com/

The site is a wonderful collection of Web sites and support activities, puzzles, and inspiration that enhance creativity in the classroom. In an era when knowledge based solely on facts and statistics is finally being cast aside, the importance of creativity is being realized. The range of sites presented here is a testimony to the variety of approaches that can be used to encourage creativity in the classroom.

Engines for Education: Ten Top Mistakes in Education

ideal for all grade levels ★★★

http://www.ils.nwu.edu/~e_for_e/nodes/NODE-283-pg.html

Every teacher should come here, not to discover what they are doing wrong, but to use these statements to keep them on track, doing what is really important. It is easy to conform to the process of teaching that we were taught, but the students of the twenty-first century require a completely different skill set and profile. This site will prod you into reflecting on just what those skills are.

ePals.com: World's Largest Online Classroom Community

ideal for all grade levels ★★★★★

http://www.epals.com/

Over 5,500 schools have used this excellent site to develop e-mail, audio conferencing, video conferencing, and CUSeeMe services. You can register and search the database for schools working in the geographical location you desire, using the technology you wish to use, or studying the topic you wish to communicate about. Making those connections is what the Internet is really good for, and this site provides all the information you need to get going.

Equal Access to Software and Information (EASI)

ideal for all grade levels ★★★

http://www.isc.rit.edu/~easi/

This site is dedicated to empowering those with disabilities to gain full access to information and software that allows them to fully participate in the education process. Excellent site for those teachers who find they have mainstreamed and handicapped students in their class.

ERIC Clearinghouse on Assessment and Evaluation

ideal for all grade levels ★★★★

http://ericae.net/

If you are looking for information on assessment and evaluation, then this collection of links and background information is the most extensive you will find anywhere. Topics such as action research, goals and standards, national testing, test construction, test preparation, pedagogy and testing, and assessment at all levels in the school are all to be found here.

FamilySearch™: Searching for Ancestors

ideal for all grade levels ★★★

http://www.familysearch.com/

This is a huge database that can be used for genealogy research, especially for American and European countries. (Two other Web sites should be noted: <http://www.rootsweb.com/> for additional global information and, for Australian births, deaths, and marriage <http:www.geocities.com/Athens/ Forum/3709/exchange>.)

Festivals.com

ideal for all grade levels ★★★★

http://www.festivals.com/

A huge range of festivals take place in every corner of the world and this site provides an insight into why they are held and who stages and participates in them. You can search by using keywords or via geographical regions.

Filamentality

ideal for all grade levels ★★★

http://www.kn.pacbell.com/wired/fil/

Filamentality is a process for teachers to design and build a Web site for education purposes. This excellent site can guide even the most techno phobic teacher through the process and allow him or her to develop a page that looks good and works.

Fun School.com

ideal for grade levels PreK–6 ★★★

http://www.funschool.com

This is an excellent site to use for introducing K–2 as well as 3–6 grade students to the Internet. The site has many fun activities and projects for students and all are excellently presented. Material here deals with various topics and curriculum areas that teachers traditionally use in the classroom.

Gander Academy's Theme-Related Resources on the World Wide Web

ideal for grade levels K–10 ★★★

http://www.stemnet.nf.ca/CITE/themes.html

This selection of Web sites provides teachers with good content for particular topics. The topics are common ones such as the environment, human body, rainforests, legends, oceanography, dinosaurs, spiders, explorers, and many more. Excellent site.

Get Your ANGRIES Out

ideal for all grade levels ★★★

http://members.aol.com/AngriesOut/index.htm

As the title suggests, this Web site provides teachers and students with strategies to constructively manage anger. If you have a student in your class or children at home that show aggressive anger toward others, this Web site can be a huge benefit to you as well as to your students or children. The site deals with letting go of grudges, anger, old hurts, and resentments. The site contains a huge range of articles dealing with all aspects of anger and anger management.

Global Schoolhouse

ideal for all grade levels ★★★★

http://www.gsn.org/

This massive site makes a great start place for educators (after teachers@work of course). Some good site listings but also some good support information on how to integrate computer information into the classroom. Check out the global schoolhouse for some great projects.

Guide to Safe Schools

ideal for all grade levels ★★★

http://www.ed.gov/offices/OSERS/OSEP/earlywrn.html

Identifying the early signs of potentially dangerous student behavior has become the responsibility of teachers. However, teachers often do not know what the early warning signs are and how to get help for children in trouble. At this Web site you can download The Guide to Safe Schools as a PDF file or straight from the Web site. Preventative action could save much grief, and this guide presents a response plan that all schools should look at having as a standard policy.

Harnessing the Web

ideal for all grade levels ★★★★

http://www.gsh.lightspan.com/web/

This is an excellent collection of ideas and classroom concepts that encourage the use of student-centered, project-based activities that incorporate the use of information technologies in the classroom. The Global Schoolnet Foundation has put the contents of their CD-ROM on the Internet and here you can find out about collaborative project-based learning, Internet research, building a collaborative Web project, references, and readings and resources, as well as find a host of Power Point workshop slides that they have made available.

History of Education and Childhood

ideal for all grade levels ★★★★

http://www.socsci.kun.nl/ped/whp/histeduc/

Presented by the University Nijmegen in the Netherlands, this is an excellent review of the history of education. Schools constitute a major sociological institution throughout the world and this site provides an excellent background dealing with educators in dating back to ancient times and in time blocks working through to the present. There are also separate sections dealing with the educational history of quite a few countries. There are also sections dealing with special education, online journals, conferences, archives, higher education, children's perceptions, and much more. Excellent material.

Hoagies Gifted Education Page

ideal for all grade levels ★★★

http://www.hoagiesgifted.org/

Teaching gifted children can be exhilarating and also frustrating. These students challenge us through their spontaneity, and keep us on our toes, forever searching for projects, concepts and ideas to challenge them further. This Web site provides an excellent collection of support articles and research, educational programs, Internet investigations, journals and magazines, online support, organizations, conferences, parent-to-parent concerns, and some humor, just in case we start taking ourselves too seriously.

HSC Online

ideal for grade levels 10–12 ★★★

http://www.hsc.csu.edu.au/

This is an excellent support page for Higher School Certificate students and teachers. The site offers links to sites that can act as good support to the various subjects offered at this level. You can also check out school home pages and a good list of professional teacher associations. Check out the study and examination techniques, which provide a good introduction for students.

Human Behavior: A Science Odyssey

ideal for all grade levels ★★★★

http://www.pbs.org/wgbh/aso/thenandnow/humbeh.html

In our attempts to understand the mind, we have had a history of using less-than inspired guess-work, creating extreme theories based on individuals, making ethical perceptions, and formulating a science based on what can be measured and observed. Although science will only ever explain part of what happens in the mind, scientists and behaviorists have come a long way in the last 100 years in explaining some of the aberrant behaviors that we observe in our communities. Take a tour through the past 100 years to see how our interpretation of behavior has changed.

Idea Box: Early Childhood Education and Activity Resources

ideal for grade levels K–2 ★★★★

http://www.theideabox.com

If you are looking for new ideas to introduce into your junior classroom, then here you can find a huge range of activities based on themes such as seasons, games, music recipes, and much more. The site also recommends reading material and has a good message board that appears to be well used. You can also subscribe and get the Idea Box free each month by e-mail.

Institute for Research on Learning's (IRL) Seven Principles of Learning

ideal for all grade levels ★★★

http://www.newhorizons.org/tech_7irl.html

This refreshing approach to learning is well worth reading. An easy-to-read and very succinct set of points that should form the basis of every school charter or vision.

InteliHealth

ideal for all grade levels ★★★

http://www.intelihealth.com/IH/ihtIH

With information gleaned from John Hopkins University, this site is a wealth of health information and support. Visit specialist zones where you can get extensive details on almost every condition known and check out the nutrition section.

K–12 History on the Internet Resource Guide

ideal for all grade levels ★★★

http://www.xs4all.nl/~swanson/history/

Although designed for the state standards in Texas, the knowledge and skills explained here are global requirements. You can find wonderful ideas for designing Internet-based lessons as well as assessment issues, good classroom practice, and an extensive lesson bank.

Kids on the Web

ideal for all grade levels ★★★★

http://www.hooked.net/~leroyc/kidsweb/

This site is an excellent collection of sites for American schools. The information is well organized into groupings and subgroupings. A well-developed site that has been around for a while and has been kept up-to-date.

Kiwi Careers

ideal for all grade levels ★★★

http://www.careers.co.nz/

A good site looking at careers for students. This New Zealand site provides details of job prospects in different occupations as well as specific careers such a snowboarding instructor! This is similar to the Quest database, but is more easily updated. It is still at the test stage, but it is growing.

Lightspan's Learning Planet.com

ideal for grade levels K–1 ★★★★★

http://www.learningplanet.com/

This is a wonderful collection of activities for K–1 students. The site makes great use of Shockwave so you need to download this if you do not already have it. (Instructions are on the site.) There is everything from space math, geography quiz, ABC, fraction frenzy, and much more. Excellent site.

Memory

ideal for all grade levels ★★★

http://www.exploratorium.edu/memory/

This is a great site dealing with something we all wish we could improve—our memories. The site includes some good online exhibits, the dissection of a sheep's brain to discover the anatomy of memory, the "memory artist" as well as articles dealing with understanding and improving the memory.

Mind Tools Bookstore: How to Get the Most Out of Your Time

ideal for all grade levels ★★★★

http://www.mindtools.com/page5.html

Unfortunately teachers are never taught how to manage their time effectively. This Web site provides an excellent introduction to managing time effectively and, in so doing, making teaching more effective. The site looks at how much your time is really worth in dollars, how to choose what to achieve, using time more effectively, creating more time, and controlling your distractions. It also provides some specific time management tools. This is a must visit site for all teachers.

Mind Tools Bookstore: Planning Skills—How to Plan Complex Tasks

ideal for all grade levels ★★★

http://www.mindtools.com/planpage.html

Failing to plan is exactly the same as planning to fail. The complexity of the teaching task is so great, that planning needs to be very effective if we are to manage the job without going insane. The site provides some excellent planning advice. It looks at the planning cycle, how to manage change, overcoming resistance to change, and completing a plan, and it provides a series of planning templates. The advice here is sensible. This information should also be passed on to students, so that they too can plan for success.

Monster.com: Jobs and Careers Online

ideal for all grade levels ★★★

http://www.monster.com/

In the ever changing employment scene, one way to get students up to date with career possibilities is to look at what is being offered at this site. This makes for a great individual study program if the teacher can develop a worksheet to accompany the search, have the student explore the possibilities, and hopefully watch the student gain some inspiration.

Muskingum College's Learning Strategies Database

ideal for all grade levels ★★★★

http://www.muskingum.edu/~cal/database/database.html

This is an excellent collection of strategies for maximizing student learning. Collected over a period of ten years, the collection is extensive and the presentations are highly readable and have good practical insights. Great site for those confronted by a difficult situation or a concept that needs clarification.

National Library of New Zealand

ideal for all grade levels ★★★

http://www.natlib.govt.nz/index1.html

This site just gets better. Check out the school library service and the heritage section that links up with the Alexander Turnbull Library. In time this will become a central resource center for information on New Zealand heritage and history.

NewsMaps.com

ideal for all grade levels ★★★★★

http://www.newsmaps.com/

There is so much information on listservs, newsgroups, and chat lines that it has become almost unmanageable. This Web site provides a map of all the newsworthy items. Information is categorized under these headings: global news, US news, business news, technology news, and press releases. Allows students to track developing news stories.

Newspapers in Education

ideal for all grade levels ★★★★★

http://www.inl.co.nz/

This is very well presented and covers a range of subjects. This page should be visited regularly to check out what is happening here. Top ten site.

Newton's Apple

ideal for all grade levels ★★★★

http://ericir.syr.edu/Projects/Newton/

This is the support material for the television show, but you do not need to watch the show to use the notes. They cover a range of topics and are very well done. Topics include solar power, cancer, sewer science, and much more.

Nutritional Educational Materials: Dairy Council of California

ideal for grade levels K–10 ★★★

http://www.dairycouncilofca.org/

This is excellent material from the US Dairy Council. The resource material here has been developed for educators and health professionals. There are online learning materials and activities focused on the importance of dairy foods and calcium in children's diets.

Online Class™ Presents

ideal for grade levels 2–12 ★★★

http://www.onlineclass.com/

This site delivers online, interactive, cross-curricular material of very good quality. Developed for grades 2–12, this is excellent material. Two excellent units are available at present—Blue Ice which focuses on Antarctica and the Student Ocean Challenge. Good material.

Oxfam's Cool Planet

ideal for all grade levels ★★★★★

http://www.oxfam.org.uk/coolplanet/teachers/index.html

This organization is making a difference in many countries around the world. Here you can see illustrated highlights of their work and these should make students realize how wealthy they really are. It may even encourage them to look past their own needs and look for ways to help others in the Third World. There is a section here for students to discover some of the lesser-known, but quite amazing facts, about our planet.

Paper Making

ideal for all grade levels ★★★★

http://www.coxes.com/paper/index.html

Paper making is an activity well suited to the classroom, because it provides a fun way to recycle used materials. This is an excellent collection of instructions, well laid out and easy to follow, making use of the pour method. (Also check out An Introduction to Making Paper by Hand at <http://www.intersurf.com/~redstic/Paper/Hand.htm>.)

Partners for Growing

ideal for grade levels 2–4 ★★★

http://www.mobot.org/pfg/preview/front.htm

This collection of fun activities for students encourages them to recognize their responsibility to the natural world. There are activities looking at leaf collecting, honey bees, the eating parts of insects, temperate rainforests, and several other topics. Good introductory material for grades 2–4.

Point.com

ideal for all grade levels ★★★

http://www.pointcom.com:80/

The Pointcom site rates a variety of other sites. There is an education section that is well worth visiting.

Public Broadcasting Service (PBS)

ideal for all grade levels ★★★

http://www.pbs.org/

This site includes supplemental education material for popular US educational programs. Although this site has been built to support the television series, it can be used as a resource on its own. Great for research and keeping up with contemporary aspects of all subjects.

PuzzleMaker

ideal for all grade levels ★★★

http://puzzlemaker.school.discovery.com/

Often we want to broaden our questioning style by including some type of puzzle in our testing strategy. This site can supply you with the ways and means to create automatic crosswords, word searches, math squares, mazes, hidden message word searches, cryptograms and many, many more. Great site with a lot of potential, but always make sure your puzzles have an educational point to them.

refdesk.com

ideal for all grade levels ★★★

http://www.refdesk.com/

This would make a great portal for the library or for any teacher wanting to gain access to a range of reference tools. This is a list site, but it includes such a great collection of tools that it is well worth having as a site on your bookmarks at the very least. There are fast facts, weather information, search engines, virtual newspapers, encyclopedias, magazines, calculators, crosswords, people search, thesaurus, dictionary, and much more.

Resources: Curriculum-Based Telecomputing Projects

ideal for all grade levels ★★★

http://www.tapr.org/~jbharris/

This is a great selection of telecomputing activities that can be used on a class-to-class or student-to-student basis. Projects are broken down into three areas: problem-solving projects, information collections, and interpersonal exchanges. There are about sixty projects listed and teachers can use one of these to introduce students to the Internet or as part of a language program.

Safety on the Internet

ideal for all grade levels ★★★★★

http://www.safekids.com/

Probably the best set of notes on this topic. These should be issued to every student before they start using the Internet and referred to regularly. They should also be part of your Internet policy statement. All teachers can gain a lot by coming here.

School Psychology Resources Online

ideal for all grade levels ★★★

http://www.bcpl.net/~sandyste/school_psych.html

For the school guidance counselor there is a plethora of new problems that students seem to have. Being aware of these and understanding their implications would require continuous skill improvement almost every day. This site provides counselors with the information and the background to these conditions. There is everything here from anxiety disorders to retardation to ADD to drug abuse.

Seven Wonders of the World

ideal for all grade levels ★★★★

http://library.thinkquest.org/23378/music.html

If you asked your students what they think the seven wonders of the world are, what would they answer? Would they say the pyramids, or maybe the huge suspension bridge connecting Alva Island to the city of Kobe in Japan? This Web site looks at the seven wonders of today's world based on a human and technological perspective.

SNOW: Special Needs Opportunity Window

ideal for all grade levels ★★★

http://snow.utoronto.ca/

This is a resource site for teachers working with special needs students, either as individuals in the mainstream class or as special classes set up to cope with the particular needs of these students. There are curricula, technical support, professional development, Web resources, and forums here.

Special Education Resources on the Internet (SERI)

ideal for all grade levels ★★★

http://www.hood.edu/seri/serihome.htm

The strength of this site is its excellent organization of the information that is available. The collection of links and reviews is extensive, including such niches as speech impairment, ADD, autism, inclusion resources, legal and law resources, medicine, and many more.

Study Guides and Strategies

ideal for all grade levels ★★★

http://www.iss.stthomas.edu/studyguides/

Often we expect our students to know how to study but in truth they need to be shown how to study successfully. This Web site provides some wonderful support to students at almost any level. The site shows what they can do in class and at home to maximize the results of their academic efforts. Primers show how students can avoid procrastination, improve concentration, improve memory, organize themselves, and reduce stress.

Sunshine Online: Teaching the World to Read with Technology

ideal for grade levels K–5 ★★★★★

http://www.sunshine.co.nz/

Brilliant collection of junior primary school information here. Have the kids join the Korky Club and receive regular news about events and themes as well as plenty of information for teachers. The theme section provides some excellent ideas for the classroom including complete lesson plans and online resources. This is a cool student site that is based on firm education foundations.

Tales from the Electronic Frontier

ideal for all grade levels ★★★★

http://www.wested.org/tales/

This is where teachers share information and new ideas on using technology in the classroom. Based on the excellent book of the same name, this site makes excellent reading. There are sections dealing with issues, tools, resources, and projects. If you are using technologies in the classroom, then this site is an absolute must see. Why reinvent the wheel? Come here and learn from other teachers' experiences.

Te Kete Ipurangi

ideal for all grade levels ★★★

http://www.tki.org.nz

This Web site is looking to become an education portal for teachers. It still has a way to go, but it does have the potential to become a great resource. Site reviews, education news for New Zealand educators, support material, etc.

Teacher Education: A Student's Perspective

ideal for all grade levels ★★★★

http://www.teachers.ash.org.au/teachereduc/Temain.html

This is an excellent site for not only teaches in training but also for teachers in the classroom. The site provides teachers and teacher trainees with excellent links to Web sites that provide pedagogical- and curriculum-based support.

TeachersFirst

ideal for grade levels K–12 ★★★★

http://www.teachersfirst.com/index.htm

TeachersFirst is a great resource site for K-12 teachers. This site includes reviewed lesson plans from around the world. The resources are grouped by subject and grade level for easy access.

Teacher's Guide to Using Cartoons in the Classroom

ideal for all grade levels ★★★★

http://www.cagle.slate.msn.com/teacher/

This is an excellent site for the study of visual language. The power of the visual image is highly evident here in a series of lesson plans, which are excellent. Lesson plans are broken into elementary, middle, and high school age groups and each age range has a wide range of topics available.

Teacher Talk

ideal for all grade levels ★★★

http://education.indiana.edu/cas/tt/tthmpg.html

This is a teacher support site that looks into contemporary issues relating to teaching, mediation, good lesson ideas, and classroom management.

TeacherVoices™.com

ideal for all grade levels ★★★

http://www.teachervoices.com

Free Internet discussion/chat room site for educators around the world. This site includes a message board and links to the most up-to-date teacher news and information.

Think Quest

ideal for grade levels 4–12 ★★★★

http://www.thinkquest.org/

This competition now offers over $1 million worth of prizes for schools. Read the fine print to see whether your students can compete. The quest is to construct a Web site that meets a series of criteria. Some of these Web sites have been so well done that they have made it into teachers@work list of top educational sites in the world. There is plenty of assistance here for would-be Web designers and teachers who want to get involved.

TimeCast: Your RealAudio and RealVideo Guide

ideal for all grade levels ★★★★

http://www.timecast.com/home/home_frm.html

The free software RealAudio allows radio and music clips to stream and play continuously over the Internet while you are carrying out other tasks. This has great applications in social science through monitoring broadcasts from the country where the event is happening, as well as in local languages through listening to radio stations that broadcast in that language. It also allows you to listen to specialist broadcasts from such stations as the BBC and CNN, that deal with science and additional subject areas, as well as listening to particular music styles as part of the school's music program.

Time for Kids.com

ideal for grade levels PreK–10 ★★★★★

http://www.timeforkids.com/

Time magazine is very much the *Reader's Digest* for international news and issues. The news context is often very relevant, but the material is too adult. Welcome *Time for Kids* as the online magazine that broaches this mismatch. The magazine has excellent, brief, and to-the-point material, and is very graphical and well designed. Excellent site to send two to three students at a time to review and report back on issues and relevant current events.

Time Zone Converter

ideal for all grade levels ★★★

http://www.timezoneconverter.com

If you are working with students around the world, it is often difficult to synchronize a time that will suit all the participants. Using this online time zone converter, you will be able to find the best possible time that allows everyone to be awake! (You can also use the site <http://sandbox.xerox.com/stewart/tzconvert.cgi.>.)

Using The Internet to Enhance Standards-Based Instruction

ideal for all grade levels ★★★

http://www.starcenter.org/documents/tassp.htm

This is an excellent article dealing with incorporating the Internet into your classroom. It is written simply and clearly with some excellent ideas. If your school uses the Internet or has access to it, read this article by Dr. Sherry.

Virtual Reference Desk

ideal for all grade levels ★★★

http://www.vrd.org/

Here you will find information and answers to your questions about school subjects, fascinating facts, research topics, and more. There is an excellent resource base here with ask an expert in numerous fields, as well as a reference to the big six skill package and the "information problem-solving approach," both of which are essential skill sets to have.

WebQuest Page

ideal for teachers only ★★★★

http://www.edweb.sdsu.edu/webquest/webquest.html

You can use the templates provided here to create your own WebQuest. There are a variety of templates including framed versions in several formats. This resource is free to download and is available for both PCs and Macintoshes. If you are looking to do a presentation on the use of WebQuests you can use the prepared set of slides available.

WGCU-TV Faculty Lounge

ideal for all grade levels ★★★

http://gator.naples.net/media/wsfp/lounge.htm#finding

This is a comprehensive teacher assistance site looking at distance learning, mailing lists, and resources on the Internet teachers as well as how to design your own Web pages. Good material.

Winged Heart: 200 Years of Ballooning

ideal for all grade levels ★★★

http://www.ungermark.se/pitalie.html

This excellent Swedish site describes the art of ballooning in the romantic as well as the scientific sense. It follows the development of the science and sport from the first hot air balloon in 1783 to some break points in Swedish ballooning to attempts to circumnavigate the globe in a hot air balloon. High-interest reading material here that would be very useful.

your homework.com

ideal for all grade levels ★★★

http://www.yourhomework.com/

The idea here is for teachers to place their homework assignments on a Web site, which then provides students with access to this material. The entire service is provided free of charge. An excellent way of promoting communication between the school, students and parents in your wired community.

Health and Physical Education

ABC of Safe and Healthy Child Care

ideal for grade levels K–8 ★★★★

http://www.cdc.gov/ncidod/hip/abc/abc.htm

This is an online handbook detailing how disease spreads in child care institutions, special needs, emergency procedures, nutrition, first aid, reporting requirements, fire safety, and more.

Adolescent and School Health

ideal for all grade levels ★★★

http://www.cdc.gov/nccdphp/dash/

This program has set its target to encourage adults to see youth as an investment. Their mental, spiritual, and their physical health need to be ensured if our community is to survive. The site works through the problem and provides some strategies and resources. Good material.

Aging and Genetics. Is it in Your Genes?

ideal for grade levels 8–12 ★★★

http://www.biorap.org/br8contents.html

Check out the research in this area and where it is taking us. Can we potentially live forever? If not, what are the implications for a world where life is extended and we have a greater percentage of the elderly that require support? Great site that provides a lot of information, a rap sheet on being a physical therapist, and a word list. There is a teacher's guide to support the work as well as a reading list and additional material for those that want to probe deeper.

Alcohol Advisory Council

ideal for grade levels 4–12 ★★★★

http://www.alcohol.org.nz/

Great material here for teachers to use in the classroom. Young people's most severely overindulged pastime is embedded in a culture that can be changed and here are all the facts that you need to develop and encourage a new culture among your students. The "Say When" and "Friends don't let friends drink and drive" campaigns are having an effect and need encouragement and support wherever and whenever possible. Good JavaScript game where the students control the amount of drink consumed by their virtual self and then observe the effects on their judgement.

Alcohol and Drug Information: The National Clearinghouse

ideal for all grade levels ★★★

http://www.health.org/kidsarea/kidsarea.htm

This is a well-designed site that is overflowing with information, statistics, support documents, programs, and some plain common sense. Join Wally bear and the Know-How Gang to investigate the issues, and educate students about the negative effects of these freely available "drugs."

Ask Noah About Nutrition

ideal for all grade levels ★★★

http://www.noah.cuny.edu:8080/nutrition/nutrition.html

This is the complete information stack on nutrition. A lot of information here on vitamins, supplements, fiber, cholesterol, and ten tips for good eating. There is also a section that deals with nutrition and disease and an article all about stopping the aging process. A good general site for research information.

Band-Aides and Blackboards

ideal for all grade levels ★★★★

http://funrsc.fairfield.edu/~jfleitas/contents.html

What happens when chronic illness occurs in your classroom? How do we deal with the student and his or her classmates? This excellent site deals with the issues by presenting two sites, one for the children themselves and one for the teacher. This is the first stop for good advice, ideas, and assurance when students in your class become chronically ill.

Baseball: Fox Sports

ideal for all grade levels ★★★★

http://www.foxsports.com/baseball/index.sml

You will find information at all levels available here—even coaching tips for the little league as well as information and tips from the top players and coaches. Highlights of the leagues as well as television coverage are all available here.

Basketball: The NBL (Australian Basketball League) and the NBA (United States Basketball League)

ideal for all grade levels ★★★★★

http://www.nbl.com.au

http://www.aball.co.nz/

http://www.nba.com/

The National Basketball Association in the US has a great worldwide following and this site does their fans proud! Great news and inside stories as well as live chat with the stars of the court. You can also catch up with the results, fixtures, and who did what, where, and when. Some good coaching tips here as well.

Bike Hub: National Bike Safety Network

ideal for all grade levels ★★★★

http://www.cdc.gov/ncipc/bike/

There is a huge amount of information for teachers and concerned parents here about the safety issues surrounding children riding their bikes in the community. If you need statistics there is no shortage here. There are sections dealing with helmets, bike safety month, biomechanics, evaluation data, education programs, and much more. Essential topic for all ages.

Biomechanics: The Magazine of Lower Extremity Movement

ideal for grade levels 11–12 ★★★

http://www.biomech.com/

This site gets technical, but it is a great site all the same. There are excellent articles here. You can subscribe, but you can also access a great deal of free material on this site. An excellent article exploring into acupuncture is included as well as other great background studies. Very readable.

Biomechanics: Worldwide

ideal for grade levels 11–12 ★★★

http://www.per.ualberta.ca/biomechanics/

This ever-increasing site is the definitive biomechanics site. Every aspect of this topic is explored in-depth and at varying levels. Good site for senior students to investigate and review. Encourage students to present oral reports on various aspects of biomechanics.

Body and Food

ideal for all grade levels ★★★

http://www.factmonster.com/ipka/A0768612.html

The site takes on an almanac approach and presents a series of articles looking at everything from what makes up your insides, what ails you, food and superstitions, smart food to junk food, and much more. The topics are well laid out and have a high-interest level.

Brain Pop: Health and Science

ideal for all grade levels ★★★

http://www.brainpop.com/

This is a wonderful collection of movie topics, as well as information sites dealing with vision, hearing, asthma, diabetes, digestion, the brain, the skeleton, blood, cells, and muscle. Each section uses video material and provides teachers with wonderful resources to demonstrate to students. You could have students prepare a minilesson to present to the class on each of the different topics using this material.

Cancer Research: The American Institute

ideal for all grade levels ★★★★

http://www.aicr.org/

There is a massive amount of information here an all aspects of cancer with the general theme of taking actions that reduce the likelihood of students growing up and getting cancer of one form or another. Excellent research and statistics here that are enough to stop anyone from smoking (hopefully), as well as a great kids newsletter (free), that you can order from the site. Huge site and well laid out.

Cancer: A Primer For High School Students

ideal for grade levels 8–12 ★★★

http://oncolink.upenn.edu/primer/

This is a disease that affects so many people and most schools will have to deal at some stage with student's suffering from some form of cancer. This Web site presents a balanced approach looking at what cancer is, the statistics about survival, and lifestyle choices that can help reduce the possibility of students getting one of the many different varieties of cancer that haunt us.

Canoe and Kayak: The E-zine

ideal for grade levels 8–12 ★★★

http://www.canoekayak.com/

This is an excellent magazine for river and ocean enthusiasts. Many articles, tips, and places to go. Good repair and maintenance articles and buying guides.

Center for Disease Control and Prevention

ideal for grade levels 4–12 ★★★

http://www.cdc.gov/

This is an excellent site looking at all aspects of health. Includes morbidity rates, scientific data, publications, travelers' health and extensive ratings and information on all manner of diseases.

Challenge of Cancer

ideal for grade levels 4–12 ★★★

http://www.biorap.org/br6contents.html

We all know someone who has died of cancer and there is a huge worldwide push to find cures for the myriad of different versions of this deadly biological hiccup. This site, another in the great series of BioRaps presents a well-balanced investigation into the subject. Check out the career rap on the epidemiologist, the research section, how to eat well to improve your chances of not becoming a statistic, and the section on cancer in your pets.

Chicken Soup for the Soul

ideal for all grade levels ★★★★

http://www.chickensoup.com/

Here you'll find a wonderful collection of short stories that will warm your heart and restore your faith in human nature. Excellent short stories that teachers can use to illustrate an ethical point or to encourage students to take care of each other and to remind them that they are not in charge of the universe!

Children's Virtual Hospital

ideal for all grade levels ★★★

http://www.vh.org/Patients/IHB/Peds/General/OrganMap/GutMap.html

There is a great collection of resources here for students investigating the human body. You can check out what your insides really look like and what each of the bits actually does. The material is well written and at a level that will interest students. You can also examine information on diseases and health conditions and explanations of what is happening when you get them.

Chronic Ill Net

ideal for all grade levels ★★★★

http://www.chronicillnet.org/

This is an useful site that looks at chronic illnesses such as cancer, AIDS, chronic fatigue syndrome, and others. Well laid out with some excellent research information and advice for caregivers.

Combined Health Information Database

ideal for grade levels 8–12 ★★★

http://chid.nih.gov/

This is a massive database dealing with every health aspect imaginable. There are more than fifteen topics that include articles, notes, advice, and warnings. This is a US federal agency site drawing on the resources of a variety of agencies. Good selection of information and research. Excellent search site.

Common Sense—strategies for raising alcohol- and drug-free children

ideal for grade levels 4–12 ★★★★

http://www.pta.org/commonsense/

These are emotive issues with a range of approaches proposed by numerous institutions and foundations. Who is providing the common sense? This site has set itself up in the commonsense frame and has provided an excellent set of resources, and a mission that very few are going to argue with. We all know that drug and alcohol abuse by teens is developing into a major school issue, but finding a set of strategies that we all can support is not easy. This site presents a straightforward and appealing set of strategies for teachers, parents, and students.

Community Violence Prevention Kit

ideal for all grade levels ★★★★★

http://www.pta.org/events/violprev/index.htm

That violence is an issue in our schools as well as our communities is beyond doubt. Dealing with violence is a much more complex task than most of us appreciate. This Web site provides schools with an excellent set of support strategies and tools that schools find very useful in preventing violence within the school. There are some good areas to view including steps for organizing the community forum, community needs assessment, and identifying problems, finding solutions, and setting goals. Excellent material.

Cybertimes of Reginald

ideal for all grade levels ★★★

http://www.mcet.edu/healthlinks/reginald/

Each week Reginald experiences a new dilemma that visitors to the site are invited to explore and discuss. Reginald's problems are mostly health- and social-related issues and you can have student's work through dilemmas such as peer pressure, smoking, healthy choices, and many other issues that poor Reginald manages to find himself stuck with.

Daily Apple

ideal for all grade levels ★★★★

http://thedailyapple.com/

This is a comprehensive site that is well laid out and is for general consumption. You can check out diseases and disorders, mental health, lifestyle and nutrition, children's health, woman's health, and much more.

Dance Online

ideal for all grade levels ★★★

http://www.danceonline.com/

This is an excellent, professionally produced online magazine dealing with all aspects of dancing. It addresses all levels from the novice to the prima donna. Excellent site.

Diabetes.com

ideal for all grade levels ★★★★

http://www.diabetes.com/

This site is well written and deals with the many facets of being a diabetic. This is a great site, especially when students in the class are diabetic. Sift through the copious amounts of information; the Kool Kids section would be a great place to start. Very good site.

Diabetes in Children

ideal for all grade levels ★★★★

http://www.childrenwithdiabetes.com/

This is an extensive and well-designed Web site to support students who are dealing with diabetes. There is plenty of information for students of all ages, including global issues, scientific information, helpful hints, surveys, as well as plenty of support through online chat and listservs, discussion groups, food and diet, and coping with diabetes at school.

Diabetes Info: For Teachers and Child Care Workers

ideal for all grade levels ★★★

http://www.diabetes.org/ada/teach1.asp

Nearly 1 in 600 children has diabetes and all teachers will eventually teach a child who has insulin dependent diabetes. We all have legal and moral responsibilities toward these children. The site presents a summary of the condition and the needs these children have as well as good advice on how to deal with the physical and emotional needs of these children.

DNA for Dinner

ideal for all grade levels ★★★

http://www.gis.net/~peacewp/webquest.htm

Information on the controversial topic of gentically altered food is balanced with pros and cons. Includes a WebQuest with resources and a rubric for grading. Other links to genetically altered food information is provided.

Dr. Rabbit's No-Cavities Clubhouse

ideal for grade levels K–7 ★★★

http://www.colgate.com/Kids-world/

Here it is—a collection of material that encourages students to clean their teeth and take oral hygiene seriously. Dr. Rabbit demonstrates how he takes care of his teeth and why students should take care of theirs.

Drug-Free and Safe Schools: An Action Guide

ideal for all grade levels ★★★

http://www.ed.gov/offices/OESE/SDFS/

This document should be printed out and used to promote staff room discussion on this subject. There is excellent background information as well as action steps that school communities can take to develop safe environments for our students. Not all the answers are here, but it includes very good material to start the discussion process.

Environmental Health and Science

ideal for grade levels 4–12 ★★★

http://www.niehs.nih.gov/kids/hottopics.htm

This is a great collection of links and articles to all those hot topics such as cloning, in vitro fertilization, health funding, genetic research, immunization, and the fight against AIDS and cancer. Great research site for students to use and then present an oral report back to the class on one of the topics.

Excellent Links to Health and Fitness Sites

ideal for all grade levels ★★★

http://www.lifelines.com/cgi-bin/mainpage.pl

A site full of excellent links to health and fitness sites on the World Wide Web.

Expect the Best from a Girl

ideal for all grade levels ★★★★

http://www.academic.org/

Expect the best from a girl and that's what you'll get. This is very practical advice and also dispels some still very commonly held myths by both teachers and the general public about the abilities and potential of girls. Excellent site. This site is designed for teachers and parents, but would be worthwhile for some students.

Fast Foods and Nutrition: The Real Truth

ideal for all grade levels ★★★

http://tqjunior.advanced.org/4485/

The Web site can be used as the basis for a journalistic investigation on the topic: Is fast food bad food? Click on the hamburger at the site and you will find out the truth about the nutritional value of fast foods.

Fire Safety Web Site

ideal for all grade levels ★★★

http://students.resa.net/stoutcomputerclass/3fire.htm

Every student needs instruction on fire safety and they need it often. This Web site can be used to increase awareness of the potential of fires through a different communication vehicle. This site is very thorough and there is a lot of information here. Students will need assistance to make sense of it all. An excellent learning center.

FitnessLink

ideal for all grade levels ★★★

http://www.fitnesslink.com/index.html

Here you can catch up with all the top stories from around the world dealing with fitness and health as well as links to hundreds of support sites in this area. There are sections dealing with the mind and body, nutrition, fitness programs, exercises, and lifestyle changes. There is even a Professional Center for those that take this area very seriously.

Fitness Management Library

ideal for grade levels 8–12 ★★★★

http://www.fitnessworld.com

The library is based on the excellent online magazine *Fitness Management* along with additional articles and a good news service based on items of interest to the fitness world. The magazine is here as well as the archives, which can be searched using the on-site search engine. The articles are well presented and at a level that would be useful to both teachers and secondary students.

Fitness Partner Connection Jumpsite

ideal for all grade levels ★★★

http://www.primusweb.com/fitnesspartner/

This site is structured more like a library with information available via their fitness library. The articles are well written and address basic fitness and health issues. Discussions on how to manage your weight effectively, the lowdown on fitness equipment as well as overall health, lifestyle, and living issues. There are sections dealing with quitting smoking and addressing the issues that occur when people do stop the habit. A calorie counter is included and the fitness forum is available to share your thoughts with other health teachers.

Food and Nutrition Information Center

ideal for all grade levels ★★★★

http://www.nal.usda.gov/fnic/

This is a massive information center! There is information dealing with food and nutritional software, healthy school meals, nutrition education and training, food borne illness education materials, and excellent nutrition education materials. There is something for everyone here at all levels.

Food Resource

ideal for all grade levels ★★★

http://www.orst.edu/food-resource/food.html

This is an extensive site, with links and content dealing with every aspect of food including such topics as vegetables, grains and cereals, dairy products, fruit, baked goods, beverages, egg products, lipids and fat replacers, recipes, and much more.

Get It Straight—the facts about drugs

ideal for all grade levels ★★★★

http://www.usdoj.gov/dea/pubs/straight/cover.htm

A very informative online book from the US Department of Justice Drug Enforcement Agency. It is very comprehensive and has a streetwise appeal that will make it very useful in the classroom. The book provides a huge amount of information on various drugs, their effects, what they look like, and how they are used. Excellent.

Golf Web

ideal for grade levels 11–12 ★★★

http://www.golfweb.com/

This is a great site with all the golf you could probably ever want. Golf Web is so large it is divided into geographical sections. It presents scoreboards from around the world, coaching tips, great courses around the world, and how to spend $20,000 on a new putter!

Health and Fitness Worldguide

ideal for all grade levels ★★★

http://www.worldguide.com/hf.html

If you are looking for a collection of tools and background information then here you will find both. There is information on anatomy, strength training, cardiovascular exercise, nutrition, and sports medicine.

Health on the Net

ideal for all grade levels ★★★

http://www.hon.ch

One of the most comprehensive health pages on the Net. There are links here and information on health and fitness, medical, and nutritional information. 243,000 visitors can't be wrong!

Health Question and Answer Service

ideal for grade levels 8–12 ★★★

http://www.goaskalice.columbia.edu/

An award-winning, interactive question-and-answer service. Students can do a keyword search of existing FAQ (Frequently Asked Questions) databases on things like sexual health and relationships, drug and alcohol concerns, and fitness and nutrition.

Healthy Lifestyles From New Zealand

ideal for all grade levels ★★★★

http://www.wce.ac.nz/sun/

This Wellington College of Education site aims to minimize the impact of cancer on our community using teachers to push home the message of being "Sun smart." The site acknowledges that people spend a large amount of time in the outdoors and encourages a preventative approach. The site also has an excellent section dealing with nutrition and smoke-free living. There is excellent background information as well as extensive material for teachers.

Healthy World Online

ideal for all grade levels ★★★★★

http://www.healthy.net/

An excellent site that integrates healthy lifestyles with well-being. The village map sets out the areas that this sites deals with including a nutrition center, newsroom, fitness center, "self-care central," library, and much more. This is an excellent resource with a lot of depth.

HeartPower

ideal for grade levels 3–8 ★★★

http://www.americanheart.org/Health/Lifestyle/Youth/heartpower/index.html

A great site dealing with integrating activities that encourage healthy nutrition and activity, smoke-free living and some very well-done presentations on how the heart works. Good fun approach that students find very appealing.

Here's Looking at You: Healthy Skin

ideal for grade levels 8–10 ★★★

http://www.biorap.org/br5contents.html

There is a complete unit of work here aimed at students in grades 8–10. The unit is complete with student information and guides, teacher's guide, and references. There is also a completely separate section, Looking Deeper, for those students who need challenging. Excellent material.

Hickok Sports

ideal for all grade levels ★★★

http://www.hickoksports.com/history.shtml

This is a huge collection of information on all aspects of most sports. Here you can check out biographies, a glossary of sports terms, books, magazines, famous quotes, trivia, software, and almost anything you can think of to do with the sports that we all follow.

HIV AIDS Prevention

ideal for grade levels 8–12 ★★★

http://www.cdc.gov/hiv/dhap.htm

As with any site of this nature, please view the site yourself first. It is factual and up-to-date with the emphasis on the disease and not on the lifestyles that can contribute to the transmission of the disease. There are some useful slides and graphics available, but please check that using these do not conflict with your school policy statements and that you use them with parental consent.

KIDDE: Home Safety Education Center

ideal for grade levels K–7 ★★★

http://kiddesafety.com/

This is a good site focused on safety in the home, most notably the topic of fire safety. With frequent reports of young children dying in house fires, this awareness and training must be a high priority. There are lesson plans here to assist you in presenting issues as well as games, puzzles, and quizzes.

Kids Food Cyber Club

ideal for grade levels 3–8 ★★★

http://www.kidsfood.org/

The goal here is to promote good nutrition and, as a consequence, improve overall health. Much effort has gone in here to develop an excellent teacher support program to go with the site. A good set of additional links to similar sites is also provided.

Life Education Network

ideal for grade levels 4–12 ★★★★

http://www.lec.org/

This organization is dedicated to persuading students to say no to drugs of all descriptions. The highlight of this site is a comprehensive and well-written section called The World of Drugs. You can learn where drugs originate, how they are propagated and prepared, and how they arrive at some school gates! There are other sections looking at how to encourage students to say no and the latest information on the latest techno drugs.

Lifestyle Cancer Information

ideal for all grade levels ★★★

http://www.wce.ac.nz/cancer/

This is an excellent, information-rich site for those investigating the links between our lifestyles and the onset of cancer. Three areas are investigated: lifestyle and the sun; lifestyle smokefree; and lifestyle and nutrition. In looking at the relationship between our lifestyle and the sun, over 20 issues are explored in detail ranging from a shady school policy to sun beds and sunlamps.

Live: Online Health Magazine

ideal for all grade levels ★★★

http://www.bbc.co.uk/education/health/magazine/index.html

This e-zine is well presented and has good contemporary content that will appeal to students. The emphasis is on anti-drugs and anti-cigarette-smoking material, but there are also many other issues that are addressed.

Locker Room: Sports for Kids

ideal for all grade levels ★★★

http://members.aol.com/msdaizy/sports/locker.html

This site features a range of sports and provides roles of the game, catching tips, interesting facts, and some ideas on how to be the next Michael Jordan of your particular sport. Presentation is excellent and sports discussed include volleyball, soccer, basketball, gymnastics, swimming, running, hockey, tennis as well as bowling. Also check out some good stretching and warm-up exercises.

Marijuana: Facts for Teens

ideal for grade levels 8–12 ★★★★

http://www.nida.nih.gov/MarijBroch/Marijteens.html

Students often see marijuana as a social drug that has few consequences. The effects and side effects of both short- and long-term use are well laid out here. Parents and teachers can get some excellent advice as to how to tell if someone is using marijuana and how it affects their children or students. There is also good advice for what to do if you find that your students or children are using this drug.

Medscape

ideal for all grade levels ★★★

http://www.medscape.com/

This is an excellent, free site dealing with all the breakthroughs and news in the medical world. Excellent material and very readable. Alphabetically organized for ease of searching.

Microbial Ecology: The Digital Learning Center

ideal for all grade levels ★★★★

http://commtechlab.msu.edu/sites/dlc-me/

Don't let the title put you off! The information here regarding microbes and health is excellent. Great sections such as The Microbe Zoo, Microbes in the News, and The Curious Microbe make excellent reading. The information is excellently presented and is very contemporary. There is material here that would make interesting reading at all levels of the curriculum. Fascinating site!

Mindtools: Sports Psychology

ideal for grade levels 8–12 ★★★

http://www.demon.co.uk/mindtool/page11.html

Plenty of information and links to other support sites. The first section on goal setting is worthwhile for all students. The materials explaining practicing in one's mind is well done and the work presented on concentration is very comprehensive. All teachers of senior students should incorporate this aspect into their courses.

National Center for Victims of Crime

ideal for all grade levels ★★★

http://www.nvc.org/

The quality of a community is reflected in the amount of crime that is committed, how we deal with the criminals involved, and how we deal with the victims. This Web site provides a good background for teachers wishing to teach the student's how to cope with crime, what their rights are, and how to reduce the chances of being involved in criminal activity.

National Football League

ideal for all grade levels ★★★★

http://www.nfl.com/

News, competitions, player profiles, rules, coaching tips, and much more. You can keep up-to-date with all the happenings at this easy-to-navigate site. All levels of competition are represented here.

National Institute of Environmental Health and Sciences (NIEH): NIEH's Kid's Pages

ideal for all grade levels ★★★

http://www.niehs.nih.gov/kids/hottopics.htm

This site includes hot topics in environmental health and science for all grade levels. There are also stories and other information about the environment and you.

New Zealand Health Statistics

ideal for all grade levels ★★★

http://www.nzhis.govt.nz/stats/statscontents.html

This is an excellent collection of statistics dealing with the health of a country. These statistics are useful for all countries, because they are somewhat generic. They look at how the health of many first world countries has changed over the last ten years. Statistics deal with mortality rates due to cancer, infant deaths, and maternal deaths; principal diseases and disabilities; accidents at home; poisonings; violence; and much more. Fascinating information that could be used by a class to develop a brochure, commercial, or radio announcement that would help decrease these frightening statistics.

Nike Sports

ideal for all grade levels ★★★★

http://www.nike.com/

Plenty of interest here for teachers and students. Catch up with the latest sports technology as well as background information on athletic training programs, coaching information, and much more.

Non Traditional Gymnastics

ideal for all grade levels ★★★

http://www.geocities.com/Colosseum/Stadium/7261/index.htm

Looking to add an extra bit of zing to the gymnastics area? Then this is the site to visit. There is a justification and introduction to this genre of gymnastics and an excellent range of activities, lessons, and assessment tasks. Very thorough and some excellent ideas even for the less adventurous.

Nutribase: The Nutrition Database

ideal for all grade levels ★★★★

http://www.nutribase.com

This is a great database with 240,000 food items and 3,000 menus from 71 different restaurants. You can find out each food item's fat, sugar, and salt content as well as any other nutrient you can imagine. This site is great for students to explore and record their daily intake of the various nutrients.

Nutrition Explorations

ideal for grade levels K–8 ★★★

http://www.nutritionexplorations.org/

Here you can find an excellent introduction to healthy eating for students in years K–8. The very graphic presentation and the animated antics of Chef Combo provide a wonderful background to this essential part of the curriculum. There is excellent teacher support as well as information and activities for the people in charge of the school food service. Find out how a journey in an alien space ship can become a focus on the food pyramid!

Orienteering: The New Zealand Home Page

ideal for grade levels 4–12 ★★★

http://www.nzorienteering.com/

Everything here from rankings, events, the national secondary school champs, clubs, as well as international links to 350 other World Wide Web orienteering pages.

Outside Online

ideal for all grade levels ★★★

http://outsidemag.com/

It would appear human beings always need to do something a little bit different and push themselves to new limits. Here you can see some of the extreme sports challenges that people set for themselves. Each month there are new features, articles, trivia sections, bookstores, places to stay, and gear to wear.

Parentsplace

ideal for all grade levels ★★★

http://www.parentsplace.com/

Parentsplace is an excellent site looking at all the problems that parents and teachers—acting in loco parentis—may face. Very good health, nutrition, and preschool section.

PE Central

ideal for all grade levels ★★★★

http://pe.central.vt.edu

This is possibly the most comprehensive physical education site available on the Web. This site has everything: health issues, coaching tips, lesson plans, assessment ideas, news and information, professional information, support, and tips and ideas for the day. This can be a default page for many PE teachers, because information is constantly added and updated.

Physical Education Digest

ideal for all grade levels ★★★

http://www.pedigest.com/

This digest is a wonderful source of information with classroom ideas, lesson plans, links to sites, and much more. The *Digest* has been in existence for fifteen years and has been online for the last three. Each 36-page quarterly magazine, contains information on coaching, research on sports and fitness, and physical education topics from around the world.

Prevention Online

ideal for all grade levels ★★★

http://www.health.org/

Here is an excellent resource from the National Clearinghouse for Alcohol and Drug Information. The facts are here as well as resources and an excellent collection of statistics and research information. There is also a newsroom highlighting mostly American news reports on drug and alcohol abuse, and programs to support those wishing to eliminate their dependence. A good set of links as well as online forums.

Promoting Fruit and Vegetables

ideal for all grade levels ★★★

http://www.dole5aday.com/

A fun site for younger children promoting fruit and vegetables in the daily diet. Nutritional information and the need for a balanced diet are presented in a fun and entertaining way.

Quackwatch! Your Guide to Health Fraud

ideal for grade levels 4–12 ★★★

http://www.quackwatch.com/

Most likely some of the articles in this Web site will pertain to either yourself, a close family member, or a friend. Dr. Stephen Barrett has set his sights on eliminating the fraudulent claims of various therapies, potions, and gimmicks that masquerade as medicine.

Real Scoop on Tobacco

ideal for grade levels 4–10 ★★★

http://www.itdc.sbcss.k12.ca.us/curriculum/tobacco.html

This is an excellent way to introduce this topic. The introduction to this site says that you have been hired by the parents of a sixth grade student (Icabod), who suspect their child is smoking. Your challenge is to create a plan to encourage him to give it up while he has a chance. You have to go through a series of processes, becoming an expert on the subject, creating an ad or visual message, writing to the local tobacco company, and then finally getting Icabod's attention through a memorable message.

Reuters Health

ideal for all grade levels ★★★★

http://www.reutershealth.com/

From this world-renowned information company comes this specialist section dealing with health and health issues. The information here is not in a medical context, but is written for the layperson interested in health. For this reason it is an excellent site to have small groups of students visit, read through the information, and then present oral reports back to the rest of the class. This weekly task can bring health issues to the fore and allow for discussion of the impact these have on the community.

Rugby Union of New Zealand

ideal for all grade levels ★★★★

http://www.nzrugby.co.nz/

All the news here on the rugby teams of New Zealand. Well-presented information with great graphics and up-to-date results, fixtures, and views of who should be doing what, where, and when!

Runner's World

ideal for grade levels 4–12 ★★★

http://www.runnersworld.com/

This is the electronic version of the top running magazine *Runner's World.* If you are into running over any distance, then this is an excellent read. There are sections here dealing with women's running, nutritional advice, injuries, and much more. Excellent site with plenty of content.

Schneid's Volleyball Page

ideal for all grade levels ★★★★

http://www.volleyweb.com

Great pages for coaches, with well laid out drills for training, serving, defense, bumping, footwork, jumping, and much more. Offensive and defensive schemes are laid out as are rules, score sheets, and statistics/recordkeeping sheets. Additional information on stretching, aerobic conditioning, as well as good background information on sports administration and nutrition.

School Health Manual

ideal for all grade levels ★★★★

http://www.state.me.us/education/shindex.htm

This is an excellent example of a school health manual. It is an extensive and well-presented manual dealing with every aspect of health in a school community. This would be an excellent system to adopt via a school health program.

School Menu: Eating in the School Environment

ideal for grade levels K–8 ★★★★

http://www.schoolmenu.com/homepage.htm

Excellent layout and approach to encouraging young students to eat well. Join DJ the animated dog in his pursuit of the best lunch. Fuel up for breakfast and learn all about the importance of the balanced approach to eating. The inevitable food pyramid is ever present but presented in a more entertaining context than usual. Check out the surround sound to go with the site.

Shape Up America!

ideal for all grade levels ★★★

http://www.shapeup.org/

Great site for people from all countries to plug into. The focus of the site is safe weight management combined with physical fitness. Check out the cyber-kitchen. There is also a good Professional Center for teachers and other trainers in this area.

Ski Net

ideal for all grade levels ★★★★

http://www.skinet.com/

For schools close to resorts and mountainous regions that have a winter program that incorporates some skiing, here is a great site to catch up on all the news stories, products, and reports from resorts around the world. You can even download and watch the video clips of people doing extraordinary loops and jumps on skis.

Skin Cancer

ideal for all grade levels ★★★★

http://www.maui.net/~southsky/introto.html

This is an excellent introduction to this scourge of humanity. Brilliant introduction that both students and the general public should be aware of. What skin cancer is, how you can determine your personal risk, precautions to be taken, as well as diagnosis, and a good glossary of terms are included. Excellent site.

Sports Illustrated for Kids

ideal for all grade levels ★★★★

http://sikids.com/

This site primarily features American sports teams and players. There are story writing exercises based on funny sports photos as well as reading material that is age-appropriate and is the sort of material that students want to read. Also check out fantasy sports and the latest snowboarding fads and fashions.

Sports Science: Where Science Meets the Olympics

ideal for grade levels 4–12 ★★★

http://whyfiles.news.wisc.edu/019olympic/index.html

This excellent site investigates the interface between technology and sport and whether technology and science play a greater part than the athletes themselves. This is an aspect of sport that is notorious and the word "cheat" is never far away. The site asks, What would happen if they held an Olympics without all modern technology? Good material from the Why Files (better that the X files).

TotalSwimm: Swimming Cyber-coaching

ideal for all grade levels ★★★

http://www.cs.sfu.ca/people/GradStudents/zaiane/personal/totalswim/

This is a great site with excellent advice offered by one of America's greatest swimming coaches. Not only is advice offered, but it is also justified through good science and research. The theme here is that technique is the focus above fitness. The site presents a series of articles and training concepts that would be great for any coach or any student who is involved in swim training.

Vibrant Life Online

ideal for all grade levels ★★

http://www.vibrantlife.com

Site includes picks from the *Vibrant Life* magazine such as the Top Stories, Open Story Archives, and The Recipe Resource.

Volleyball: World Wide

ideal for all grade levels ★★★

http://www.volleyball.org/index.html

This site contains information on coaching, rules, and international competitions as well as providing information on national and international leagues. The site is very useful to teachers and aspiring players, because it offers good general fitness advice as well as good skill development programs. Great site; great sport.

Information and Communication

Amazing Picture Machine

ideal for all grade levels ★★★

http://www.ncrtec.org/picture.htm

Whenever you create Web pages, the picture that says a thousand words can be hard to find, scan, and add to your document. This site is full of ready-to-use pictures. There are copyright restrictions, so read that section carefully. A search on the word *dinosaur* yielded fourteen graphics, all of which were very useful. A search engine will assist you to find what you need from a good selection of units of work.

Anywhere

ideal for all grade levels ★★★

http://myhotlist.com/

One of the most annoying issues when using more than one computer is storing a hot list of Web sites that you can access from anywhere. Here you can download, free of charge, an excellent tool that allows you to access your hot list from anywhere, anytime. It also allows you to make your hot list available to other people. Simple but effective.

Apache: Web Server Software

ideal for all grade levels ★★★★★

http://www.apache.org/

This free software is the most widely used software to serve Web pages on local intranets or the Internet. It comes complete with operation manuals and is an excellent product. You can download it from the site.

AppleCare Service and Support

ideal for all grade levels ★★★

http://www.apple.com/support/

This is an Apple page (and no, they are not going out of business). Come here for all the technical support and up-to-date information on both hardware and software. This site is well-designed and easy to follow.

Ask Jeeves for Kids

ideal for all grade levels ★★★★

http://www.ajkids.com/

Ask Jeeves (for adults) has been around for a while, but the one problem with using it happened when students occasionally received inappropriate qualifying questions back from it. Now we have Ask Jeeves for Kids which allows students to use natural language to find information on the Internet. They can now type in What is the moon made of? and Jeeves will ask a qualifying question and then return a list of sites for them to investigate. Not the most accurate search engine in the world, but great for themes—and no Boolean search skills are required.

Beginning HTML

ideal for all grade levels ★★★★

http://www.htmlgoodies.com/

This site contains a fantastic set of tools for both the beginner and the intermediate Web site developer. You can find out about the latest trends, as well as plenty of how-to sections that makes even the most complex Web site development easy to follow.

Brain Spin

ideal for all grade levels ★★★

http://www.att.com/technology/forstudents/brainspin/

This offering from AT&T presents a collection of education units on communications themes, such as fiber optic communications, building networks, and an investigation on the shortfall in telephone numbers. Students are encouraged to investigate these issues and provide solutions. There is also an excellent historical piece on Alexander Graham Bell.

Builder.com

ideal for all grade levels ★★★★

http://www.builder.com/

This is an excellent site for students and staff who are using HTML and Web tools either to build their intranet or home page or to teach digital art. There is a huge range of support information, tools, and ideas here for everyone from the novice to the experienced. This site is used regularly by the author, and it never fails to supply that little extra information when answering a critical question.

CD-ROM Evaluations

ideal for all grade levels ★★★

http://www.becta.org.uk/information/cd-roms/

This is a great site that evaluates CD-ROMs for their classroom applications. There are over 1,000 classroom appropriate disks evaluated, and the evaluations are very thorough and include applications as well as suitability guidelines.

Child Safety on the Internet

ideal for all grade levels ★★★★

http://members.home.net/cranmer2/censorship.html

This is an issue that needs to be handled with care and planning. Policies need to be put into place to ensure that the Internet environment is as safe as possible. This is an excellent site that addresses all the issues in this field and does it well. All schools need to look through this before allowing students anywhere near the Internet.

CliptooNZ

ideal for all grade levels ★★★★

http://www.cliptoonz.com/

The site not only provides a wonderful collection of cartoon images, it also provides a great collection of New Zealand images covering all aspects of culture, sport, geography, employment, people, items, farms, classrooms, and much, much more. Purchase each image for $1 and use it all you want or purchase the CD. You can also create scenes by using supplied backdrops and adding characters, items, and furniture.

Computer Lessons for Kids and Small Adults

ideal for grade levels K–8 ★★★

http://www.magmacom.com/~dsleeth/kids/lessons/starter.htm

This is an excellent introduction to how a computer works, what the major parts do, the DOS operating system, and an overview of the peripherals. The material is well laid out, simple to understand, and very suitable for younger students.

Cool Tool of the Day

ideal for all grade levels ★★★

http://www.cooltool.com/

This site presents a new tool, plug-in, or support piece of software each day. You can also view a database of over 700 reviews of tools and links that are useful for both the Internet and other classroom software.

Criteria for Evaluation of Internet Information Resources

ideal for all grade levels ★★★

http://www.vuw.ac.nz/~agsmith/evaln/index.htm

This is a set of criteria that can be applied to Internet sites. While very few will review a Web site for all these criteria, they serve an important service in providing a framework for good decision making. Aspects considered important include scope, content, design, purpose, workability, and cost.

CU-SeeMe Schools

ideal for all grade levels ★★★

http://globalschoolhouse.org//cu/_cfm/statelist.cfm

This software is fast becoming the established means for schools to communicate with each other via desktop videoconferencing. With the cost of this technology well within the reach of most schools, the increase in traffic has become exponential. Come here to download the software, see some demonstrations, or find out what events are happening. You can also list your school and receive invitations to events.

CU-SeeMe Software

ideal for all grade levels ★★★★

http://www.cuseeme.com/software/index.htm

Download updates or order the latest version of this very popular videoconferencing software. Check out the new software improvements along with the improvements in the new cameras, which are now able to deliver twenty-five frames per second. This technology is opening up huge potential for teachers and students.

Developer.com

ideal for all grade levels ★★★★

http://www.developer.com/

This is an excellent and extremely comprehensive site for teachers and students interested in the mechanics of computing and the software that operates inside the gray box. There are articles here dealing with operating systems, new technologies, and tips and tricks for almost every program available.

Digital Beat: Topics

ideal for teachers only ★★★★

http://www.benton.org/DigitalBeat/

This daily newsletter has released some excellent reports dealing with a range of information technology applications within the realm of education. Topics include professional development for teachers, the future of broadband Internet access, education technology, the digital divide, and media and the Internet.

Education with New Technologies

ideal for all grade levels ★★★★★

http://learnweb.harvard.edu/ent/welcome/index.cfm

This Web site is designed to help educate and assess effective ways of using new technologies. The site is divided into five sections. The Learning Center provides a rationale and philosophical base for the use of technologies within education. The Gallery highlights examples of where technologies have been effective in the classroom. The Workshop provides skill development for teachers. In the Meeting Hall teachers can communicate with each other. There is also a huge collection of reference Web sites and materials to support the site's conclusions.

EdWeb Exploring Technology and School Reform

ideal for grade levels 11–12 ★★★

http://edweb.gsn.org/resource.cntnts.html

Good material here including an interactive HTML course, a debate over the information highway, and an excellent section looking at just what schools are doing with computers in the classroom. There is also a section called WWWEDU (pronounced WE DO), which is a discussion group looking at the place of the World Wide Web in education.

eGroups

ideal for all grade levels ★★★

http://www.egroups.com

Yes, another Internet term is birthed! An e-group is a group of individuals who want to start a newsgroup or listserv without all the hassles of having a specific computer tagged to manage the system. You can register your group here and then use this Web site to log in and check your group mail. This is very easy to set up and is an excellent vehicle for small special interest groups to communicate simply and effectively.

Electronic Elementary

ideal for grade levels K–6 ★★★★

http://www.inform.umd.edu/EdRes/Topic/Education/K12/MDK12_Stuff/homepers/emag/

Online magazine highlights Internet projects, activities, and creations of K–6 students from around the world. Published four times a year, each magazine highlights features encouraging younger students to get involved in activities based in a variety of countries around the world. There is a section dealing with teacher resources as well as a special section encouraging writing.

Electronic School Online: Reading the Future

ideal for all grade levels ★★★★

http://www.electronic-school.com/

This journal is must read material and the entire journal is presented here online. There are the usual journal themes and articles as well as conference lists, news, and technology information.

Electronic Technology in Education

ideal for all grade levels ★★★

http://www.newhorizons.org/technology.html

This is an excellent article (with links to other articles) that deals with the fundamentals of implementing technology into schools. Here you can discover how computers can stimulate and develop writing skills, encourage students to collaborate with international peers, help students do authentic research, and allow students to carry out problem solving in contexts they can relate to. This is an excellent article and the research and information is invaluable when attempting to convince peers that these technologies have a place in the classroom.

Enhancing Learning Through Imaging

ideal for all grade levels ★★★★

http://www.kodak.com/US/en/digital/edu/education.shtml

This is an excellent set of sites that Kodak has prepared to assist schools in using the new electronic imaging tools, such as the digital camera and the digital video. Check out the K–12 solutions page for some excellent ideas on how to use these tools in the classroom to support learning and to engage students in higher-order thinking activities.

Finding Data on the Internet

ideal for all grade levels ★★★

http://nilesonline.com/data/

This is a fantastic site that outlines simply some of the golden rules for finding information on the Internet. Well presented, a must see site for getting started on the Internet.

From Now on Subject Index

ideal for all grade levels ★★★★

http://www.fno.org/fnoindex.html

There is a great selection of well-written articles here on all topics associated with the introduction of technologies into the classroom. Everything is here, including the following topics: Internet use policies, libraries of the future, networking and connectivity, research, technology planning, and Web site development.

FrontPage Editor© Tutorial

ideal for all grade levels ★★★

http://www.siec.k12.in.us/~west/online/website/

Tammy Payton continues to produce excellent resources for teachers with this latest tutorial on creating Web pages using FrontPage. It is typical of the high-quality work she presents, free of charge, to teachers around the world.

Future of Networking Technologies for Learning

ideal for all grade levels ★★★

http://www.ed.gov/Technology/Futures/overview.html

This site is a must-see and must-print-out-and-read for all teachers working in this area. This is a series of reports written for the US government to point the way of the future. These articles try to do some crystal ball gazing to see what the future holds. Very well written. Once you have viewed the abstracts, set some time aside to read the full documents.

Gaggle.NET: safe e-mail for students

ideal for all grade levels ★★★

http://www.gaggle.net/

If you are tempted to provide your students with an Internet e-mail address but concerned that they may be inundated with inappropriate mail, then this site may meet your requirements. This free service provides a screening program that removes all offensive and spam e-mail before the students see them.

Harnessing the Web

ideal for all grade levels ★★★

http://gsh.lightspan.com/web/

The Global Schoolhouse has put together an excellent tutorial on how to make the most of the Internet in the school. It is an excellent introduction for all staff and would be a great way to introduce staff with little experience to the Web. There are sections dealing with the relationship between the Web and school reform, exemplary Web projects that students have developed, planning projects, and learning to use the tools.

Highway 1

ideal for all grade levels ★★★

http://www.highway1.org/

This nonprofit organization is dedicated to providing independent advice on the latest in information technologies. Good articles dealing with everything from networking to digital imaging.

HighWired.com

ideal for grade levels 11–12 ★★★

http://www.highwired.com/

This is an online community linking together high schools from around the world. The site provides a collection of free publishing tools that allow you to build your own Web site and interact with schools across the globe. This is an excellent site that can be used to form the basis of a class Web site encouraging effective communication in all the different Web-based formats.

Homestead: Building a Home Page

ideal for all grade levels ★★★★★

http://www.homestead.com/

There are two issues schools face when attempting to build a home page: (1) Where can we find a simple but flexible software package that allows us to construct a site that looks good and reflects our culture? and (2) Where can we have the site hosted without costing us too much? Homestead offers a solution to both of these issues. The software they provide is free, easy to use, and flexible. Homestead also allows you to store your efforts on their server for free! This is a good offer, but you will need a Pentium 100 or greater with a 28.8 kbps modem and 32Mb of RAM.

How Chips Are Made

ideal for all grade levels ★★★

http://www.intel.com/education/chips/

The chip that has allowed the computer revolution to take place, but very few of us actually understand what is in the chip and how it is made. The site looks at the chip that we find inside our computers, coffee makers, traffic lights, space shuttles, and almost every electronic item we use each day. You will need Shockwave to see the animations, but it is well worth the effort to download Shockwave.

ICYouSee: A Guide to the World Wide Web

ideal for all grade levels ★★★★

http://www.ithaca.edu/Library/Training/ICYouSee.html

This is a great set of Web pages that can be used by teachers and students to assist in their understanding of what the Web is, how it works, and how you can get the best from it. The site answers seven fundamental questions concerning the Web and deals with them authoritatively and succinctly.

Idiot's Guide to Creating a Home Page

ideal for all grade levels ★★★★

http://www.voyager.co.nz/~bsimpson/html.htm

Voyager is offering some great advice here as well as space on their server for you to put up your page. This is very well done and can form a great introduction to HTML and the Internet.

Inspiration Software

ideal for all grade levels ★★★

http://www.inspiration.com/

The author rarely recommends software, but this is great for developing semantic fields and brainstorming concepts with students. It allows you to quickly link ideas in a flowcharting process and establish links between ideas. Go to the site and download a thirty-day free trial and use the free guide to get going. Great software.

INTEC: Professional Development—Inquiry-Based Math/Science

ideal for all grade levels ★★★★

http://www.concord.org/intec/topics/content.html

This is great material using the Internet to teach math and science in middle and high schools. There are five sections as well as a practice session. This is supported by the National Science Foundation and provides an excellent vehicle for teachers to improve their skills.

International Society for Technology in Education

ideal for all grade levels ★★★★

http://www.iste.org/

Includes guides to resources, education technology news, special interest groups, and some good material on distance learning applications. There is also a good reference section looking into some of the papers that have examined the benefits of online education.

Internet Detective

ideal for all grade levels ★★★

http://sosig.ac.uk/desire/internet-detective.html

This is an interactive tutorial that investigates and evaluates the quality of Internet resources. Developed with funding from the European Union, this is an excellent introduction for teachers looking to teach the students how to evaluate the quality of the information they find on the Internet.

Internet Tutorial and Guide

ideal for all grade levels ★★★

http://www.microsoft.com/magazine/guides/internet/

This is an excellent set of tutorials dealing with all aspects of the Internet. The site explains all about Internet Explorer and how it works, how to conduct searches on the Internet, how to get online, all about e-mail, and also includes sections dealing with online banking, security, and investment. For the more advanced, there are sections dealing with creating a Web site as well as putting multimedia on the Internet.

Iz and Auggie and the Invention Snatchers

ideal for grade levels 4–12 ★★★★★

http://www.headbone.com/derby

Excellent context for teaching information literacy and Internet searching. There is a full teacher's guide and site access is free. If you are looking for a site to provide students with some investigative initiatives then this is an excellent site that will teach them searching, sifting, scanning, and evaluation skills.

JavaScripts

ideal for all grade levels ★★★★

http://www.javascripts.com/

JavaScripts are the most efficient way of adding interactive information to a Web site. This site has hundreds of ideas and animations available for free. Great place to look through, but try to be selective! Be sure to avoid creating pages that take too long to download—visitors will quickly lose interest.

Java Technology

ideal for all grade levels ★★★

http://java.sun.com

All you wanted to know about this latest addition to the Net. There are applets galore here to download and use, as well as advice on how to use them.

K–5 CyberTrail

ideal for all grade levels ★★★

http://ernie.wmht.org/trail/mainlink.htm

This site provides a trail for teachers and students to follow that introduces them to the Internet. There are trails for different age groups with different foci. There are great ideas here as well as places to visit and things to pick up along the way.

Kids Connect

ideal for all grade levels ★★★

http://www.ala.org/ICONN/kidsconn.html

This free access service is provided by the American Association of School Librarians. It allows students to provide direct assistance to any student who is looking for resources for school or personal interest. The site is also looking for volunteer assistants, so keep this in mind. Great service that cuts the teacher out of the loop and provides an incentive for students to persevere with their searches.

Learn the Net

ideal for all grade levels ★★★

http://www.learnthenet.com/english/index.html

Knowledge when you need it may not be an educationally sound mission, but the site provides an excellent set of tools to assist teachers. The tools allow teachers to access data and information which—if the skills are in residence—they will be able to build into knowledge and wisdom. Good page here for ideas when introducing students to the Web, various tools, conferencing, Web publishing, newsgroups, and more. Nontechnical language with good developmental pathways ensures this site will be well used.

Learn to Use the Internet as a Curriculum Resource

ideal for all grade levels ★★★★

http://www.ala.org/ICONN/onlineco.html

This is a great selection of online courses for teachers designed to improve your skills in using the Internet in the classroom. The courses investigate such aspects as telecollaborative projects, integrating the Internet into the classroom program, the effect on the information management within the school, how to use search engines effectively, and other issues that need to be addressed when introducing the Internet into the classroom.

Learning with Technology Profile Tool

ideal for all grade levels ★★★★★

http://www.ncrtec.org/capacity/profile/profile.htm

Too often teachers make decisions about their information telecommunication requirements with very little understanding of what is available, where the future is going, what processes they should be going through, and what integration issues they need to resolve. This Web site provides a profile tool that allows the school to develop an strategic plan, identifying strengths and weaknesses. This computer program is available for Macintoshes and PCs and is also available as a PDF file.

Long-Range Plan for Technology 1996–2010

ideal for all grade levels ★★★★

http://www.tea.state.tx.us/technology/lrpt/index.html

This is a great resource available in PDF format from the Texas Education Agency. Planning past the end of the year seems impossible at times, let alone through to 2010, but this program provides some excellent pointers on how to future proof your information and communications investment.

M&M Software Online Catalog

ideal for all grade levels ★★★

http://www.mm-soft.com/catalog.asp

Here is a very good collection of public domain, shareware, and freeware available to schools. There are programs here that are suitable for every age group and in every curriculum area.

Macintosh Tips and Tutorials

ideal for all grade levels ★★★

http://home.earthlink.net/~ohora/index.html

This site is dedicated to less-experienced users and approaches problems from the perspective that the user knows nothing or very little. The site does the job very well and is cleanly laid out. There are fifty step-by-step lessons, reviews of products, twenty-seven Claris Works tutorials, freeware, shareware, and Mac links. Great site for Macintosh owners who are still on the learning curve.

MacWindows Tutorial

ideal for all grade levels ★★★★

http://www.macwindows.com/tutorial.html

A common problem in schools is how to convert one type of file to another in a mixed computer platform. The tutorial looks at all aspects of this problem, providing tips on everything from using and formatting PC floppies on Macs and opening Windows files with a Mac to network protocols and much more. Great site, well laid out; a mine of free information.

Microsoft

ideal for all grade levels ★★★★

http://www.microsoft.com/

This is a mammoth Web site with all the possible software, software patches, how tos, networking advice, giveaways, and much more. The size of this site is overwhelming; you need to be quite sure of what you want before you start entering ideas into the search engine. Great educational support and ideas for the classroom.

Museum of Modern Technology

ideal for all grade levels ★★★

http://www.actden.com/skills2k/

Although this is an advertisement for Microsoft, it *does* have good material that is worth sharing. There are a series of tutorials looking at the operating systems Windows 95, 98, and 2000, e-mail through Outlook Express, the World Wide Web through Internet Explorer, and Windows NT. (*Note:* You can find an excellent tutorial on FrontPage at <http://www.actden.com/fp/>.)

National Center for Technology Planning

ideal for all grade levels ★★★★

http://www.nctp.com/

Planning is often the missing term when it comes to schools and information technology and telecommunications technology development. This site is a great resource for all schools. Many of the promotions are relevant only to American schools, but much of the material is generic and provides excellent information to school administrators for successfully developing technologically sustainable information systems. In particular, do not miss the Technology-Based Needs Assessment Instrument and the Guidebook for Planning.

National Educational Technology Standards for Students

ideal for all grade levels ★★★★

http://cnets.iste.org/splash.htm

This is a collection of standards that can be used by schools as a starting point for creating their own standards within the school. Plenty of background information and assistance are offered here.

NetDay

ideal for all grade levels ★★★

http://www.netday.net.nz/

This excellent concept, borrowed from the US, is all about having a focus within the community to get the school for access to information technologies. Plenty of information here for schools who are in the planning stages and need some cheap and reliable support information. (Go to <http://www.sofweb.vic.edu.au/itb/netday/index.htm> for the Australian site.)

Net Guide

ideal for all grade levels ★★★★

http://www.netguide.co.nz

This is one of the best and most readable Internet magazines available. Short, crisp, and relevant articles provide an excellent magazine for teachers starting out with the Internet. This great site mirrors the quality magazine.

NetMechanic

ideal for all grade levels ★★★★★

http://www.netmechanic.com/

If you have your own Web site, here is an excellent collection of tools that allow you to tune up and service your site. You can check out the load time for your pages, reduce the size of your graphics, check your site for dead links, check for bad HTML tags and syntax, or you can sign up for a full service, 24 hours a day, seven days a week.

Netscape Communications

ideal for all grade levels ★★★

http://home.netscape.com

Most teachers will probably end up here every day without even asking. But just in case you don't, here is where to find it. Teachers should read this page every now and then to keep their surf tools honed. There are plenty of giveaways and some great information regarding trends and technical information.

Networking Schools: For What Purpose

ideal for all grade levels ★★★

http://www.fno.org/jun97/purpose.html

Another excellent article from this great journal for teachers of information technology. The article asks teachers and administrators to ask themselves a series of key questions before they are caught up in the hype of getting networked. The starter questions look into access issues, rationale, communication within the schools, and vision. All schools should visit here before they even start thinking of networking.

Parachat: Chat Software

ideal for all grade levels ★★★

http://www.parachat.com/

Schools can now incorporate chat opportunities on their Web sites. This can be useful for student discussion sessions, homework sessions, chatting with other schools about particular topics, or for teachers to chat with other schools. The software is easy to incorporate into your existing site and costs $50 a year. Download from here and start experimenting.

PBS TechKnow

ideal for all grade levels ★★★

http://www.pbs.org/kids/fungames/techknow/

This is a great site for getting students up and running on the Web. The theme of the site is to encourage students to be Net savvy and not to believe everything they see and hear in this medium. They can do some work and be issued with a Net license or they can judge for themselves what makes a good Web site. Good material and well-presented information.

PC Technology Guide

ideal for all grade levels ★★★

http://www.pctechguide.com/

This is very much for the technically minded who want to delve into the inner workings of their PCs. There is information here describing the components inside that gray box; storage facilities and how to expand, speed up, and rearrange them; the issues surrounding multimedia; and the issues pertaining to peripherals (zip drives, printers, etc.).

Quick Guides

ideal for all grade levels ★★★

http://depts.washington.edu/catalyst/quick/index.html

This is a series of tutorials and guides that cover such issues as putting existing course material online, creating Web sites, putting course readings on the Internet, working with digital images, creating PowerPoint presentations and putting them on the Internet, as well as much more.

Revenge of the Lunar Fringe!

ideal for grade levels 4–10 ★★★★

http://www.headbone.com/derby/fringe/

This is an Internet adventure where students learn how the Internet works and how to manage information. Students immediately relate to the highly graphical presentation and the upbeat language. The content and concepts are excellent.

Safety on the Internet

ideal for all grade levels ★★★★★

http://www.ou.edu/oupd/kidsafe/warn_kid.htm

This is probably the best set of notes on this topic. These should be issued to every student before they start using the Internet and referred to regularly. They should also be part of your school's Internet Policy Statement. All teachers should come here.

Shockwave

ideal for all grade levels ★★★

http://www.macromedia.com/shockzone/

This is an excellent example of the potential of this emerging software. Shockwave is an excellent tool, and this site is an example of what will be available in the near future.

Short Courses in Digital Photography

ideal for all grade levels ★★★

http://www.shortcourses.com/index.htm

If you or your school has recently purchased a digital camera, then this is the ideal place to get some background information and excellent classroom applications. The digital camera can be an excellent technology for schools, and the site will assist you in refining those skills and making the most of this new technology.

Sun Microsystems

ideal for grade levels 11–12 ★★★

http://www.sun.com

Java "lives" here so expect a lot of applets and information. If you are looking for high-end material this is the place to shop. Sun World is also worth looking at.

Sydney Morning Herald Information Technology

ideal for all grade levels ★★★

http://www.it.fairfax.com.au

The Australians do it well here, and this daily update is well worth reading. The material is not too technical, which allows teachers a chance to read something they understand without reaching for next year's technical dictionary.

T is for Thinking!

ideal for all grade levels ★★★★

http://www.ithaca.edu/Library/Training/hott.html

What you see on the Web may not always be what it should be. Critical thinking is an essential skill when it comes to assessing what is a credible site on the Web. This site looks at five suggestions for ensuring that you and your students are able to discern what is a reputable and useful site and what should be ignored. This is an essential skill for all those using the Web, and this is a good and succinct set of guidelines.

Teaching Guides

ideal for all grade levels ★★★

http://depts.washington.edu/catalyst/method/index.html

This is an excellent set of guides encouraging educators to promote student collaboration over the Internet, strategies to encourage discussion, how to manage students' diverse learning styles, and how to enhance your presentations in the classroom. Here is some excellent training for the twenty-first century teacher.

Tech Talk: Audio Net

ideal for all grade levels ★★★

http://www.broadcast.com/technology/

Listen to information technology news broadcast each week. You can listen live or play back the archived material via a RealAudio plug in. Excellent way to keep up with all the happenings in this field.

Technology Source

ideal for all grade levels ★★★★★

http://horizon.unc.edu/TS/

This is an excellent monthly online magazine that looks at the integration of information technology tools into education. The articles range from the practical applications of new technologies to future predictions by major industry players. There are also articles dealing with information literacy, computer systems, project management, and Web sites that provide teachers with guidance on applications and use of the Internet.

Technology Strategic Planning

ideal for all grade levels ★★★★

http://www.iteachnet.com/DRBROWN/Dbrown.html

One of the largest problems in the application of information and communication technologies in the classroom is the lack of strategic planning. This has led to an ad hoc approach and a lack of good leadership and planning. This Web site presents some excellent planning strategies that can assist teachers in ensuring that they get the maximum possible outputs from the money that they invest in information and telecommunication technologies. The process may seem time consuming, but in the long run it will save you enormous time and possibly a lot of embarrassment.

TechWeb

ideal for all grade levels ★★★

http://www.techweb.com/

This site takes an encyclopedic look at the issues in technology in any environment. There are reviews of new products and enhancements as well as support information on Web developments and applications of new technologies. News stories, e-mails newsletters, and service providers are all here.

Telecommunication Networks

ideal for all grade levels ★★★

http://teleeducation.nb.ca/it/module4/

This is an excellent introduction to telecommunication systems using the telephone system. There are both theory and practical assignments dealing with both digital and analogue components of this system. Excellent contexts used in this far from boring presentation.

U Wired Tools

ideal for all grade levels ★★★

http://depts.washington.edu/catalyst/tools/index.html

This is a wonderful collection of tools that have been developed to enhance student learning through collaboration and communication. These Web-based tools are simple to learn and easy to operate. You can create and conduct online surveys and questionnaires, send anonymous e-mail, allow students or colleagues to view the same online document and make comments on it, and use templates that have been designed and developed with teachers as the focus.

Using Power Point in the Classroom

ideal for all grade levels ★★★

http://www.actden.com/pp/

This is an excellent online guide to using a PowerPoint in the classroom. You are shown how to create slides, use images, movement and sound, and how to present your final product. PowerPoint is not just for teachers. Students can use it to create storybooks and to make their own presentations.

Videoconferencing: It's Place in the Classroom

ideal for all grade levels ★★★

http://www.becta.org.uk/technology/desktopvc/desktop_vc/vcresrc.html

Plenty of links to a great selection of sites as well as in-house information. From the simplest systems to full screen, full motion—it is all explained here. The information is well presented and examines both the technology and its application to the classroom.

VocalTec: Using the Computer as a Phone

ideal for all grade levels ★★★

http://www.vocaltec.com

This is the great development in the online communication trend. VocalTec has been the leader in providing software that allows your computer to act as a phone. The software is very cheap and easy to use. They offer duplex (two people can talk at once) systems. This service is not free, but international phone calls are $1.20 per hour. (*Note:* For free software check out Voxware on <http://www.voxware.com>.)

Web Graphics 101

ideal for all grade levels ★★★★

http://www.builder.com/Graphics/Graphics101/

This is an excellent introduction to using graphics on the Internet or the school Intranet. You can download images here as well as the illustrations. The tutorial deals with color and channels, scaling an image, adding transparency, reducing colors, taking a screen shot, modifying a GIF, and resaving a JPEG. There are also extended tutorials dealing with animating GIFs, tweaking your graphics for extra speed, and using image editors.

Web Monkey for Kids

ideal for grade levels K–8 ★★★★★

http://hotwired.lycos.com/webmonkey/kids/

If you want to introduce young students to producing Web sites on the Internet, then this set of tools is the ideal way to do it. By following the simple online instructions, students can create simple HTML projects such as creating a birthday invitation, doing a self-portrait, or making a simple slide show. They can get used to moving images and text as well as use the tools that the site has available for creating pictures and putting a site online.

Web Side Story: Top 1,000

ideal for all grade levels ★★★

http://w20.hitbox.com/

Do you need to know or want to know how many people visit your site each day, week, month, or year? This free service provides you with a graphical presentation of those that visit, stay, and return. Excellent service in return for a small graphic advertisement on your page.

webTeacher

ideal for all grade levels ★★★

http://www.webteacher.org/winexp/menu.html

The site has excellent primers and tutorials on browsers, inputting addresses, how to use e-mail, and navigating the vast information sea. You can also find out how to locate and get involved in newsgroups and mailing lists. The well-paced modules are very thorough.

Web Workshops for Teachers

ideal for all grade levels ★★★★

http://www.webworkshops.com/intro.htm

This is a series of twelve online courses that use the theme of ecosystems of the world in order to prepare teachers to integrate technology into daily classroom activities. The courses are not free, but if you're looking for some good professional development, this material is well laid out. It goes through concepts, step by step, and introduces new ideas along the way, including designing databases and spreadsheets and developing classroom projects using Hyperstudio.

Wingate

ideal for all grade levels ★★★★

http://wingate.deerfield.com/

This software has risen to the highest level of appreciation in schools around the world. Why? Because the software allows one phone line to be shared by up to eight machines. There is some loss of data transfer, etc., but the software works well enough to make it a good interim solution. This latest version (2.1) provides fire wall protection and has some good management features.

Wnet for School

ideal for all grade levels ★★★

http://www.wnet.org/wnetschool/JustForYou.cgi

If you are looking for applications of the Internet in the classroom or tutorials to assist teachers who are coming to terms with information and communication technologies, then this Web site will provide an excellent place to start.

Writing HTML: A Tutorial for Creating Web Pages

ideal for all grade levels ★★★

http://hakatai.mcli.dist.maricopa.edu/tut

This site was created for teachers to assist them in creating learning resources that access information on the Internet. In this exercise, you can create a lesson called Volcano Web. Because this Web site is designed with teachers in mind, pedagogical issues are addressed as well as good onscreen layout. You can use any text editor with this tutorial.

Yale Style Tutorial: Web Style Guide

ideal for all grade levels ★★★★

http://info.med.yale.edu/caim/manual/contents.html

This is the online edition of the classic Web style guide for those who wish to construct their own Web sites or school intranets. Topics covered include graphics, topography, design, and navigation. The book is well written and provides a standard for Web site design.

Youth Tech Entrepreneur

ideal for grade levels 4–12 ★★★

http://www.yte.org/

The concept is to teach students a formal program of instruction dealing with how to manage the computer systems within the school. This includes teaching them to be technicians but also teaching them to teach other students the skills that they have learned. The third strand to this program is encouraging the students to be entrepreneurs. The program is set out at this Web site. All schools should consider developing a Youth Tech Entrepreneur program.

Music and Performing Arts

African Music and Dance

ideal for all grade levels ★★★

http://www.cnmat.berkeley.edu/~ladzekpo/

There are some excellent sections at this site looking at sacred rituals, drumming sequences, sound tracks, links to various ensembles, and an excellent montage from CK Ladzekpo entitled "Sounds of Africa." You can also do the foundation course in African dance-drumming!

All Music Guide

ideal for all grade levels ★★

http://allmusic.com/index.html

A general music and entertainment site that includes a good search tool to finding various songs, genres, and musicians on the Web, as well as providing a significant quantity of its own content. The information is great and there are some excellent essays. Contemporary music dominates the content.

American Ballet Theater Group

ideal for grade levels 4–12 ★★

http://www.abt.org

The purists may not agree with the melding of drama and ballet, but the result is an excellent dance vehicle for the stage. This site provides some inspiration. No how-to here but some great exemplars.

Aotearoa Traditional Maori Performing Arts Festival

ideal for all grade levels ★★

http://www.atmpas.org.nz

Get all the information and background to this major cultural event as well as past winners, judging formats, regional competition dates, and all the support information.

Beatles

ideal for all grade levels ★★

http://www.liv.ac.uk/ipm/beatles/

No matter your view of their music, the Beatles had a huge impact on the music style, its culture, and its popularization with the youth market. You can catch the history here along with biographies, origins of some of the more popular songs, and the people that managed and married into the group.

Blue Highway

ideal for grade levels 4–12 ★★★★★

http://www.thebluehighway.com/

This site tracks the history of music known as the blues. It is very powerfully done. It is not just a chronology of the music of the time, it also explains where the music came from—the institutionalized savagery of the US Deep South—and it explores the music's development within the confines of America's largest cities. There is a Java-based chat room, listings of radio stations that play the blues, plenty of blues music, blues news, links to blues Web sites, and RealAudio blues music.

Brief History of the Power of Dance

ideal for all grade levels ★★★★

http://www.sonymusic.com/artists/MichaelJackson/museum/lowband/floor_2/lowband_inq.html

Excellent site dealing with the history of dance dating from 30,000 BC through the present. Everything here from dance raves to the renaissance period for dance to dance in the twentieth century. The site provides depth using both links and its own considerable content. This is well-presented, fascinating material!

BRS Web Radio

ideal for all grade levels ★★★

http://www.web-radio.com/

This is probably the most extensive collection of online radio stations available on the Internet. The site is divided into geographical areas. This is an excellent way of demonstrating the international nature of music and also the variety of music that is available. Tuning into Indian, Arabic, Russian, West Indian, and Spanish stations demonstrates the variety of popular music around the world.

Bulletin Boards for the Music Classroom

ideal for all grade levels ★★★★

http://members.aol.com/jasontracy/bulletinboards.html

This is a great collection of bulletin boards for teachers of music. There are many of them here dealing with all aspects of music. Some attempt to teach, some allow you to brag about how wonderful your students are, and some feature themes and topics. New bulletins are added often. Join a bulletin board, and you'll receive incoming mail every day!

Catalog of Classical Composers

ideal for grade levels 8–12 ★★★

http://www.classical.net/music/mstrindx.html

This is a great site that investigates composers through classifications of their styles. Composers are from the medieval era, the renaissance period, baroque etc. Each week the site highlights a composer and provides extensive information on a particular composer. Great biographies and interesting career highlights.

Children's Music List: Online Song Books

ideal for all grade levels ★★

http://www.montyharper.com/MHP/Songbook.html

This is an extensive listing of songs that are available online. Some include the music. A good range from Muppet songs to Schoolhouse Rock to Christmas songs. Read the warning under The Digital Tradition Folk Song database!

Cine Media: The Internet's Largest Film and Media Directory

ideal for all grade levels ★★

http://www.afionline.org/CineMedia/CineMedia.home.html

This is a huge collection of over 18,000 Web sites that deal with this field. The sites vary from poor to excellent. Material dealing with every film genre you could imagine as well as sites featuring video, television, and camera work.

Cinema: How Are Hollywood Films Made?

ideal for grade levels 4–12 ★★★★★

http://www.learner.org/exhibits/cinema/

This site provides a wonderful insight into the process of making a film. Students can use this hands-on approach by carrying out a series of activities, working through the process of screen writing, correcting, producing, acting, and editing. The material presented provides a very strong context and is a powerful learning tool. This would make a wonderful teacher-guided unit of work or as a stand-alone learning center for students to work through at their own pace.

Clarinet Family

ideal for all grade levels ★★

http://hem.passagen.se/eriahl/clarinet.htm

There are twenty-seven different types of clarinets. At this site you'll find information about many of them and how they are used in today's music.

Classics World

ideal for grade levels 4–12 ★★★★

http://www.bmgclassics.com/classics/beg-guide/

This sites presents a journey through the history and background that underpins the music we now call contemporary. The site avoids the use of jargon and presents an easy-to-read and highly interesting introduction that appeals to students.

Classics World: Opera Stories and Background

ideal for all grade levels ★★

http://www.bmgclassics.com/classics/index.html

As children we may have heard some these operas, but had no idea what they were all about. Now you can click on Aiida or Julius Caesar and you get a full rundown of what is happening and being said. There are twenty-five reviews here of the most popular operas on the stage. Students are starting to listen to classical music, so who knows, they may start liking opera!

Costume Page

ideal for all grade levels ★★★

http://users.aol.com/nebula5/tcpinfo2.html

When performing onstage it is important that the costumes are representative of the era being played out. Here you can investigate ancient costumes from varying parts of the world: medieval, renaissance, Elizabethan and Shakespearean, and seventeenth through twentieth centuries.

Country Weekly

ideal for grade levels 8–12 ★★

http://www.countryweekly.com/

This magazine deals with all things country including the culture, the music, and the musicians. Although it has a tendency toward US material, this site includes interesting articles and a good exposé for teachers who are trying to provide a wide exposure to all forms of music.

Creative Drama and Theater Education Resource Site

ideal for all grade levels ★★★★

http://www.suu.edu/resource/theater/index.html

Wonderful teaching resources here. The site includes creative drama information and links, plays for performance, a book list and discussion section, but best of all is the classroom ideas section. There are many excellent ideas here for all levels of the school.

CultureKiosque

ideal for grade levels 8–12 ★★

http://www.culturekiosque.com/

This is the European guide to arts and leisure. Here you can find news, reviews, and interviews about art, classical music, opera, jazz, movies, pop music, dance, celebrities, compact discs, cuisine, arts and entertainment guides, and much, much more. Very European!

Curriculum Studio

ideal for all grade levels ★★★★

http://artsedge.kennedy-center.org/cs.html

This is an excellent collection of tools to assist in the design of curriculum, setting standards, assessment guidelines, and materials available. There is a showcase of some models in this area as well as a considerable collection of lesson outlines, program planners, and additional resources targeted at performance arts.

Cyber Film School

ideal for all grade levels ★★★★★

http://www.cyberfilmschool.com/

This huge site has a lot to offer for both teachers and students. There is a range of articles dealing with all aspects of filmmaking as well as background on how movies are made. There are links to the magazines that deal with issues on the moviemaking culture as well as reviews of films. There are guides to doing research, information on the relationship between the viewer and the product, and much more. The technology for making our own films is getting closer, and soon we will all be Spielbergs. Great site with a lot of information and support for the classroom.

Dance and Technology Zone

ideal for grade levels 8–12 ★★★

http://www.art.net/Resources/dtz/

This is a resource for artists who are particularly interested in using new media and information technologies for the creation and performance of dance, dance theater, and related live performance works. If you are looking for new ideas to challenge your students, then this will be a good place to find that inspiration.

Dance Magazine Online

ideal for grade levels 8–12 ★★★

http://www.dancemagazine.com/

Each month this site features a new collection of reviews, dance links, information on what is happening in the dance world, discussions, dance news, and interviews with dance celebrities. If you wish to have your dance curriculum to stay contemporary, then this is a good Web site to visit on a regular basis.

Dance Online

ideal for all grade levels ★★★★

http://www.danceonline.com/

This Web site has undergone a considerable makeover and now presents the information in a highly entertaining and artistic form. You can catch up with the dance news from around the world, tour the excellent photographic exhibition, read the chronicles of dancer "X," catch up with talk about dancing, read the reviews, and follow the links.

DataDragon: Music Education

ideal for all grade levels ★★

http://datadragon.com/education/

Excellent music education site from the larger DataDragon site. There are articles and support here that deal with learning to read music, hearing what the various instruments sound like, information on music genres, a good anecdotal site for teachers entitled This day in Music, and links to other sites.

Didaskalia: Ancient Theater Today

ideal for grade levels 8–12 ★★★

http://www.warwick.ac.uk/didaskalia/

This is a great site that explores the theater genres that were perfected in the Greek and Roman eras and are still practiced today. The site deals with the drama, music, and dance of this period including historical references and links to present troupes and groups who practice this style of theater today.

Disney Music Page

ideal for grade levels K–7 ★★

http://dismusic.com/

This is a simple page with a collection of MIDI files that play the various theme songs used in Disney films. Useful site to introduce music to students, because the site provides music they know and can relate to.

Drama Teacher's Resource Room

ideal for grade levels 4–12 ★★★★

http://www3.sk.sympatico.ca/erachi/

This is a wonderful resource for all teachers of drama. There are resources dealing with technical issues such as stage productions, lighting, and scripts. Other sections include texts and seminars and a substantial collection of lesson plans, some of which are useful to teachers in need of inspiration and new ideas. There are also links to other sites and some lovely quotes.

Eadweard Muybridge: The Father of Motion Picture

ideal for all grade levels ★★★★

http://www.kingston.gov.uk/museum/muybridge/

If you are looking into visual language or a study of film as a communication vehicle, then this material can provide an excellent insight into how it all began. Beautifully presented site showing the times and the thoughts that drove this man.

Electric Guitar

ideal for all grade levels ★★★★

http://www.si.edu/lemelson/guitars/index.htm

Without doubt, the electric guitar has been the most influential instrument in the last forty years of contemporary music. During that time there were many youngsters who wished they could play in a band and play the lead guitar. The history and development of the electric guitar is well chronicled here.

Electronic Music Interactive

ideal for grade levels 8–12 ★★★★

http://nmc.uoregon.edu/emi/

You need Shockwave to download this file. (This will take about four minutes using a 28.8 modem.) For your wait, you will get 80 original diagrams, 50 original interactive animations with sound, and 150 interactive glossary terms. You will also be able to access a multimedia primer for the study of electronic music. Excellent material for secondary school students and their teachers.

Elementary General Music

ideal for all grade levels ★★★★

http://www.generalmusic.org

This is a wonderful Web site for all teachers of music. There is a huge collection of resources for the primary and intermediate classrooms as well as plenty of research, a virtual lounge, and additional Web sites and curriculum materials. A very comprehensive and worthwhile site.

Energy in the Air: Sounds from the Orchestra

ideal for grade levels K–10 ★★

http://tqjunior.advanced.org/5116/

This is a well-designed site dealing with the main instruments found in the orchestra. As you click on each of the instruments you are provided with a history of the instrument, activities you can do, information on the instrument, and pictures of the different styles of each of the instruments. A good bibliography and glossary are also provided.

First Music: Guide to Music on the Internet

ideal for all grade levels ★★★

http://www.firstmusic.com/

This generalist site is very comprehensive. If you are looking for contemporary music to support a curriculum initiative, then this is a good place to start. There are some excellent profiles, music e-zines, concert information, and a great selection of radio stations from around the world organized in a geographical basis.

Gilbert and Sullivan

ideal for all grade levels ★★★

http://diamond.idbsu.edu/gas/index.html

This prolific pair wrote many of the classic plays and operettas that are performed in schools today. This site provides teachers with background information to many of their works as well as audio and video files. There is also a tribute and links to other sites. A lot of background information to assist in selecting the right theatrical event for your next production.

Graphical Timelines of Composers

ideal for all grade levels ★★★

http://www.classical.net/music/composer/dates/comp10.html

There are two timelines available at this site (in Acrobat PDF and HTML) dealing with the major composers from 1100–1700 and 1600 to the present. Often students have little understanding of the sequence of events and the time periods that each composer actually lived in. This resource provides teachers with an excellent handout for students to place in the inside covers of their music books.

Guitar World.com

ideal for grade levels 11–12 ★★

http://www.guitarworld.com/

Guitar World primarily features contemporary guitar work from the leading rock bands from around the world. This site provides young musicians everything they could possibly want to know or hear about in regard to music news, advice about equipment, and online lessons from the experts.

History of Country Music

ideal for grade levels 4–12 ★★★

http://www.roughstock.com/history/

The Web site tracks the history of country music starting in the 1920s and moving through the present era. It looks at some of the influential artists and songs and includes numerous rare images, sound clips, and digital movies. For teachers wanting students to appreciate this genre of music, this is an excellent site to present in the classroom.

History of Drama

ideal for grade levels 4–12 ★★★

http://www.emory.edu/ENGLISH/DRAMA/HistDrama1.html

If you are looking for background information on drama or investigating dramatic styles, then you can find a great collection of information here. The site is divided into five sections: Greek, Roman, Medieval, Renaissance, and neo-classical drama. Excellent resource for investigative study.

History of Modern Ballroom Dancing

ideal for grade levels 8–12 ★★

http://www-staff.mcs.uts.edu.au/~don/pubs/modern.html

From the country that gave us "Strictly Ballroom," here is a history of modern ballroom dancing. The site goes back in history to look at the evolution of ballroom dancing from a technical and a social perspective.

Hop Pop Town

ideal for grade levels 8–10 ★★★

http://www.kids-space.org/HPT/

This highly interactive site has been developed to assist students is developing musical sequences. The interface uses both live audio and Shockwave to produce a kid-friendly interface that allows students to take their creative ideas and express them musically.

Improv Page

ideal for all grade levels ★★★★

http://ece.uwaterloo.ca:80/~broehl/improv/

Improvisation is a great form of theater that requires both good oral language and drama skills. The site here is full of ideas for the classroom and some great games to get students to loosen up and be ready to participate fully. Other features include suggestions for getting an improv group going, a history of this art form, descriptions on books about improv, and links to other resources. Great site. Suitable for all ages.

Instrument Encyclopedia

ideal for all grade levels ★★★★

http://www.si.umich.edu/CHICO/MHN/enclpdia.html

The Instrument Encyclopedia is an excellent site where you can search the database or have students browse through the site. The Sachs-Hornbostel system of classification is used throughout for ease of searching. The encyclopedia contains information on the history and the development of almost all modern instruments. This is a great site for senior music students, and is very useful for finding information when introducing new instruments.

Instrumental Music Teacher Resources

ideal for all grade levels ★★★

http://lrs.ed.uiuc.edu/students/cunningh/project

There is a lot of information here on teaching methodology, rehearsal techniques, motivation, and conducting, as well as great resources on topics such as mainstreaming in music, at-risk students, gender issues, and music across disciplines. This is one of the most useful sets of Web pages for music teachers.

International Theater Design Archive

ideal for all grade levels ★★★★

http://www.siue.edu/PROJECT2000/

The aim of this site was to collect 2000 scenic, costume, and lighting designs by the year 2000. You can search the database through scene design, costume design, or lighting design. When you need to design period costumes, and you cannot even find a picture of the era, let alone the particular character, then this is the place to visit. Good lighting suggestions for special effects and an excellent collection of scenes for different aspects and eras.

Introduction to Lighting

ideal for all grade levels ★★

http://www.bath.ac.uk/~su2bc/infoguides/lighting/index.shtml

This is an excellent introduction for those teachers and students involved in local theatrical or musical productions. The basics are explained in simple-to-understand language, with good visual support.

J S Bach

ideal for all grade levels ★★★★

http://www.jsbach.org/

This well-designed, extensive site feaures the biography of Bach, the incredibly talented composer and musician. You can read a biography of his life, check out his complete works, or just simply enjoy the music he created.

Jack's Harmonica Lessons

ideal for all grade levels ★★★★

http://www.jps.net/harmonica/

This is an excellent series of ten lessons that the author encourages you to copy and distribute to friends or classes so that the whole world will be playing the harmonica. The author's enthusiasm and passion for his instrument is patently obvious. The lessons provided are well laid out and easy to follow.

Jazz Online

ideal for grade levels 4–12 ★★★★

http://www.jazzonln.com/

Jazz is experiencing a great revival and this site reflects the energy and enthusiasm of this revival. A lot of news and views here along with reviews of releases both new and old. Jazz 101 is an online course for those that want to gain some appreciation of this style. There are even some video clips of jazz greats doing what they do well. There is also a search engine to find info on your favorite album, player, or jazz group.

Learning Musical Elements Through Listening

ideal for all grade levels ★★

http://www.ed.uiuc.edu/students/yyang/HTML/prj.html

This is a great page on this topic and is well worth a look for all teachers. The material is graded for students. There are different strategies, musical elements, composers, and genres.

Live Concerts over the Web

ideal for grade levels 8–12 ★★

http://www.liveconcerts.com/lobbybodyframe.shtml

Through the use of RealAudio and RealVideo you can listen to, and in some cases watch, concerts from around the world. No matter what your taste, there is bound to be something for everyone at this site. In the classroom this can allow for making short recordings of particular music styles, digitally storing them, and using them when appropriate.

Marching.com

ideal for all grade levels ★★★

http://www.marching.com/

Marching bands have often been a part of a school's dramatic musical program. This Web site focuses primarily on the US, but is fascinating in the depth, scope, and talent that is evident in the bands displayed at this Web site. Maybe it is just the pageantry or the precision, but marching bands always come across as groups who truly enjoy their pursuits.

Mark Shepard's Flute Page

ideal for all grade levels ★★

http://www.markshep.com/flute/index.html

This site offers some tips on how to play the flute and some modern approaches. The highlight is The Plumber's Pipe—a simple instruction sheet for making a flute from PVC pipe. (PVC pipe is available from the local hardware or plumbing store.)

Math and Music

ideal for all grade levels ★★★

http://tqjunior.advanced.org/4116/Music/music.htm

There seems to be a strong connection between success in mathematics and appreciation and ability in music. This site attempts to confirm that link and develop the concept. The site investigates such aspects of music as pitch, rhythm, and tone and examines the math that underpins these musical qualities.

Media Production

ideal for all grade levels ★★★★

http://www.cnrt.scsu.edu/media/index2.html

This extensive site has something to offer all production and media teachers. Everything here from the Media Awareness Network to the *Videomaker* magazine to online course outlines and handouts. Excellent resource site with links to additional useful sites.

Media Unplugged

ideal for grade levels 4–12 ★★★

http://library.thinkquest.org/11360/

Excellent student-designed site looking at television, the process behind the production of what you see, and advertising and its effects. Students are given the chance to create their own television broadcast. This can be done simply using a video camera and the support that this site offers. Let the funky rabbit take your students through the process. This excellent site can be used by the whole class to direct a unit of work on this topic.

Motion Picture Industry

ideal for grade levels 4–12 ★★★★

http://library.thinkquest.org/10015/

The highlight here is a Script Buddy—a utility that assists students in writing scripts for short plays and films. There is also a behind-the-scenes look at movies and information about watching movies. You can check out the filmmaking reference library as well as take part in an interactive filmmaking simulation. There is an excellent material here for any teacher or student who is involved in making his or her own films.

Mozart's Magical Musical

ideal for all grade levels ★★★★

http://www.stringsinthemountains.org/m2m/1once.htm

This excellently crafted site deals simultaneously with Mozart and Steamboat Springs, Colorado, but mostly it is about Mozart. The story is told via some excellent cartoon images and a well-told story line. It is a great story full of drama and this site tells it well. Great introduction at any level to this genius.

Mudcat Café

ideal for all grade levels ★★★★

http://www.mudcat.org/

Only a blues music site could have a title such as this. The site is very extensive and has a large database as well as forums and an online record shop. There is an excellent history of the blues as well as links to radio stations that play the blues and traditional folk songs. There are also articles and background information on the singers, their bands and where they hang out.

Musical Genre

ideal for all grade levels ★★

http://dir.yahoo.com/entertainment/music/genres/

A great place to start. Yahoo does well here with a global look at music of every genre you could imagine from new age to rave to house to techno. Also check out disco, folk, blues, metal, and and ska.

Musical Instruments Encyclopedia

ideal for all grade levels ★★★

http://www.Lehigh.edu/Zoellner/encyclopedia.html

Download RealAudio and this site comes alive with the sound of music. You can click and see the instrument, check its history and current status in the music world, and then hear what it sounds like. There is a good variety of instruments from the common to the very obscure.

Musical Notes

ideal for all grade levels ★★★

http://library.thinkquest.org/15413/

You will find sections dealing with theory on note reading, intervals, chords, and other useful information, as well as sections on music history, musical styles, careers in music, musical instruments, and even some challenging interactive games with music as the theme. There is also a good selection of links to other music sites. This is a good Web site for nonmusically inclined teachers to find lesson ideas and materials.

Music Education at DataDragon

ideal for all grade levels ★★★

http://DataDragon.com/education/reading/

This is a good collection of information for music teachers, both for themselves and also for their students. They can hear and learn about the different musical instruments, learn to read music, discover information on the various musical genres, find out what happened on this day in musical history, and link to other music education sites.

Music Education from the Garden State Pops Youth Orchestra

ideal for all grade levels ★★★★

http://www.gspyo.com/education/

This site features some great material for introducing young students to the various musical instruments with photographs and the sounds of each instrument as well as an introduction to learning to read music. For the more musically inclined, check out This Day in Music History.

Music Education Online

ideal for all grade levels ★★

http://www.geocities.com/Athens/2405/index.html

This is the music educator's home page. There are a huge number of links to other music sites, as well as some good bulletin boards here for music teachers to post sale items or questions about resources, performers, or performances. Some online lessons can also be accessed.

Music Emporium

ideal for grade levels 4–12 ★★★★

http://library.thinkquest.org/3656/html/index2.htm

The highlight here is the section dealing with how instruments work. This is excellent material that would be an invaluable accessory to any music program. There is also a section that shows students how to compose their own music (for the more advanced MIDI students), a good section dealing with the teaching and appreciation of music on the Net, and a very useful glossary.

Music Graphics Galore

ideal for all grade levels ★★★

http://www.geocities.com/Nashville/Opry/1809/

This is a huge collection of graphics that can be used by all teachers, but especially music teachers. When purchasing graphics for education, you usually receive only 20–30 that are relevant to the teaching of music, but here you will find 140 guitar graphics and 195 music backgrounds, as well as thousands more dealing with almost every musical instrument or style.

Music History 102

ideal for grade levels 4–12 ★★★★

http://www.ipl.org/exhibit/mushist/

This is a wonderful tour though the ages looking at the development of the music styles that we see today. There is an excellent selection of RealAudio clips to back up the written and visual presentation. The various musical epochs are explored including medieval, renaissance, baroque, classical, romantic, and the twentieth century.

Musicianship Basics

ideal for all grade levels ★★

http://www.dragnet.com.au/~donovan/mb/music.html

There is enough free information here to make the site well worth the visit. There is a collection of Java-based activities that students can engage in. The activities are well designed, intuitive, and build on previous understanding. You may wish to purchase the program from here.

Music in the School: World Band

ideal for grade levels 11–12 ★★

http://co-nect.bbn.com/WorldBand/CoNECTMusic.html

Register your school and join in this innovative concept. Schools connect with each other over the Internet, collaborate to produce compositions, assist each other with sequencing works, and ceate a collaborative environment.

MusicNet: The Online Guide to Music Education

ideal for all grade levels ★★★★★

http://library.thinkquest.org/3306/

This is a very extensive site with an online MusicNet encyclopedia, an excellent section featuring professions in the music industry, and a section highlighting music education games and contests. You can spend hours here mining this site for relevant, up-to-date information. Encourage your senior students to use the chat and message boards. This site is very inspirational.

Music Online: Telecommunications Environment for Teaching

ideal for grade levels 8–12 ★★★★

http://nsn.bbn.com/motet/CurriculumIndex.html

Students can study contemporary music as well as interacting with musicians and composers via the scheduled online performances featured on this site. This is a great application of the Internet doing what cannot be done traditionally and providing excellent educational outcomes. All the information and sound files are here at the site.

MusicSearch: A MusicSearch Engine

ideal for all grade levels ★★★

http://www.musicsearch.com/

Increasingly we are seeing a niche for search engines that cater for specific interests. If you're involved in music then here is the search engine for you. MusicSearch only searches music-orientated sites. You can do a quick search or you can use the meta–search engine for more involved and complex searches.

Music, the Universal Language!

ideal for all grade levels ★★★★

http://home.earthlink.net/~bluesman1/text.html

Not only is this a clever Web page, but it also contains some excellent material. The info link on the front page leads information on African lessons ideas, fun music ideas, information on the Kodaly method, and much more. There are also sections here that contain songs, music games, and a good collection of links to other sites. Make sure you also check out the great leadership quotes.

Online Guitar Community

ideal for all grade levels ★★★★

http://itp.nyu.edu/wholenote/

This is an excellent collection of information and support for students and professionals who play the guitar. There is a great series of online lessons and tools that allow you to share your knowledge with others. You can also join in the online discussions or check out the resources available here.

Opera for Children Project

ideal for grade levels 4–12 ★★★★★

http://www.kidsop.com/

If you like the idea of your students staging a contemporary opera written for their age group, then come here and pick up the music and the story. Chose from *Wizard Things, Coyote and the Winter that Never Ends,* or this year's work. There are ideas for the setup and the production of the performance as well as many helpful suggestions for a successful show.

Phantom of the Opera

ideal for grade levels 4–12 ★★★

http://www.geocities.com/Broadway/2149/

The haunting melodies of this production come flooding back. This site would be a great introduction to the production before students go to see it. The story is laid out along with all the lyrics of the songs, including sound files and photos. Very comprehensive.

Piano Education Page Just for Kids

ideal for grade levels K–9 ★★★

http://www.unm.edu/~loritaf/pnokids.html

This is an excellent series of resources for teachers teaching the piano to K– 9 students. You can listen to music, travel through time to meet a famous composer, learn to have more fun with your piano lessons, get a tip or two to help you play better, or even ask a piano teacher a few questions. The Note Brothers guide you through the site.

Pipsqueaks: Fun with Music

ideal for grade levels 4–8 ★★★★

http://www.childrensmusic.org/Pipsqueaks.html

Do you need some silly songs for the classroom? Check out these audio resources—you can hear online radio shows for kids and learn how to make your own! Sing, hear, and create your own music using the resources that are based at this site. This site is for teachers who want to extend the possibilities of what they can do, engender a passion for music, and have fun at the same time.

Playbill Online

ideal for all grade levels ★★

http://www.playbill.com/

The consummate theater home page, Playbill has everything from theater listings to gossip sections to travel packages for theater lovers.

Playwriting Seminars

ideal for grade levels 8–12 ★★★

http://www.vcu.edu/artweb/playwriting/

This is an excellent set of online seminars dealing with the essential basics of playwriting from the basic content to the structure, format, and the business of submitting the script. The seminars are very thorough and professionally produced.

Reader's Theater Editions

ideal for grade levels 4–12 ★★★

http://www.aaronshep.com/rt/RTE.html

These are a series of scripts written by Aaron Shepard. The short plays are very useful in the classroom and highlight a range of issues. Some are humorous and others are stories retold from other cultures. The plays are copyright-free for school use. Each play includes a brief summary and lists the time it takes to perform, the reading level, and the required number of actors.

Rock'n'Roll Hall of Fame: Lesson Plans for Teachers

ideal for grade levels 4–12 ★★★★

http://www.rockhall.com/programs/plans.asp

This is an excellent collection of lesson plans that are well laid out, include good background notes, and are highly entertaining. There is an emphasis on developing high-order thinking skills and promoting interdisciplinary learning. Some of the material may be considered controversial and it would be wise to filter through the lesson plans before using them.

RollingStone Magazine

ideal for all grade levels ★★★★

http://www.rollingstone.com

This magazine is online with great effect. The online version contains all the articles and pop culture news, as well as live virtual concerts, live music broadcasts, and charts of who is where and how long they have been there. There are also RealAudio clips featuring a variety of artists.

School of Drums

ideal for all grade levels ★★★★

http://www.catalog.com/drummers/bphome01.html

Here you can find an excellent treasury of drum lessons, drum set tips, percussion techniques, and drumming tricks. If you have a set of drums and a soundproof room, then here you can find some wonderful support material, exercises that students can work through, and extensive background information. The author insists that anybody can play the drums after only one or two lessons. His enthusiasm may spur some students to take this much further.

Search for Lyrics

ideal for all grade levels ★★

http://www.lyrics.ch

This is a great database where you can search for song lyrics based on either a line from a song, the artist, or the album. Great for that song that you keep humming the first line to and then can never remember the rest of the song. Quite comprehensive; includes more modern songs and fewer pre-60s lyrics.

String Pedagogy Notebook

ideal for all grade levels ★★★

http://www.uvm.edu/~mhopkins/

For those who do not play stringed instruments, the title of this site is meaningless. But for those involved in teaching students to play stringed instruments, this is a great collection that examines the teaching practices involved in this art. There is information for both right- and left-hand playing, ear training, care and maintenance, and quick time movies of some of the techniques.

TapDance

ideal for all grade levels ★★★

http://www.tapdance.org/tap

This is an extremely comprehensive Web site dealing with every aspect of tap dancing. Included here is a tap dance calendar, information on special events, a list of who is who in tap dancing, films that feature tap dancing, a good glossary, and an excellent history. You can also subscribe to list-servs and discussion groups here.

Teaching Academic Skills Through the Exploration of Music

ideal for all grade levels ★★

http://www.cis.yale.edu/ynhti/curriculum/units/1995/2/95.02.11.x.html

The site highlights the teaching of music through an interdisciplinary approach. This teaching unit explores ways to teach music in a holistic sense. The focus is the use of film to achieve a better understanding of how music is not a separate entity, but rather, is part of the bigger picture of communication.

Teoría

ideal for grade levels 4–12 ★★

http://www.teoria.com/

The site is dedicated to the study of music theory. There are software reviews, books, exercises, music theory questions, and links to good music sites. This site has been developed for teachers of music theory and provides some excellent resources.

Value of Music in Education

ideal for all grade levels ★★★★

http://pionet.net/~hub7/

All teachers, at some stage or another, question the value of what they teach. This site is an excellent place to visit when you ask that question of yourself. The site deals with the value of music, how music affects brain development, and effective teaching practices that can take music beyond being just a subject. There are also plenty of links here and interesting material on the effect of music on children.

Vintage Rock

ideal for all grade levels ★★★★

http://www.vintagerock.com/

It is almost worrisome that rock and roll has become mainstream; there is something innately appealing about it being a little bit radical. When you hear teenagers comparing the Beatles to Beethoven and Bach, you start to realize that the rock and roll era is now over forty years old. The site provides an excellent gallery of information and reflection on the good old days when rock and roll was considered an insult to society.

Virtual Museum of Music Inventions

ideal for all grade levels ★★★

http://www.op97.k12.il.us/schools/longfellow/lrexford/base/

This is a different approach to motivating students to have an interest in music and how it is produced—encourage them to invent their own instrument. This page provides many ideas and pictures of what can be achieved. Sections include How Sound Is Made and Teaching About Sound; and Tips for Teachers.

Welcome to Stage Hand Puppets

ideal for grade levels K–3 ★★★

http://www3.ns.sympatico.ca/onstage/puppets/

This site provides a range of activities to help your young students perform their first puppet show. Ideas on how to make puppets from scrap materials and tips on presentation. You can catch the online theater and get patterns for some of the puppets.

Young Playwrights Inc.

ideal for all grade levels ★★★★

http://www.youngplaywrights.org

This is an online playwriting adventure. You can work through the ever-growing collaborative play that students can be involved in writing. You can also enjoy the online collaborative workshop, check out this week's news, meet some young playwrights and investigate playwriting as a career. There is also a section dealing with the one-minute play, which is an excellent tool to use in the classroom.

Technology in Education

See the information and communication section as well as the science section for additional sites that will be suitable for teachers and students studying technology in education.

Title URL	Rating	Page
Access Excellence	★★★★★	
http://www.gene.com/ae/		200
Advertising Age's 50 Best Commercials	★★★	
http://adage.com/news_and_features/special_reports/		200
Aero Design Team Online	★★★★	
http://quest.arc.nasa.gov/aero/index.html		200
Amazon Interactive	★★★★	
http://www.eduWeb.com/amazon.html		200
Atomic Age at 50	★★★	
http://www.techreview.com/articles/aug95/atomic.html		200
Bad Human Factors Designs	★★★	
http://www.baddesigns.com/		200
Best Manufacturing Practices Center of Excellence	★★★	
http://www.bmpcoe.org/		201
Big Six	★★★★	
http://www.socoHHo.k12.tx.us/schools/edresources/bigsix/bigsix.html		201
BioRap: Product Safety, What Are Your Safety Chances	★★★	
http://www.biorap.org/br7contents.html		201
Biotechnology Graphics	★★★	
http://www.gene.com/ae/AB/GG/		201
Bomb Squad: Robots to the Rescue	★★★★	
http://www.pbs.org/wgbh/nova/robots/		201
Britten Motorcycle	★★★	
http://www.britten.co.nz/main.html		201

Technology in Education

Technology in Education

Access Excellence

ideal for all grade levels ★★★★★

http://www.gene.com/ae/

This is a top ten site. Access Excellence is an educational program sponsored by Genetech. Primarily for high school age students this site has activities, e-mail exchange, biotechnology news, competitions, a look at what biotechnology is, and much more. A great site and teachers of all levels should start here.

Advertising Age's 50 Best Commercials

ideal for all grade levels ★★★

http://adage.com/news_and_features/special_reports/

This is a collection of the top fifty commercials of all time. Why were they so successful at the time? What social issues and stereotypes were in play? Why did so many people identify with the ideas or concepts presented? These questions and much more are investigated at this site.

Aero Design Team Online

ideal for all grade levels ★★★★

http://quest.arc.nasa.gov/aero/index.html

There is a lot of information here on the design process as it is applied to aeronautical engineering. The information is designed for students by the team at NASA and has excellent graphics as well as material that encourages students to experiment with the ideas suggested. Find out what aeronautics is and how design teams overcome the specifications that apply to different types of planes such as military, cargo, rescue, and civilian transport. Students can join in on regular chat sessions as well as look at the tools that engineers use to develop new models.

Amazon Interactive

ideal for all grade levels ★★★★

http://www.eduWeb.com/amazon.html

The focus here is the Quichua people who live in this part of the world. This goup of people is looking at setting up an ecotourism project. This group of people is using great technology to meet their needs and to find opportunities and processes to ensure their viability.

Atomic Age 50

ideal for grade levels 4-12 ★★★

http://www.techreview.com/articles/aug95/atomic.html

This is an excellent site to review how a particular technology—atomic power—has greatly impacted the world. Twenty-one experts, including Japanese survivors and military observers, recorded the impact of the first atomic explosion.

Bad Human Factors Designs

ideal for all grade levels ★★★

http://www.baddesigns.com/

This is an excellent scrapbook full of equipment designed for extraterrestrials. Great material. Highly entertaining, but each item has a real point to make. Check out the can opener, the paper towel dispenser, the staplers, and much more.

Best Manufacturing Practices Center of Excellence

ideal for grade levels 4–12 ★★★

http://www.bmpcoe.org/

This is an excellent site aimed at encouraging best practices. Plenty of news and background information. The focal point of this site is the Virtual Factory. Excellent material here and plenty of it.

Big Six

ideal for all grade levels ★★★★

http://www.socoHHo.k12.tx.us/schools/edresources/bigsix/bigsix.html

This is essential reading for all teachers involved in using information access tools. Not only a good conference speaker, Mike Eisenberg, Director of ASK Eric, has denoted a set of six essential skills that define an overall process that all students and teachers need to be aware of. This is essential reading and makes for a great introduction to the whole area of information management and interpretation.

BioRap: Product Safety, What Are Your Safety Chances

ideal for all grade levels ★★★

http://www.biorap.org/br7contents.html

Excellent approach to this topic from BioRap. There is a student's issue, teacher's guide, and plenty of references and material to keep the gifted child going. Check out the research that has been done in this area, the career rap on being a toxicologist, the extensive word list, information on product testing, and some quizzes. Excellent site.

Biotechnology Graphics

ideal for grade levels 8–12 ★★★

http://www.gene.com/ae/AB/GG/

Here you will find a selection of biotechnology graphics and labeled diagrams complete with explanations representing the important processes in biotechnology. Each diagram is followed by a summary of information, providing a context for the process illustrated.

Bomb Squad: Robots to the Rescue

ideal for all grade levels ★★★★

http://www.pbs.org/wgbh/nova/robots/

Excellent site dealing with the applications of robots to the defusing of bombs. The site includes interviews with robotics experts from Carnegie Mellon University and information about the development of unique robots to deal with land mines, terrorist attacks, and nuclear disasters. There are also video clips and links to additional resources.

Britten Motorcycle

ideal for all grade levels ★★★

http://www.britten.co.nz/main.html

When this motorbike made its debut, the engineering world was turned on its head. John Britten threw away the textbook on how to build a motorbike and radically changed the design and the mechanics of these high-speed machines. With virtually no funding and using homegrown technologies, he challenged what a motorbike could be. This Web site is a tribute to his talent, his vision, and the endurance (and love) of his family.

Build-It-Yourself: Wild Things

ideal for all grade levels ★★★★★

http://northshore.shore.net/~biy/

The theme here is to encourage students to build their own toys. Each month students are given a different mission based on building particular objects ranging from cuckoo clocks to submarines. The information is wonderfully presented and is very motivational. Each mission provides a list of parts needed as well as a complete set of plans that will bring the mission to its fruition.

Canadian Youth Business Foundation

ideal for grade levels 4–12 ★★★

http://www.cybf.ca/

This site has been upgraded; you can now access a host of support and resources for technology education. There is the Entrepreneurs X-change (small business success stories, a selection of hot tips, and forums), Insights (providing good support links to professional advice regarding business development), and the Resource Station. There are also a range of online events that use chat and other communication technologies.

Center for Alternative Technology

ideal for grade levels 11–12 ★★★

http://www.cat.org.uk/

Based at Machynlleth, Powwys (Wales), this site (and their bimonthly magazine) is an excellent resource for teaching technology. It is mostly concerned with alternative energy and in particular tidal and wind energy. The home page is good with plenty of information and good links.

Center for Polymer Studies

ideal for grade levels 8–12 ★★★★

http://polymer.bu.edu/

This is a wonderful site that looks at the developments taking place in the field of polymer chemistry. The results are a whole new range of materials for constructing buildings, toys, and spacecraft. The opportunities that these developments present are considerable, but only if our students are aware of the properties and the possible applications.

Cereally Speaking

ideal for all grade levels ★★★

http://www.geocities.com/Athens/Ithaca/1018/cereally_speaking.html

The aim here is to encourage children to become more aware of the marketing and propaganda that is fed to them every day. The theme of approach is breakfast cereals. This is great material that would be at home in almost any classroom at any level. Have children take the taste test. Can they tell the difference between the branded and the generic brand? How many boxes of cereal would they have to consume to get the prize? Advertising, crunch tests, food value, and many more great ideas here.

Children and Technology

ideal for all grade levels ★★★

http://www.edc.org/CCT/ccthome/message.html

This is the home page for the Center for Children and Technology. There is some great research posted here as well as some experimental pages. Teachers using the computer and the Internet need to read some of this research and to realize the strengths and weaknesses of the computer in different situations.

Clearinghouse for Infrastructure: Bridge Information

ideal for all grade levels ★★★

http://iti.acns.nwu.edu/clear/bridge/index.html

What technology program would be complete without some bridge building? This site has all the background you could possibly want. There is every manner of information here from bridge artificial intelligence to bridge foundations, corrosion, fatigue, disasters, and much, much more.

Composting in Schools

ideal for grade levels 4–10 ★★★

http://www.cfe.cornell.edu/compost/schools.html

This is a great site looking at the science and technology of composting organic material. The site has a great slide show introduction that is suitable for downloading and showing offline, as well as information on systems and research projects that students can get involved in.

Creativity Web

ideal for all grade levels ★★★

http://www.ozemail.com.au/~caveman/Creative/

The importance of being creative and innovative is central to what technology education is all about and this site is a great place to find out the best ways of developing creativity within the classroom. Everything here from Edward de Bono to recording methodologies, creative thinking, and mind mapping.

Design and Technology Times

ideal for all grade levels ★★★

http://www.salford.ac.uk/d&t-times/

This excellent magazine supports the UK technology curriculum. The section on Making Design and Tech Work looks at what schools are doing and what ideas they are putting into practice. Also the section on Talking Points deals with issues within technology education. A good selection of technology and design resources.

DNA for Dinner

ideal for grade levels 4–10 ★★★★

http://www.gis.net/~peacewp/Webquest.htm

While the title is somewhat misleading, the contents of this Web site are very good. In 1998 there were more than fifty million acres of genetically engineered crops grown worldwide and yet most people know little, past the hype of the newspaper headlines. This Web site introduces the concept of genetically engineered foods and the issues that surround this controversial topic. This site makes a wonderful research site or learning center for students to investigate.

Dr. Fizzix: Mousetrap Challenge

ideal for grade levels 8–10 ★★★

http://www.docfizzix.com/plans.htm

This is the standard mousetrap challenge of using a mousetrap to power a vehicle. Records are kept from schools around the world that have entered the challenge. You can enter and receive a certificate if you make the top ten. A good site for providing an international aspect. It could be used for introducing e-mail.

DuPont

ideal for all grade levels ★★★

http://www.dupont.com/

This is the home page for DuPont, a company that has been the source of numerous technological innovations. Many of the latest are outlined here in considerable detail. To keep up with the materials section of the curriculum, this is a must-see site. Technical reports are available here as well.

Edu Stock

ideal for grade levels 8–12 ★★★

http://library.thinkquest.org/3088/welcome/welcome.html

http://library.advanced.org/3088/welcome/welcome.html

This series of educational pages attempt to introduce students to the stock market and how it works. The focus is a free to access stock market game that students can enter. It pays to do the online tutorial before you start your trading.

Edward de Bono's Six Thinking Hats

ideal for all grade levels 

http://www.edwdebono.com/

From the man that invented the term *lateral thinking* this concept of six hats empowers users to develop an understanding of the process of critical thinking. These pages provide an insight into how to encourage thinking, including the lateral sort. (The books featured are available from SkyLight Professional Development at <http://www.skylightedu.com>.)

Electric Guitar

ideal for grade levels 11–12 

http://www.si.edu/lemelson/guitars/index.htm

Struggling to find a theme that will keep your students interested in technology education? At this site you can investigate the invention and the development of the electric guitar, follow its commercial success, discover innovative designs, and learn how guitars actually work. Excellent site with innovation as the theme.

Electronic Engineering Times

ideal for grade levels 11–12 

http://www.eetimes.com/

Excellent newspaper here for the more senior students and their teachers. If you want to keep up with what is happening in electronics, then this is the place to visit. A great site for students to review and then present an article or give an oral presentation back to the class on a particular technology, whether it be a process, product, or environment.

Energy Quest

ideal for all grade levels ★★★★

http://www.energy.ca.gov/education/index.html

This is an excellent site looking at the issue of energy, including recycling from an educational stance. This is an excellent site for looking into the environmental issue and also for looking into the technologies associated with energy.

Engines of Our Ingenuity

ideal for all grade levels ★★★★

http://www.uh.edu/admin/engines/

Here you can listen to over 1,450 audio presentations that deal with innovation and ingenuity. Each of these audio vignettes tells the story of how our culture is formed through human creativity and how technology has shaped the world that we live in. Fortunately the whole site is searchable.

Enterprise Education Database

ideal for all grade levels ★★★

http://www.curriculum.edu.au/enterprise/index.htm

This is a database of resources that exist to support enterprise education both in Australia and throughout the world. Via the search facility you can choose the country you wish the information to originate in, the level at which you are working, and curriculum areas. You can also choose from a set of criteria and specify the type of data you want (e.g., activity, resource, etc.).

Exploratorium's Science of Cycling

ideal for grade levels 4–12 ★★★★★

http://www.exploratorium.edu/cycling/index.html

The humble bicycle has come a long way and recent Olympic events have shown the advantage that new technologies can bring to the sport of bicycle racing. This is an excellent site that looks into each section of the bikes and investigates the innovations in both design and materials used. Excellent material that is very well presented.

Exploring Leonardo

ideal for grade levels 4–12 ★★★★

http://www.mos.org/sln/Leonardo/LeoHomePage.html

Leonardo daVinci was one of the most brilliant minds we have on record. The records he left us are extensive in many areas. Not only was he one of the greatest painters of the Italian Renaissance, he was also a vegetarian who despised war. As well as making important scientific discoveries, his inventiveness and lateral thinking are still used as a benchmark today. Check out the Inventor's Workshop and Leonardo's Perspective and gain some insight as to why the this one man gave the world so many wonderful ideas and yet at the same time finished so few of them and published almost none.

Fabriclink

ideal for all grade levels ★★★★

http://www.fabriclink.com/

This is the best collection of information on fabrics around. This encyclopedic collection of information and applications is great for those teachers who are working with fabrics and their applications to needs and opportunities. Check out the What's New section to see the latest fabrics and what they are being used for. The Consumer Guide and the Fabric University both contain excellent material. Put an hour aside to just get a glimpse of this site.

Flights of Inspiration

ideal for all grade levels ★★★

http://www.fi.edu/flights/index.html

There is some dispute as to who actually managed to make the first powered flight (Pearce in NZ or Wright in the US), but this Web site produces good insight into the flight made by Wilbur and Orville Wright. It follows up with the first transatlantic flight and an excellent section dealing with the forces and the challenges of flight. There is also an excellent teacher's section that should be viewed.

Food Science Sites

ideal for all grade levels ★★★

http://www.kku.ac.th/~supnga/food/index.html

The food technology area of the curriculum is well serviced by this site. It includes a huge range of food science institutes from around the world, resources, businesses, and much more.

Frog Design

ideal for all grade levels ★★★★

http://www.frogdesign.com/

This design institution has an excellent home page that takes a broad look at the design process and how they go through the process with their clients. Far from tedious, they present the process very succinctly and with style. Six phases are identified: investigation, exploration, definition, implementation, preparation, and production.

Future Problem Solving

ideal for all grade levels ★★★

http://www.fpsp.org/

This is a wonderful service that supports students who are looking at providing solutions to needs and opportunities that they have identified. The program provides a structured process, that is both efficient and effective and needs to be taught in the classroom.

Get a Grip on Robotics

ideal for grade levels 4–12 ★★★★

http://www.thetech.org/hyper/robots/contents/

This excellent presentation from TheTech explains the basics of robotics and how movement and sensory responses are controlled and executed. There is quite a lot of detail on the movement of arms and fingers as well as information on motors and controllers. A good section dealing on today's applications rounds off an excellent site.

GirlTech

ideal for all grade levels ★★★★

http://www.girltech.com/index.html

There is a lot of information here for both the student and the teacher. Great support and encouragement for girls to pursue a course of study in technology education in a format that has appeal. The teacher section is fascinating with good articles dealing with the different ways that girls and boys play and interact with each other. There are some good recommendations for classroom practice and much, much more. Check out the invention page, the kooky inventions, and some excellent female inventor role models.

Global Ideas Bank

ideal for all grade levels ★★★

http://www.globalideasbank.org/

This site calls for ideas to be submitted and also presents all the ideas that have been presented so far. The ideas have been categorized into groups such as housing innovations, as well as social innovations under titles such as Crime and the Law. This is a good site for students and teachers to see that ideas do not necessarily have to be products but rather they can be the root of social change via new systems or environments.

Graphics Design Module

ideal for all grade levels ★★★★

http://www.stemnet.nf.ca/eastwest/main/graphicspecs.html

Excellent resource for all teachers of technology. The module on this topic comes complete with four assignments. Section one investigates traditional technologies as applied to graphics and the second section looks at graphics principles, layout, and typography. Section three investigates design and technological problem solving for graphics. Section four investigates formats, tools, and applications for graphics on the Internet. Activities are included with each lesson. Excellent for both senior student work and for teacher skill improvement. You will need Paintshop Pro to do the exercises.

Great Buildings Collection

ideal for grade levels 4–12 ★★★★

http://www.greatbuildings.com/

This is a gateway to architecture from around the world and across history. The documents here catalog hundreds of buildings from leading architects using three-dimensional models, photographic images, architectural drawings, commentaries, bibliographies, Web links, and much more. If you are looking at structure in a technological context, then this is a wonderful site.

Green Design Initiative

ideal for all grade levels ★★★

http://www.ce.cmu.edu/GreenDesign/

There has been a trend in recent years to develop environmentally friendly solutions to problems as we start to realize some of the consequences of the excesses of the last 150 years. Carnegie Mellon University has been at the forefront of environmentally aware design and development. This site works through some good examples as well as looks at the relationship between the stakeholders in this type of development.

Hello Dolly

ideal for grade levels 11–12 ★★★★

http://powayusd.sdcoe.k12.ca.us/dolly/main.htm

The cloned sheep has metamorphosed this song title into a debate of huge magnitude. This site has been developed for students to track and debate the efforts of US Representative Ehlers who wishes to pass a piece of legislation prohibiting cloning. A wonderful study follows, dividing students into groups to research the debate and then develop their own ideas and beliefs. Excellent self-directed learning unit for the entire class.

History of Advertising

ideal for grade levels 4–7 ★★★★

http://www.hatads.org.uk/home.html

This site features the history of advertising on television from the 40s to the 90s. This is an excellent site for students to explore and see the changes in how advertising has been used as a sales tool. There are some hilarious reminders of what we took so very seriously not all that long ago. This site can be used to predict what the trends will be in the twenty-first century. Good demonstration of the changing trends in society and the changing approaches advertising has used.

History of Biomedicine

ideal for grade levels 8–12 ★★★

http://www.mic.ki.se/History.html

The context of medical technology is a fascinating for older students and this site provides a wonderful support to teachers looking to follow the development of medical technology over the past 2,500 years. The site is divided into various time eras starting with ancient times and working toward the present, but it also examines particular cultures where medical technology flourished such as Mesopotamia, India, China, Egypt, and Europe.

Honey.com

ideal for grade levels PreK–8 ★★★

http://www.honey.com/kids/index.html

This is an excellent site designed for those young technologists looking into honey and its production, collection, processing, and packaging. You can ask students to look into packaging this product using alternative materials that reflect its natural image. You can ask students to develop logos or images that could be used to market this product to children their own age.

How Stuff Works

ideal for all grade levels ★★★★★

http://www.howstuffworks.com/

This is one of the most amazing Web sites for technology teachers. It is so extensive that it defies proper description. This site provides wonderful cutaway drawings and explanations for how each object works. Objects that are dealt with include car engines, gas turbine engines, diesel engines, two-stroke engines, steam engines, rocket engines, electric motors, television, VCRs, cell phones, GPS systems, radios, compact discs, tape recorders, chess computers, telephones, refrigerators, pendulum clocks, smoke detectors, thermometers, toilets, tire pressure gauges, batteries, microwaves, airplanes, hydraulic machines, and much more.

IBM Patent Server

ideal for all grade levels ★★★★

http://patent.womplex.ibm.com/index.html

From this site you can access twenty-six years of patents and trademarks that have been registered. This site is very large, but its saving grace is its efficient search engine and alternative search tools. If your students are looking for information on a possible solution, then part of their answer may lie here (although a lot of the patents are very wordy). The other feature of the site is the Gallery of Obscure Patents. Excellent site.

ID8. The Industrial Design Research Page

ideal for grade levels 11–12 ★★★★

http://www.io.tudelft.nl/research/IDEATE/

This great site looks into industrial design. Here are some great design projects that deal with concepts as well as material projects. Included here are such things as the importance of visual imagery, the history of form, concepts in domestic appliances, and much more. It may sound very dull but it is anything but dull!

Institute of Electrical and Electronic Engineers

ideal for grade levels 8–12 ★★★

http://www.ieee.org/

This very comprehensive site is great for teachers as support information. The thirty-seven specialized fields of interest contain a huge amount of information. These groups include components packaging and manufacturing technology, education society, control systems society, and many, many more.

Institute of Food Science and Technology

ideal for all grade levels ★★★

http://www.ifst.org/

There is so much information here both for members of this institute and those with an interest in this field. Everything from definitions of what food science and technology is, to policy information on genetic modification, food and safety issues, diseases spread using food as a vector, as well as links to international declarations, commentaries on micronutrients, and food additives. The site also features extensive links to other useful sites.

Institution of Professional Engineers New Zealand

ideal for all grade levels ★★★★★

http://www.ipenz.org.nz/

This is a rich source of information featuring the IPENZ online magazine. This magazine is an excellent source of information and background for all teachers of technology. A top ten site.

International Centre of Excellence for Information Technology, Singapore

ideal for all grade levels ★★★

http://www.nus.edu.sg/

One of the prerequisites for a successful technology curriculum is a culture of technology. Singapore has led the world in many areas and in particular in developing a nationwide culture of innovation and ingenuity. This site highlights the support provided to schools and workplaces. Their annual Innovation Festival is one that many countries could emulate.

International Technology Education Association: List of Listservs

ideal for all grade levels ★★★

http://www.iteawww.org/B3a.html

ITEA has a range of listservs that are useful to many teachers of technology. The listservs range from Changing from Industrial Arts to Technology Education, to Designing Facilities for Technology Education to Implementing Elementary School Technology Education to Standards for Technology Education. It's a great service and association to belong to.

Invention and Design

ideal for all grade levels ★★★★

http://jefferson.village.virginia.edu/~meg3c/id/id_home.html

This great site is supported by the National Science Foundation in the US. This is a very comprehensive unit starting with a good introduction linking design and invention and followed by five invention and design modules. The modules encourage lateral thinking and are based on various themes including reinventing the telephone, following the development of the solar water heater, the relationship between inventing and the environment, and a good section investigating search strategies. Designed for grades 6–10, but the ideas are suitable for all ages.

Inventions

ideal for all grade levels ★★★★★

http://www.nationalgeographic.com/features/96/inventions/index.html

This is a wonderful Web site from *National Geographic.* Join Professor Lou Knee as he explores the process of inventing using his wonderful invention machine. This is an excellent introduction to the technological process with an emphasis on innovation and ingenuity. This site is an excellent way to introduce fundamental concepts such as problem solving, lateral thinking, planning, and decision making.

Inventions and Technology

ideal for all grade levels ★★★★★

http://www.twingroves.district96.k12.il.us/Renaissance/University/Inventions/Inventions.html

This is a wonderful approach that shows students the technologies and the times called the Renaissance. Vincenzo shows students the technologies that existed during this time and what was about to be developed. The site looks at technologies such as clocks, gunpowder, spectacles, printing presses, flush toilets, the microscopes, telescopes, submarine, and matches. Vincenzo also explains the nature of the times and how people who stepped outside the norm were laughed at or locked away.

InventNet

ideal for grade levels 8–12 ★★★

http://www.inventnet.com/page1.html

This site has set itself up as the self-help site for would-be inventors and as such has provided some great introductory information for technology students and teachers. The focus here is on design and marketing with a lot of work presented on the patenting process. Site is well-suited for students in grades 8–12.

Inventor of the Week Archives

ideal for all grade levels ★★★

http://Web.mit.edu/invent/www/archive.html

This is a great collection of famous inventors and the inventions they brought about. Arranged in alphabetical order, you can check everyone from Edward Binney (Crayola crayons) to Alexander Graham Bell to Patricia Bath (the inventor of the apparatus to remove cataracts). Use this great site when introducing the concept of how inventors invent. The site assists in overcoming stereotypes that students may have of inventors wearing white coats and working in laboratories.

Inwit—Writings, Links, and Software Demonstrations

ideal for grade levels 8–12 ★★★★

http://www.algorithm.com/inwit/funstuff.html

This is a wonderful collection of writings from people involved in or associated with Algorithm Inc. Here we have a collection of essays and scientific readings dealing with everything from lightning to why a golf ball has dimples. Fascinating site.

IT: Intermediate Technology

ideal for all grade levels ★★★

http://www.oneworld.org/itdg/index.html

The term *intermediate technology* was coined by E. F. Shumacher when present technologies in third world countries were unable to meet the needs of the people but at the same time imported technologies were inappropriate. This resulted in the search for intermediate technologies that breached this gap. This is an excellent site examining the consequences of the inappropriate application of technologies and the search for intermediate solutions.

Journal of Technology Education

ideal for all grade levels ★★★

http://scholar.lib.vt.edu/ejournals/JTE/jte.html

This is a new address for this excellent site. All the past issues are archived here and, in a very pleasing development, the latest editions are now available in an Acrobat format.

Kid's Inventor Resources

ideal for all grade levels ★★★

http://www.inventored.org/k-12/

Here is a collection of resources and support information for students wanting to investigate the process of being an inventor. The site shows you how to be an inventor, how to invent safely, and how to be prepared to march to a different drummer. There is also excellent section looking at the history of invention as well as a special section that encourages girls to be inventors. This is an excellent resource for teachers to introduce the process of technology to students and also for students who are doing their own research.

KIE Curriculum

ideal for all grade levels ★★★

http://www.kie.berkeley.edu/KIE/curriculum/curriculum.html

The KIE program is excellent for introducing problem solving based around needs and opportunities. There is a series of lesson plans here that use the Internet and problem-solving strategies to find solutions to needs and opportunities. Most of the examples here are science-based so this site could fit in either of these two curricula. Particularly interesting is the Aliens on Tour lessons that ask students to design clothing and dwellings for cold-blooded aliens with different needs. Great site.

Lemonade Stand

ideal for all grade levels ★★★

http://www.littlejason.com/lemonade/index.html

This is the classic online version of a lemonade stand set up and operated by the pure supply and demand relationship. An excellent way to introduce the effects of limiting supply, the increase in cost price, and the subsequent effects on profitability. A few additional advantages of the Web version of this game are that you can advertise (using some of your capital) and you have to pay rent on your lemonade stand. Excellent activity.

Mammoth Net

ideal for grade levels PreK–8 ★★★

http://www.dkonline.com/twtw2/private/index.html

The characters on the page may well be familiar from the Mammoth books of the same series. The site contains such resources as Inventor of the Month, The M Files, Inventors Club, classroom ideas, and, of course, the books. Good site for the younger innovator.

Media Literacy Online Project

ideal for all grade levels ★★★

http://interact.uoregon.edu/MediaLit/HomePage

Without an understanding of the power of the media, the technology process goes nowhere. This is a great site that examines all aspects of media literacy including accessing information through technology. A very thorough site that provides teachers and students with great background material in this area.

Medical Ethics: Where Do You Draw the Line?

ideal for grade levels 8–12 ★★★★

http://www.learner.org/exhibits/medicalethics/

There are innumerable new cures, genetic therapies, cloning possibilities, and even surrogate motherhood. Are all these options good options? Who decides who gets what as the cost and the ethics of these therapies come into debate? This site does a great job of introducing the ethical issues through three issues. Excellent material.

Medieval Technology Timeline

ideal for all grade levels ★★★

http://scholar.chem.nyu.edu/~tekpages/Timeline.html

This is a wonderful resource for technology teachers. You can investigate the major technological innovations in 200-grade epochs, starting in 500 AD. For each 200 grades there is a summary of the major innovations and links to supporting Web sites. Students can be asked to put the innovations into chronological order prior to seeing this information and argue the case for their particular viewpoint.

MIT's Magazine of Innovation Technology Review

ideal for all grade levels ★★★★★

http://www.techreview.com/

Technology Review is a good magazine and along with *Popular Mechanics* these two would be excellent source magazines to assist you in keeping up in this subject area where everything changes so quickly.

NASA Commercial Technology Network

ideal for all grade levels ★★★★★

http://nctn.hq.nasa.gov/

This is the start point that takes you through the Tech Briefs section, which includes technical information that has been summarized and written in a not-too-technical format on many new technologies. The site also links to the latest Spin Offs online book that investigates the most recent applications of some of NASAs research that applies to more earthly needs and opportunities. Sections here also deal with success stories in business applications of NASA technology and you can pick up a free screen saver.

NASA Human Spaceflight

ideal for grade levels 4–12 ★★★

http://spaceflight.nasa.gov/

NASA is one of the world's greatest generators of patents, inventions, and new ideas. Spaceflight is a whole area that is being challenged through the use of far cheaper robotic explorers. However, human's ability to adjust and be innovative in a huge range of situations means that humans will always be the first choice if the cost is not prohibitive.

Office of Naval Research

ideal for all grade levels ★★★★

http://www.onr.navy.mil/sci_tech/

This extensive site looks into products, systems, and environments and the technologies the US Navy has either developed or is developing to meet the needs and opportunities that have been identified. Excellent information on materials science, human systems, systems and sensing, and electronics amongst many others. Weapons and traditional technologies are also here and may form a good background to discussions on technology and society.

Plastic Bag Information Clearinghouse

ideal for all grade levels ★★★★

http://www.plasticbag.com/

The plastic bag companies have gone to town here to convince the world that plastic bags are environmentally friendly. Believe it or not this site looks in some detail at the plastic versus paper issue and is similar to the polystyrene versus paper cup arguments. The choice is not straightforward. This site is an excellent one around which teachers could provide a unit at any level. Great site.

Problem-Solving Cycle

ideal for all grade levels ★★★

http://www.cit.state.vt.us/educ/vtea/problem.htm

This is a must-see site for all technology teachers. Download it and read it. The paper uses an excellent example to demonstrate the process and it is entertaining reading. Students will find this process critical for success.

Progress of Nations 1999

ideal for all grade levels ★★★

http://www.unicef.org/pon99/

Whenever a technology program is taught, it is imperative that the social consequences of technology decisions are also taught. UNICEF has produced an excellent review of the well-being of the peoples of the world. The report examines health, nutrition, education, and the opportunity to earn a fair reward for labor. Technological decisions always have sociological impact but these impacts are not always that obvious. This report also provides a wealth of needs that the poor and the unempowered have and these can be presented to students for them to find solutions to.

Project Management

ideal for all grade levels ★★★

http://www.tcdc.com/dmgmts/dmgmt1.htm

Project management is the discipline of defining and managing the vision, tasks, and resources required to complete a project. Excellent set of links that combine to provide a range of free resources that constitute a great basis of instruction in the field of project management. Huge amount of worthwhile information located here.

Project Management Institute: A Guide to the Project Management Body of Knowledge

ideal for all grade levels ★★★★

http://www.pmi.org/publictn/pmboktoc.htm

Two essential precursor courses for technology education teachers are those dealing with time management and project management. The Project Management Institute has now made available, free of charge, their handbook on this topic. The guide is well laid out with very relevant content; the key chapters are 1, 2, 6 and 11. For senior teachers, all chapters will be of great use. Essential site.

Quartz Watch: Symbol of Technology in a Changing World

ideal for all grade levels ★★★★

http://www.si.edu/lemelson/Quartz/contents/

This great Web site deals with the influence of the quartz watch on the watchmaking community. Discover who invented it, the history of trying to sell the idea to the Swiss, the sale to Japan, and the crunch that followed. The story of the watch wars is essential for all technology teachers to read and then use in the classroom.

Robotics at Space and Naval Warfare Systems Center, San Diego

ideal for all grade levels ★★★

http://www.nosc.mil/robots/

This is a comprehensive and up-to-date look at the developments in robotics from this center. This has great application particularly in the area of the use of sensors and remote operations. The sophisticated movement of these robots and their tiny size are features that are propelling possible new opportunities for these objects in everyday life. Very comprehensive site.

Roman Technology Handbook

ideal for all grade levels ★★★

http://www.unc.edu/courses/rometech/public/content/art_handbook.html

Most of the chapters of the handbook are available online with more to come in the near future. Investigate survival in these times looking at food, shelter, and clothing that the Romans used and developed. How did they get around and get things done in the time before electric motors? Check out the transport section for technology of the times and the great section dealing with civil engineering (bridges, sewerage, etc.).

Science Seminars Archive

ideal for grade levels 4–12 ★★★★

http://www.gene.com:80/ae/TSN/SS/

Science Seminars is a monthly seminar on biotechnology topics. The seminars are very comprehensive. Topics include Microbial Fermentations: Changing the Course of History. Included here are the seminar, student activities, a seminar discussion panel, and a suggestion box. This is really good interactive technology.

Simple Machines

ideal for grade levels PreK–10 ★★★

http://www.fi.edu/qa97/spotlight3/spotlight3.html

The site features the concepts that are basic to the application of mechanical systems to the development of solutions for many everyday needs and opportunities. This site sets out the basics of what simple machines are, and combined with Marvelous Machines <http://www.galaxy.net/k12/machines/index.shtml>, it makes an excellent theory and practical introduction for students.

Space Food and Nutrition

ideal for grade levels 4–12 ★★★★

http://spacelink.nasa.gov/products/Space.Food.and.Nutrition/

Use Adobe Acrobat Reader to download a complete unit of work dealing with space food research and how it has met the challenge of providing food that tastes good, is nutritional, and travels well into space. This hands-on unit has plenty of practical activities and an excellent teacher guide is provided. This would make an excellent unit of work looking at food technology.

Super Bridge

ideal for all grade levels ★★★

http://www.pbs.org/wgbh/nova/bridge/

This is an excellent presentation from the *Nova* television program. The Web site provides a good range of resources for teachers who wish to incorporate bridge building as part of the technology program. You will need Shockwave to benefit from this site. The site looks at the different types of bridges and the strengths and weaknesses and includes a good resource guide.

Syllabus Web

ideal for all grade levels ★★★

http://www.syllabus.com/

From the same people that publish the magazine, Syllabus Web is a great site for the latest information in using technology in the classroom. Teachers can also subscribe to the magazine. This is a well-written site with some excellent reviews, ideas and plans. A good place to start looking when developing your information technology plan for the next five years! Although aimed primarily at the tertiary level, the same concepts apply.

Tech Museum of Innovation

ideal for all grade levels ★★★

http://www.thetech.org/

The Tech Museum of Innovation is an excellent site for investigating the innovation process and the people who have developed innovative solutions. There is an excellent interactive exhibit here looking at robotics—the next best thing to having it in the classroom.

Technology Education: DeLuca's TechnoSchool

ideal for all grade levels ★★★★

http://courses.ncsu.edu/classes/ted430/intro.htm

Brilliant! This site deals with an introduction to manufacturing, and it is designed for students and teachers. There is an excellent introductory unit followed by a complete unit on manufacturing system design. The unit is ideal for older students and perfect as background information for teachers. There is also a Java-based Analyze and Decide section that takes students through a brainstorm, decide, labor cost, and break even analysis. This is great material suitable for all levels.

Technology: A Science Odyssey

ideal for all grade levels ★★★★★

http://www.pbs.org/wgbh/aso/thenandnow/tech.html

This is a fascinating site for all technology teachers. The site reflects back on the last 100 years and the technologies that have revolutionized how we produce objects, systems, and environments. The site covers Marconi, the development of flight; Henry Ford, the 1920s, and the new manufacturing methods evolved; the age of plastics; the invention of the transistor; and the impact of the telecommunications age.

Threads: Inside the AT&T Labs

ideal for all grade levels ★★★

http://www.att.com/technology/attlabs/

One of the most powerful aspects of the Internet is the ability to bring to the public's attention what is happening at the leading edges of science and technology. The site looks at the development of products, systems, and environments at research and development laboratories. Divided into three sections, the site looks at a time line of research and development at the labs. In The Attic you will find great ideas that never quite caught on, and in the Sprockets section you will find short video clips on the development of influential technologies.

TIES (The Magazine of Design and Technology Education)

ideal for all grade levels ★★★

http://www.tcnj.edu/~ties/

TIES magazine is a premiere technology education magazine well worth receiving for its research and curriculum ideas. This magazine is very useful to teachers of technology, drawing on worldwide experiences of leading teachers and technologists.

Toys: How Our Favorite Playthings Came To Be

ideal for all grade levels ★★★

http://www.discovery.com/stories/history/toys/toys.html

Toys are often the first place that new technologies appear in the public arena. This site is about some of the breakthrough technologies that allowed these toys to develop and appear on store shelves around the country. The site looks at the Frisbee, the Barbie doll, the Slinky, the skateboard, and video games. Each of these toys depended on revolutionary technology for their production and successful marketing.

Turning Students into Inventors

ideal for all grade levels ★★★

http://jefferson.village.virginia.edu/~meg3c/id/id_sep/id_sep.html

This report summarizes the design course run at the University of Virginia. What is excellent about this site is the very thorough report and recommendations that are here and the implications for technology teachers. There are samples of the work completed that are useful because they include standards, expectations, and interviews. The syllabus for the course is also here.

UBUYACAR

ideal for grade levels 8–12 ★★★

http://www.mcli.dist.maricopa.edu/pbl/ubuystudent/index.html

Students are given the task of working out what their salary will need to be in order to purchase the car they want (as opposed to need). The site takes a problem-solving approach and allows students to work through the process, to assess their decisions, and discover the implications of their decisions.

Vermont Technology Education Association

ideal for all grade levels ★★★★

http://www.cit.state.vt.us/educ/vtea/index.htm

The state of Vermont has an excellent Technology Education Association. This is their home page and it is full of good information. They have a strategic plan, they are concerned with standards and learning opportunities, and they even have a lending library (postage extra). This definition prefaces the site: "Technology is a human process where people use tools, knowledge, and other sources to extend human capability in order to solve."

Willie Wonka's Invention Room

ideal for grade levels PreK–3 ★★★★

http://www.wonka.com/InventionRoom/invention_room.html

Here is an excellent theme that can be used to introduce younger students to the invention process. *There is a wonderful* Java-driven invention room where students can experiment, as well as other resources that encourage students to use their imaginations. Teachers might like to preface the use of this material by reading the book (or sections of it) to the students.

Visual Arts

AltaVista Photo and Media Finder

ideal for all grade levels ★★★★

http://www.altavista.com/cgi-bin/query?mmdo=1&stype=simage

If you need a photo for a unit of work to highlight a discussion point, or if you would like a video clip or audio clip of a famous speech, then this site should be the first place to look. There are over seventeen million searchable images, audio clips, and video files from the Web and private collections that should provide you with what you're looking for. This is a massive collection and a wonderful resource for teachers, especially for art teachers.

Amazing Picture Machine

ideal for all grade levels ★★★

http://www.ncrtec.org/picture.htm

Schools are now starting to include Web site development in their art programs. One of the most important aspects of Web site development is layout and style. This search engine can be used by teachers and students alike to find suitable images to include in their page layout. The most important aspect of layout is simplicity and the importance of visual language, as opposed a lot of explanatory text.

Antonov Art: Oil Paintings, Education Tips, Classical Realism

ideal for grade levels 8–12 ★★★

http://www.1art.com/

This is a wonderful Web site dealing with contemporary and classical portraits, still life, and florals. This self-confessed artist workaholic has an excellent Web site full of little gems. Although a bit disorganized, it is like rummaging around in someone's attic. There are valuable resources stashed away here.

ART Capades

ideal for all grade levels ★★★

http://www.kn.pacbell.com/wired/capades/

What an excellent site! How does art make you feel? How does the artist's style and skill transform a picture into a living work that evokes passion and empathy with the figures or the imagery in the paintings. Try the swapping style activity to see the effect different styles have on the same subject.

ArtCyclopedia

ideal for all grade levels ★★★★

http://artcyclopedia.com/

This is described as the definitive index of every artist, drawn from hundreds of art galleries and museums. The material on each of the artists varies considerably with the better-known artists having extensive listings. The less well-known have more succinct biographies. Fortunately the site has an effective database search engine that allows for quite easy searching to find the topic, theme, or artist you want information on. The most requested artist is van Gogh followed by Monet, Picasso and Dali.

Arthur

ideal for grade levels K–3 ★★★

http://www.pbs.org/wgbh/arthur/

If you are looking to do facial expressions or portrait work then this site will provide your students a context they will be well familiar with. Based on the television program of the same name, all the characters are here and students can enjoy learning how to draw faces that express particular emotions.

Art Images for College Teaching

ideal for grades levels 8–12 ★★★★

http://www.mcad.edu/AICT/index.html

This is a wonderful collection of royalty-free images available to the educational community. Although the site is designed for college students, many of these images provide a wonderful introduction to a variety of styles and approaches that could be used in grades 8–12. The site is divided into five sections: ancient art, the medieval era, renaissance and baroque, eighteenth through twentieth centuries, and non-Western.

Art Journey

ideal for all grade levels ★★★★

http://library.thinkquest.org/3059/

You need to enter your name and a password to get started. From here you can pick a character for yourself and away you go. You can choose an artist and he will introduce himself, and then you can choose questions to ask from the selection that appears underneath the picture. The artists are organized in chronological order but you can also visit the public gallery, and you can even add your own masterpiece to this gallery.

ArtMetal: Resource to Metalworking

ideal for all grade levels ★★★

http://wuarchive.wustl.edu/edu/arts/metal/AM_res.html

If you want to expand your range of materials in art to include metal then this site is superb. There are great ideas here as well as information on types of metals to use, fabrication, forging and casting, finishings, and even some business advice. Great resource site.

ArtNetWeb

ideal for all grade levels ★★★

http://artnetweb.com/index1.html

This is an excellent site with a particularly good link to the Guggenheim Museums collection of African art. This site would serve as an excellent inspirational site for teachers at all levels. Contemporary art collections are generally held here.

Art of China

ideal for all grade levels ★★★

http://pasture.ecn.purdue.edu/~agenhtml/agenmc/china/china.html

At any level of the school, the Chinese style of art can be introduced and worked on as a theme. this site provides an excellent source of information and ideas as well as providing images that students can draw on and then integrate into their own cultural heritage.

Art of the First World War

ideal for grade levels 8–12 ★★★★

http://www.art-ww1.com/gb/index2.html

This is a wonderful exhibition of 110 paintings brought together by the major history museums of Europe. The quintessential point of interest is that the thirty-four different artists included fought for many different countries and on both sides of the battle. An excellent set of paintings that communicates extraordinary passion and commitment.

Art on the NET

ideal for grade levels 8–12 ★★★

http://www.art.net/

This is a very good site if you are looking for sample work from a variety of artists. There is a good collection of resident artists and galleries, as well as links to studios and galleries from around the world. Also included are resources for artists and recorded sound bites from different artists.

@rt Room

ideal for all grade levels ★★★★★

http://www.arts.ufl.edu/art/rt_room/index.html

One of the best sites for art teachers, the @rt Room serves up great ideas for the classroom at every level. The ideas are practical and will inspire all those that teach art as part of an overall curriculum as well as the specialist. There is an excellent section encouraging people to think @rtrageous—think like an artist and see art everywhere! There is also a great demonstration on papermaking.

Art Safari: An Adventure in Looking

ideal for all grade levels ★★★★★

http://artsafari.moma.org/

Seeing and looking—there is so much difference between the two. This Web site encourages students to look at the visual world around them. The safari encourages learning about art by looking and sharing interpretations. The Quest has students make up stories based on four different works of art. The focus of the site is the natural curiosity of the child and the often surprising and insightful interpretations of what they see.

ArtsEdge Teaching Materials

ideal for all grade levels ★★★

http://artsedge.kennedy-center.org/teaching_materials/artsedge.html

Here is a suite of resources for all art teachers that includes curriculum standards, frameworks, and guides for designing curriculum. There are also subject area resources covering all the arts and discussion sites for teachers of the arts. Be sure to look through the showcase. Although whole programs may not attract you, elements of all of these have merit, and they provide a great stimulus for ideas and improvements for your own curriculum.

ArtsEdNet

ideal for all grade levels ★★★

http://www.artsednet.getty.edu/

A good general art site with great teacher resources and gateways to great art sites. Very comprehensive.

ArtSource

ideal for all grade levels ★★★

http://www.ilpi.com/artsource/welcome.html

This is a huge site with an excellent collection of referenced sites. Check out everything from fabric art, metal, or any other imaginable medium. Check out art from ancient Greece or look into the developing merger between art and architecture. This site also has a complete set of links to art journals and electronic exhibitions.

Art Teacher Connection

ideal for all grade levels ★★★

http://www.inficad.com/~arted/

This site encourages innovation in art education through new technologies. Great material here with art lessons supplied online, links to over 200 sites, and lesson connections that links themes to crosscurricular units of work with an emphasis on art. Plenty of online handouts and even a bit of photography! Good handbook for newbies that will assist in getting the rest of the art department using these technologies.

Asian Art

ideal for all grade levels ★★★

http://www.asianart.com/

What a great way to introduce this huge range of styles into the classroom. There are links here to collections as well as some excellent articles dealing with the development of the various forms and current thinking and debates. There are also plenty of links to galleries and exhibitions that feature various styles.

Carmine's Color

ideal for grade levels K–3 ★★★

http://www.sanford-artedventures.com/play/color1/color1.html

If you are looking for a way to introduce the idea of color to young students, then this Web site will provide you with many ideas and a self-paced tutorial. The site looks at color in young children's lives as well as what happens when colors combine.

Case of Grandpa's Painting

ideal for all grade levels ★★★★

http://www.eduweb.com/pintura/

This is brilliant! Join A. Pintura, art detective, as he tries to solve the problem of the missing painting. Through the investigation students learn all about composition, style, and the great masters. Excellent Web material; best art site.

Chagall Windows

ideal for all grade levels ★★

http://www.md.huji.ac.il/chagall/chagall.html

Marc Chagall, the inspirational artist that works in glass, displays his works from the Hadassah-Hebrew University Medical Center. The stained glass windows displaying Reuben, Asher, Judah, and Gad as well as many more are here in full color. See the artistry that makes these windows major art works.

Cities of Art

ideal for grade levels 8–12 ★★★

http://www.mega.it/cities/ecities.htm

There are cities around the world that conjure up notions of romance and art, and this site has provided a gateway to sites that explore the cities that are famous for their art. This would be a unique context to introduce senior students to art via an atlas. Cities highlighted include Alexandria, Sofia, St. Petersburg, Prague, Basel, Florence, and many more.

Clay Times: The Journal of Ceramic Trends and Techniques

ideal for all grade levels ★★★

http://www.whistlepig.com/claytimes/

Substantial parts of this excellent journal are available online. Anything to do with ceramics can be found here. There are a couple of very good articles online addressing setting up a studio, diagnosing problems with an electric kiln, and developing one's own style. These well-written articles are well-suited to the classroom teacher.

Clayworld

ideal for all grade levels ★★★

http://www.Clayworld.com/

A very informative site that looks into different aspects of clay and ceramic work. The section on industrial ceramics is for those who do not believe art and science can work together. There are plenty of reviews of some top artisans in this field as well as the Potter's Studio that presents articles, contests, and news.

Communication Arts: The Essential Creative Resource

ideal for grade levels 8–12 ★★★

http://www.commarts.com/index.html

Communication arts uses graphic images to communicate ideas. This site provides both teachers and students with a lot of ideas, not only on the artistic side but also in the job opportunity area by highlighting jobs and career opportunities. There is plenty of information here on new technologies available in this field as well as sections dealing with innovations and the *Communication Arts* magazine. Very comprehensive.

Contemporary Arts Museum

ideal for grade levels 8–12 ★★★

http://www.camh.org/index2.html

Excellent material available online here from one of the best contemporary art museums. The strength of this museum is that it does not collect pieces, but specializes in exhibits instead. There is a collection, not surprisingly, of online exhibits, archives of past exhibits, and a good section for teachers and students.

Creative Impulse: The Artist's View of World History and Western Civilization

ideal for grade levels 8–12 ★★★★

http://history.evansville.net/index.html

This is a very comprehensive collection of information and links that allows you to study history through the examination of the creative products of those times. What better way to see the history of the world than through the art, music, drama, and literature from the minds and hearts of those who lived during those times?

Dave Chihuly: Dancing on Glass

ideal for all grade levels ★★★★

http://www.chihuly.com/

The artwork here is stunning. This artist takes glass and breathes a depth of life into it that is rarely seen. Beautiful large and small pieces combine fire, earth, gravity, and human breath to form stunning color combinations and breathtaking effects. Great inspiration for students.

Egyptian Art and Archeology at the University of Memphis

ideal for all grade levels ★★★★

http://www.memst.edu/egypt/main.html

This is a huge collection of artworks of all forms and media reflecting the development of mostly ancient Egyptian art. You can also take a tour of Egypt that highlights the sites of the empires that ruled the various kingdoms and shows where pieces of art were discovered.

Egyptian Galleries

ideal for all grade levels ★★★

http://members.aol.com/egyptart/index.html

The use of Egyptian art as a theme is a very common one. This Web site focuses on the work of Richard Deurer who has photographed many Egyptian paintings and works of art. The site also provides a virtual tour of Egypt and looks at the major Egyptian works of art. There is an excellent section entitled the Children's Gallery and you can see some of the work other students around the world have done on this theme.

Elements of Design

ideal for all grade levels ★★★

http://www.iron.k12.ut.us/schools/chs/art/homepage.html

This site is a result of the master's thesis completed by Susan Gonzalez. It includes hundreds of lesson plans detailing ideas for the classroom based on the themes of color, texture, space, shape, and form. The site features excellent ideas and supporting Web sites and literature.

Everything Art

ideal for all grade levels ★★★★

http://www.wwar.com/

This is a massive site with links to almost anything you could possibly imagine in the art world. It is a well-established site and is a comprehensive registry of visual arts information worldwide. This includes all arts such as performance and antiques, as well as what you would normally expect. Great site.

Explore the Art World

ideal for all grade levels ★★★

http://martinlawrence.com/explore_sub.html

This is the home page of the Martin Lawrence Galleries and their Web site has a fantastic collection of art. The focus here is on fine arts, but also of interest are the Internet auction of important works of art and the fine art bookstore. The site has greater interest to teachers in a professional sense, rather than as a site to be used in the classroom.

Face to Face: Portraits from the Past

ideal for all grade levels ★★★★★

http://www.sanford-artedventures.com/play/portrait2/a1.html

Let Carmine the chameleon introduce your students to the idea of creating portraits. The context is engaging and very well done. Your students can learn what makes a good portrait, view some of the famous portraits from the past, and try making portraits.

Fine Art Forum: Art and Technology Net News

ideal for grade levels 8–12 ★★★

http://www.msstate.edu/Fineart_Online/home.html

This is a great site that reviews art sites for the fine art connoisseur. There are some great sites on the Web dealing with this style and this site provides links to them.

Florence Art Guide

ideal for grade levels 8–12 ★★★★

http://www.mega.it/eng/egui/hogui.htm

For students that appreciate art and art history and for art teachers, this site is a real blessing. You can cruise on your virtual gondola around this wonderful city and explore various monuments, historic periods, artists, and art works that make this city so famous. Click on the map and explore the passion of art.

George Eastman

ideal for all grade levels ★★★★

http://www.eastman.org/

George Eastman was one of the cofounders of the Eastman-Kodak company and this Web site is a wonderful tribute to the art of photography. There is a great time line of photography as well as good collections of historical photographs, motion pictures, and technology collections that catalog the development of the camera. You can also catch up with the latest research in photography.

Global Children's Art Gallery

ideal for all grade levels ★★★

http://www.naturalchild.com/gallery/

Often art teachers need ideas that they can use as a springboard. This site provides a wonderful palette of ideas from children's art from around the world. Not only is this good art, but it is also an excellent inspiration for our students showing what they can aspire to. There is a good search engine that allows teachers to view particular styles and topics.

GraphicsDEN

ideal for grade levels 8–12 ★★★

http://www.actden.com/grap_den/index.htm

Complete the free registration and come in and learn all about being an artist. There is an excellent collection of lessons dealing with electronic art, as well as an art box and a gallery of pictures. This is a good starting point for teachers wanting to incorporate electronic media into their art curriculum.

Illustrator's Source

ideal for grade levels 8–12 ★★★

http://www.illustrators.net/

This is an excellent site if you are looking for styles of illustration as well as examples and exemplars. A host of illustrators are showcased here that teachers can use to highlight various styles and approaches. Students can gain an insight into the relationship between literary content and the chosen illustration style.

Incredible Art Department

ideal for all grade levels ★★★

http://artswire.org/kenroar/

Great site for all art teachers. From here you can link into numerous other Web pages dealing with art, check out the lesson plans receive news in the art world (mostly US), discover some good ideas for the art room, and find a variety of other good links.

Inside Art

ideal for all grade levels ★★★★★

http://www.eduweb.com/insideart/

While on a trip with his class to the art museum, a bored and daydreaming student finds himself captured by a momentary vortex and sucked into a painting. Help find who painted it and why, so that our prisoner can escape back to join his class. Great interactive site with a detective theme. Investigates color, use of brush strokes, style, and passions. Highly recommended as a learning center.

InterGlaze: Glazing Recipes

ideal for grade levels 8–12 ★★★★

http://www.sonic.net/~wang/interglaze.html

What a useful site! Enter the information you know about the glaze you want to make, including such possible things as name, color, type, and opacity and the database will do a search and present you with the recipe that matches your requirements. There is also an excellent collection of links to other pottery and clay sites from around the world.

Italian Sculpture

ideal for all grade levels ★★★★

http://www.thais.it/scultura/default.htm

The excellent collection of sculpture available at this site makes it well worth the visit. Even for very young artists this site can be used to show what can be done in sculpture.

Jacques-Edouard Berger Foundation

ideal for all grade levels ★★★★★

http://sgwww.epfl.ch/BERGER/index.html

This is one of the best sites on the Web for both its quality of images and the concept behind its presentation. It is supported by 10,000 slides collected through the Jacques-Edouard Berger Foundation. Rather than showcasing a huge database on the collection, the site features a series of programs based on a specific concept such as following Seti through his pilgrimage to Abydos. The programs are designed to provide a "true experience through the new technology." They have succeeded.

Japanese Art Resources

ideal for grade levels 11–12 ★★★

http://artsedge.kennedy-center.org/student/japan.html

The art of Japan is quite unique and its stylized form is an excellent vehicle for teaching students appreciation of not just technical aspects of art but the impact of cultural influences. There are reviews of links here to many sites that highlight visual arts, performance arts, and traditional crafts as well as the interplay between culture and art.

Joseph Wu's Origami Page

ideal for all grade levels ★★★

http://www.origami.vancouver.bc.ca

Straight from Japan, this site is very well done and has many different animals to make. The scaled dragon will be a major challenge to even the most keen paper folder.

Kinder Art

ideal for grade levels K–3 ★★★★★

http://www.kinderart.com/

This site contains a great collection or art news, resources, lesson plans, and support for art teachers of grades K–3. There are over 150 lesson plans dealing with every aspect of art imaginable at this level, including multicultural art, sculpture, printmaking, and much more. The art library contains art puzzles and quizzes, articles of interest, art trivia, and links to additional sites. Also included is children's art from around the world.

Kinder Art: Lessons

ideal for grade levels K–10 ★★★★★

http://www.kinderart.com/lessons

This ever-evolving and expanding Web site has been upgraded. It is much more comprehensive and its presentation is now exemplary. There are over 160 lesson plans here and many are very well thought out. The Art Library and the New this Week sections are always full of inspirational ideas.

Kinetosaurs

ideal for grade levels K–7 ★★★

http://www.childrensmuseum.org/kinetosaur/c.html

All children are fascinated with dinosaurs and here are some wonderful ideas for using this as a theme in your art program. There are online instructions in PDF format as well as excellent photographs and examples. You can make papier-mâché dinosaur sculptures, dinosaur wire sculptures, a dinosaur mobile, an imaginary dinosaur, and many other excellent art projects.

Krannert Art Museum

ideal for all grade levels ★★★

http://www.art.uiuc.edu/kam/

The famous Krannert Art Museum is home to over 8,000 works of art dating back to the fourth millennium BC and this home page is testimony to this collection.

Leonardo: An Online Electronic Art Almanac

ideal for grade levels 8–12 ★★★

http://mitpress.mit.edu/e-journals/LEA/home.html

This is an excellent journal dealing with issues in the art world. The journal deals with digital reviews, featured profiles of artists, features, and an archive of previous articles.

Leonardo da Vinci

ideal for all grade levels ★★★

http://www.island-of-freedom.com/DAVINCI.HTM

The gallery has sections dedicated to da Vinci's oil paintings, his engineering and futuristic designs, his drawings and sketches, and his life and times. It is simple to use and easy to read and the illustrations are excellent.

Lewis Wickes Hine: Photographer

ideal for grade levels 8–12 ★★★

http://www.nypl.org/research/chss/spe/art/photo/hinex/empire/empire.html

Lewis Wickes Hines's photographs of the construction of the Empire State Building have become legendary. Many of them are online here and they show his ability to capture the essence of the times, while ostensibly photographing the construction of a building. There are many lessons that can be passed on through these works. The essence of a good photograph never changes, only the context and elements change.

Life and Letters of Vincent (van Gogh)

ideal for grade levels 8–12 ★★★

http://www.vangoghdisc.com/narr1.htm

This is an excellent background on this renowned painter. His life recorded in the letters he and others wrote reveals a temperamental artist driven by passion. A fascinating and disturbing picture, as well as good gallery material.

Louvre Art Museum

ideal for all grade levels ★★★

http://www.paris.org/Musees/Louvre

A great introductory site to the Louvre. Check out its history as well as the main exhibitions on display and some of the great works that are housed in this famous museum. You can take a virtual tour of some of the museum here as well as book a ticket for your next visit.

Magic of Painting

ideal for grade levels 11–12 ★★★★★

http://www.geocities.com/~jlhagan/lessons/mainmenu.htm

This is a wonderful collection of painting lessons from the London International Art School. The lessons are excellent and are aimed at high-performing students. Lessons start with perspective and work through color, transparency, light and shade, and texture and design and then look at analyzing paintings.

Make a Splash with Color

ideal for grade levels 8–12 ★★★

http://www.thetech.org/exhibits_events/online/color/

This site deals with three aspects of color. The first aspect is the various ingredients in color, including its shade or its hue. The second section deals with the way light is received and reflected from different surfaces. The third section deals with the eye and its ability to receive the incoming light and turn this light into a set of images that allow us to make sense of the world we live in.

Masks.org

ideal for all grade levels ★★★

http://www.masks.org

The use of masks in art is very common, but often it repeats last year's approach with little innovation. This site provides all the innovation you require. There are many ideas as well as links to masks from almost every region on earth. A good site to print out some color examples and laminate them, and place them on the classroom walls to act as a motivation to students.

Mediterranean Art and Architecture

ideal for grade levels 11–12 ★★★★

http://rubens.anu.edu.au/

This is a site held by the Australian National University. With over 16,000 images in a variety of styles, this is really an exceptional site. Join 300,000 other visitors who take a look at some of this collection every day!

Memory of Stephen Dimitroff, Fresco Master

ideal for all grade levels ★★★

http://www.artswire.org/Community/afmadams/afm/fresco.html

What is great about this site is the excellent set of lessons on how to produce a fresco. This could be done in a modified form at almost every level of the school.

Museum Dictionary

ideal for all grade levels ★★★★★

http://www.kyohaku.go.jp/mus_dict/hdtce.htm

This is a wonderful Japanese site that investigates a range of Japanese art forms. This has been done very creatively using a range of stories describing the artistic genre. The site is divided into stories about ceramics, paintings, metalwork, textiles, calligraphy, sculpture, laquerware, and architecture.

National Gallery of Art, Washington D.C.

ideal for all grade levels ★★★★

http://www.nga.gov/

This is a huge collection of information on paintings, sculpture, and graphic arts from the middle ages to the present. The collection contains over 100,000 objects listed and available through the Web. There is an excellent search engine where you can enter an artist's name, a style, a period, or a title.

Native American Indian Art

ideal for all grade levels ★★★★

http://www.kstrom.net/isk/art/art.html

This site contains a huge range of Native (North) American Indian art works. In-depth information is presented on the techniques used in creating traditional paintings, pottery and sculpture, as well as the legend of painting and much more. The history of Native American Indian art is looked at and the site also provides some excellent photographic essays.

North Texas Institute for Education on the Visual Arts

ideal for all grade levels ★★★

http://www.art.unt.edu/ntieva/artcuhh/

The curriculum and the content are all available here and there are some great ideas and concepts for the visual arts teacher. There are numerous sections that investigate such aspects as art production, art history, art critiques, aesthetics, interdisciplinary curricula resources, investigating art through questioning strategies, technology for art resources, and much more. If you are serious about art education, then this is the place to come.

Photo Interactive

ideal for all grade levels ★★★★

http://library.thinkquest.org/11355/html/index.htm

Photo Interactive is a superb student-developed site for Think Quest. There are three main sections—Education (what photography is all about), Gallery (displays students' photographs from around the world), and Virtual Photography (basics of virtual photography). Great site especially for introducing students to the basics of photography.

Pole to Pole

ideal for all grade levels ★★★★

http://www.clpgh.org/cmnh/exhibits/pole_to_pole/index.html

This is an exceptional site where the photographer Donald Robinson has placed part of his extensive collection on the Internet. His work is artistic in its interpretation of these last frontiers. These two regions are extremes in temperature, majesty, and beauty. Wonderful site.

Refrigerator Art Contest for Kids

ideal for grade levels K–8 ★★★

http://www.artcontest.com/

This is a great concept. Students send in their artwork, then each month five pictures are selected, and finally students from around the world vote on them.

R2001 Gallery

ideal for all grade levels ★★★★

http://r2001.com/r2001gallery/gallery.html

This testament to art styles and their producers is a sweep through all art forms and possible materials. The photographs bring to life the rich works of Seiji Uedca, Alexi Aaltonen, Gerald O'Connell, Frans Fransson, and many, many more. This is a great selection of works demonstrating all forms and styles.

Salvador Dali

ideal for grade levels 8–12 ★★★

http://daligallery.com/

This is the official, premiere site. Even if you are not a fan of Dali, you can still appreciate the site as an art form in its own right. This site gives an historical perspective that would be great for looking at societal influences on a painter and the resulting art forms. There pictures of his works as well as some refreshing information on some of his contemporaries and their works.

San Francisco Fine Arts Museum

ideal for all grade levels ★★★

http://www.thinker.org/

Thinker is the largest image database in the world. If you are looking at art of any kind and want some samples, then this is the place to go. The database holds 60,000 images and is searchable, making what you need easy to find.

Sandcastle Central

ideal for all grade levels ★★★

http://www.sandcastlecentral.com/index.html

Art can be many things to many people, but sand is an excellent vehicle for allowing young students to produce three-dimensional sculptures in a cheap and easy-to-replace medium. Even if you do not have a beach on your doorstep, you can also always have a sandpit close by for the students to use. This Web site will provide you with beginners' tips, advice on carving tools, a photo gallery, and even sandcastle news.

Scream Design.com

ideal for all grade levels ★★★

http://www.screamdesign.com/

The site contains hundreds of original animation buttons, bullet points, and backgrounds. There are many reviews, tips, and ideas for potential Web designers here. The site is crammed with information and contests.

Sebastian Márquez: Pixel Painting

ideal for all grade levels ★★★★

http://www.users.wineasy.se/snmz/chano2.htm

It's hard to believe that these paintings that look like old masters were created using paint programs on the computer screen. Using Painter and Paint Shop, Sebastian Marquez has constructed beautiful paintings with three-dimensional effects, giving them a rich look of oils. Learn how he does it and then give it a go.

Sistine Chapel

ideal for grade levels 11–12 ★★★★

http://www.christusrex.org/www1/sistine/0-Tour.html

This as an amazing tour of the Sistine Chapel. You really need a 23-inch monitor to get the full impact of these photographs and their detail. An excellent virtual trip of a lifetime.

Spider School: Building Art Audiences and Communities on the Web

ideal for all grade levels ★★★

http://www.artswire.org/Artswire/spiderschool/spider.htm

This is a great site if you have a Web site based around art. There is advice here on how to best plan, design, and organize your Web site. It also includes a great selection of sites and content for you to link to.

Surrealism: A History

ideal for grade levels 8–12 ★★★

http://www.bway.net/~monique/history.htm

Whether or not you agree that surrealism and abstractionism have been replaced by the new term *modernism,* is really not important. What is important is that the artists who broke new ground to introduce a style of art be remembered for their innovation and the messages they were trying to communicate through this style. This site chronicles the development of surrealism and highlights the artists who were at the forefront and challenged the old ways.

Vincent van Gogh

ideal for grade levels 8–12 ★★★★

http://metalab.unc.edu/wm/paint/auth/gogh

This great expressionist painter only painted for ten years, yet he was prolific and also very good (by all accounts!). This site has a great collection of thumbnails of many of his works that can also be viewed as full-screen versions. Accompanying each picture are excellent background notes and interesting biographical material.

Vincent van Gogh Information Gallery

ideal for all grade levels ★★★★★

http://192.41.62.196/

This is a very extensive Web site based exclusively on the works of van Gogh. There are more than 2,500 pages of material here and more than 2,500 graphics. The Web site contains every single work that van Gogh produced in his lifetime. This is an amazing labor of love and is not only content rich but is well presented and is easy to navigate. An excellent art Web site.

Virtual Ceramics Exhibit

ideal for grade levels 8–12 ★★★★

http://www.ilpi.com/artsource/vce/welcome.html

Looking for some world class examples of ceramic art? This site presents an exhibition that is second to none. Over sixty pieces of contemporary ceramic art. Some beautiful pieces here complete with judge's comments and artist's profile.

Vision and Art

ideal for all grade levels ★★★★

http://psych.hanover.edu/Krantz/art/

This is a tutorial on visual information and how it is used. The site attempts to provide the learner an understanding of depth perception, color perception, and form perception. You can follow through the tutorial looking at how we are cued to perceive depth, how interposition assists in understanding relativity, how texture gradients provide depth, and much more. This provides teachers with an excellent understanding, as well as ideas for teaching these principles within their art classes.

Web Gallery of Art

ideal for grade levels 8–12 ★★★

http://sunserv.kfki.hu/~arthp/index.html

This online gallery presents more than 4,000 digital reproductions of European paintings created during the years 1150–1750. There are short biographies and summary for most of the art works. It is a good art dictionary of styles and artists of this period.

Why Is the Mona Lisa Smiling? Learning About Leonardo

ideal for grade levels 8–12 ★★★

http://library.thinkquest.org/13681/data/davin2.shtml

This site demonstrates a great democratic principle of the Web: it does not matter who you are, it is the quality of the work that is important. This site is put together as a team effort of Swedish and American students and it is excellent. A great art site, introducing some fundamental, though not simple, concepts behind the success of great paintings. There are links to other Leonardo da Vinci sites to go with the good original work on the site.

World Artist Directory's Art Teacher

ideal for all grade levels ★★★★

http://worldartistdirectory.com/ArtTeacher/

This is a huge Web directory linking you to almost any artist you could imagine. You can also search the database using art forms, artist's name, a site, title, or location. It can also be searched based on art activities and tutorials.

World Art Treasures: Edward Berger Foundation

ideal for all grade levels ★★★★

http://sgwww.epfl.ch/BERGER/

This extremely rich collection of art is available online via a series of artistic contexts. These include such topics as The Dizzying Grandeur of Rococo, Pilgrimage to Abydos, Discovery of Painting: Titian, Borbodour, and many more. This is not your average site and there is work here that can be drawn out for art studies at all levels.

Notes

Notes

Two Ways to Keep Your *1001 Best Internet Sites* Current

#1 For Free

Check SkyLight Professional Development's Web site every month for additional new Web sites recommended by the author. Go to

http://www.skylightedu.com

#2 Update Subscription Service

If you wish to receive 100 additional Web sites for educators each month and keep up-to-date with articles on information and communication technologies in the school environment, sign up for the teachers@work updating service.

The updating service provides 100 Web site reviews each month that can be printed out and distributed to every teacher in the school or added to your school Intranet. In addition to the reviews, there is also a monthly newsletter that contains suggestions for the classroom and articles on pedagogical issues, safety on the web, technical help (written in nontechnical language), suggestions for cabling and distribution of the Internet, software reviews, and news on emerging and new technologies. You will find the information at the teachers@work Web site at

http://www.teachers-work.com/

Printed in the United States
By Bookmasters